T0113638

"This is a rough and raw book, highly entertaining and deeply moving. We live, eat, breathe, laugh, and shiver with these GIs. This book lets you hear the voices of the men of Easy Company so you can actually see the tracer bullets and hear the incoming shells."

—Robyn Post,
coauthor of the *New York Times* bestseller
Brothers in Battle, Best of Friends

"I've always thought it was too bad that Ambrose's book and the HBO series selected only a few people to profile. . . . Easy Company was made up of a hell of a lot more guys than those of us who got all the notoriety. . . . This book gives an opportunity for some of those men to share their stories. That's a good thing. These are all top flight men. I was honored to be included in their ranks."

—Lt. Lynn "Buck" Compton,
member of Easy Company and author of *Call of Duty*

"This book adds valuable and fascinating information from men in E Company, 506th PIR, 101st Airborne. . . . These are men who volunteered for their duty because they wanted to be the best in the army. They are some of the finest men I know—both then, and today."

—Tech. Sgt. Don Malarkey,
original member of Easy Company
and author of *Easy Company Soldier*

"A distinct honor in my life was to have had the privilege of personally meeting many of these great men of Easy Company and having the opportunity to listen to their stories firsthand. A more courageous and humble lot I have never met—nor ever will. Their stories of joy, sacrifice, and suffering are America's stories and shall forever be cherished and preserved thanks to this wonderful and timely publication."

—Pete Toye,
son of Joe Toye, Easy Company member

"Imagine being able to sit down and listen to twenty veterans of one of the most fabled American military units of World War II tell their personal war stories—stories full of pain and fear and camaraderie and pride that most of them, like a lot of veterans, probably never even told their families. That priceless opportunity is here in Marcus Brotherton's fascinating collection of oral histories by a remarkable group of American heroes. Be amazed, be humbled."

—Flint Whitlock,
Pulitzer Prize–nominated author of
The Fighting First: The Untold Story of the Big Red One on D-Day

WE WHO ARE ALIVE AND REMAIN

UNTOLD STORIES FROM
THE BAND OF BROTHERS

MARCUS BROTHERTON

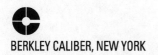

BERKLEY CALIBER, NEW YORK

THE BERKLEY PUBLISHING GROUP
Published by the Penguin Group
Penguin Group (USA) Inc.
375 Hudson Street, New York, New York 10014, USA
Penguin Group (Canada), 90 Eglinton Avenue East, Suite 700, Toronto, Ontario M4P 2Y3, Canada
(a division of Pearson Penguin Canada Inc.)
Penguin Books Ltd., 80 Strand, London WC2R 0RL, England
Penguin Group Ireland, 25 St. Stephen's Green, Dublin 2, Ireland (a division of Penguin Books Ltd.)
Penguin Group (Australia), 250 Camberwell Road, Camberwell, Victoria 3124, Australia
(a division of Pearson Australia Group Pty. Ltd.)
Penguin Books India Pvt. Ltd., 11 Community Centre, Panchsheel Park, New Delhi—110 017, India
Penguin Group (NZ), 67 Apollo Drive, Rosedale, North Shore 0632, New Zealand
(a division of Pearson New Zealand Ltd.)
Penguin Books (South Africa) (Pty.) Ltd., 24 Sturdee Avenue, Rosebank, Johannesburg 2196,
South Africa

Penguin Books Ltd., Registered Offices: 80 Strand, London WC2R 0RL, England

The publisher does not have any control over and does not assume any responsibility for author or
third-party websites or their content.

Copyright © 2009 Marcus Brotherton
Cover design by Rita Frangie
Cover photo courtesy of Shifty Powers
Book design by Kristin del Rosario

All rights reserved.
No part of this book may be reproduced, scanned, or distributed in any printed or electronic form without permission. Please do not participate in or encourage piracy of copyrighted materials in violation of
the author's rights. Purchase only authorized editions.
BERKLEY CALIBER and its logo are trademarks of Penguin Group (USA) Inc.

PRINTING HISTORY
Berkley Caliber hardcover edition / May 2009
Berkley Caliber trade paperback edition / May 2010

Berkley Caliber trade paperback ISBN: 978-0-425-23419-8

The Library of Congress has catalogued the Berkley Caliber hardcover edition as follows:

Brotherton, Marcus.
    We who are alive and remain : untold stories from the band of brothers / contributors, Rod Bain . . .
[et al.].
        p. cm.
    Includes bibliographical references and index.
    ISBN 978-0-425-22763-3
    1. United States. Army. Parachute Infantry Regiment, 506th. Company E.   2. World War, 1939–
1945—Personal narratives, American.   3. World War, 1939–1945—Regimental histories—United
States.   4. World War, 1939–1945—Campaigns—Western Front.   5. United States. Army—
Parachute troops.   6. Soldiers—United States—Biography.   I. Title.

D769.348506th .B76 2009
940.54'12730922—dc22

                                                                                            2008047668

146119709

CONTRIBUTORS

Rod Bain
Don Bond
Roy Gates
Forrest Guth
Ed Joint
Joe Lesniewski
Dewitt Lowrey
Clancy Lyall
Al Mampre
Earl "One Lung" McClung

Norman Neitzke
Ed Pepping
Frank Perconte
Darrell "Shifty" Powers
Frank Soboleski
Herb Suerth Jr.
Amos "Buck" Taylor
Ed Tipper
Bill Wingett
Henry Zimmerman

With the families of:

George Luz Sr.
Robert Burr Smith
Herbert Sobel

The contributors wish to dedicate this book

*To the men of the 506th Regiment, 101st Airborne Division,
many of whose acts will never be known*

To those who made the supreme sacrifice and never came home

*And to the men and women of the American Armed Forces, all generations,
who have served, and continue to serve, to uphold our freedoms*

ACKNOWLEDGMENTS

This book would not have come to light had it not been for author Robyn Post, who, while completing her book about Bill Guarnere and Babe Heffron, began to contact men to discuss another project about the remaining members of Easy Company. Simultaneously, Robyn was busy researching a different book. She knew the clock was against the Easy Company project's success, so she phoned my agent, Greg Johnson, knowing he had championed Buck Compton's and Don Malarkey's memoirs, and asked if he knew a writer who would be able to develop the project. I had just worked with Buck Compton on his book and jumped at the chance.

Editor Natalee Rosenstein at the Berkley Publishing Group saw the strength of this project immediately and contracted the book based on a simple, five-page pitch sheet, which I'm ever grateful to her for doing. Thanks are also due to assistant editor Michelle Vega, who was her usual terrific self in keeping things organized and smooth, and to all the team at Penguin, including Peter Horan, Catherine Milne, and Michele Langley.

When the project began, I had three men who wanted to tell their stories, with hope of four others. I knew their stories would be intrinsically valuable even if the book was only about seven men, yet because the war chronology of Easy Company had been covered already in several books and the Band of Brothers DVD series, I wasn't certain how this book would be unique.

Over time, my vision for this book began to form. I didn't want to create another book that focused on what the company did as a whole. Rather, I wanted to spotlight the men as individuals: who they were when they were young, why they enlisted, what situations each encountered in combat, what lives they made for themselves after the war. I knew the strength of the story would emerge as readers imagined sitting down in living rooms with these men, listening to their stories, hearing their voices, grammar, and word choices, experiencing living history firsthand.

I contacted Herb Suerth Jr., president of the Men of Easy Company Association. He liked the idea, particularly the angle of giving voice to the men who hadn't told their stories yet. Through Easy Company rosters, my agent and I began to cold-call and write letters to the men asking if they were interested in participating.

Some of the men were hesitant at first, even skeptical. A few phoned Buck, wondering if I was legit. Humility also played a role in the men's decisions: the men didn't want to talk about themselves. Health and age prevented several from participating. Over time, trust won out.

I was helped and encouraged by several of the adult children of Easy Company members. Thanks go to Susan Finn, George Luz Jr., Lana Luz Miller, Donna Bain Farquhar, Dr. Nancy Crumpton, Garry and Grace Alley, Tracy Compton, Syndee Compton, Tracy Gordon Goff, Michael Sobel, Gary and Marcy Carson, and Ann and Bruce Winegarden. Thanks also go to Janet Jacobsen, Rod Bain's sister.

At the end of this book, I invited three adult children of deceased Easy Company members to tell about their fathers. Many similar essays could be written, yet I felt that Herbert Sobel, Robert Burr Smith, and George Luz Sr. comprised a good cross representation of the company. They are key in understanding more about the men: Sobel, because he continues to be a controversial figure; Smith, because of the life of adventure he led after the war; and Luz, because he was so universally admired.

I was privileged to talk with many of the wives of the Easy Company men. Renee Soboleski was fabulous in organizing her husband's materials. Thanks also go to Grayce (Peg) Wingett, Donelle Bain, Patricia Bond, Lucille Clark, Sally Joint, Phyllis Lesniewski, Isabel Lyall, Virginia Mampre, Rose Maynard, Jean McClung, Lucille Neitzke, Dorothy Powers, Monna Suerth, Elaine Taylor, Rosalina Tipper, Mildred Zimmerman, Delvina Luz, and the late Harriet Guth.

Rich Riley, a World War II 101st Airborne historian and friend of Easy Company, proved a great resource. Thanks go to historian Jake Powers for his dedication to Easy Company, and to attorney Vance Day, who cares deeply for the troops.

I gratefully acknowledge that this project stands on the shoulders of those who first brought Easy Company to light, including Stephen Ambrose and Ronald Drez, Tom Hanks, Steven Spielberg, and Merav Brooks at HBO (the men all speak highly of you).

Thanks extend to Major Dick Winters and Colonel Cole Kingseed, the late David Kenyon Webster, Larry Alexander, Don Malarkey and Bob Welch, Christopher Anderson, Forrest Guth and Michael de Trez, and many other authors, writers, and historians for faithfully chronicling Easy Company and the 101st throughout the years. Included in this list are Donald Burgett, George Koskimaki, Charles Whiting, Mark Bando, Michael Haskew, Lance Jones, Robin Sink McClelland, James D. Sutton, John Taylor, Arthur Northwood Jr., and Leonard Rapport. Special thanks extend to Ross S. Carter, author of *Those Devils in Baggy Pants* (504th PIR, 82nd), a truly exceptional book.

Thanks go to the administrators of tribute Web sites who work to preserve the history and community surrounding Easy Company, including Peter van de Wal in Holland, Valor Studios, www.majordickwinters.com, www.wildbillguarnere.com, www.frankdeangelis.com, www.carwoodlipton.com, www.davidkenyonwebster.com, www.menofeasycompany.com, www.joetoye.com, and more.

Gratitude is expressed to the late Walter Gordon, a neighbor of Stephen Ambrose's. Gordon is credited with being the vital link in birthing the current renown of Easy Company. Much credit goes to Bill Guarnere, the catalyst behind organizing company reunions for so many years and compiling and maintaining rosters.

I am ever grateful to my wife, Mary Margaret Brotherton, for her strong support in this project and her love always, to journalists Dorothy Brotherton and H. C. Jones, my readers on this project, to intern Ty Johnson from Seattle Pacific University, and to David Kopp, my mentor and friend.

CONTENTS

An Elite, Experimental Fighting Unit

Someone had driven a bulldozer up the side of Mount Currahee, the three-and-a-half-mile-long incline at Camp Toccoa, Georgia. In the bulldozer's wake lay a jagged swath of gulley. Rocks and furrows pressed up into the cut. Whenever rain fell, which wasn't often in the summer heat, a creek gushed down Camp Toccoa's newest running track.

One company of soldiers—about 140 men—grunted up the path early one morning in August 1942, led by Captain Herbert Sobel, Easy Company's commander. The men jogged in formation, one behind another, equidistant from each other side to side. If a rock reared up in a man's path, he was not allowed to swerve. He leaped over the obstacle, muscles taut, hoping he didn't roll his ankle or bloody his shin.

Private Ed Tipper, a young Irishman from Detroit, ran Currahee that morning. He gasped with the other recruits, sides aching, legs pounding, wondering if he had the necessary stuff to make it into the paratroopers. Ahead of him ran one of the senior citizens of the bunch, Jack Ginn, already an old man at twenty-five. Ginn had been out drinking the night before and stank, Tipper reported. As the sweet, ugly smell wafted back, Tipper felt a strange sense of determination. Ginn continued to run, hangover and all, and Tipper figured that if Ginn could make it to the top, boozy as he was, then certainly he would be able to make it, too.

In that same pack ran a Virginia coal kid named Shifty Powers. A fabulous rifle shot since his days in the Clincho backwoods, he dreamed of making it into the Airborne. The paratroopers were simply the best. It was an all-volunteer program. A man could quit any time he wanted. The majority of men didn't withstand the arduous training and washed out into other military branches. Sixty-six years later Powers described the hope: "At the time the army didn't have specialist units like they have now. The paratroopers were the best-trained soldiers America had. We were the equivalent of today's Green Berets or Navy SEALs. All the training we had—you got so you knew what the guy next to you was going to do—and he knew what you were going to do."

Powers noted that the army was trying something new at Toccoa. Until then, men went to basic training first, then were sent to various units. But the army decided to lump the 101st's basic training and paratrooper training into one place and time, and train the entire division together. The end result, so army officials hoped, would be to produce a group of men unparalleled in their cohesiveness. The paratroopers of the 101st would be deadly, efficient, unmatched on the battlefield. "So that's what we did," Powers said. "We started together in Toccoa, and went all the way through the war together. And at the end, those of us who were left, we were still together."

In that same pack ran Rod Bain, the son of a World War I veteran. Ask Bain to describe Easy Company today and he thinks for a moment: "Average age, probably twenty. Very young, very eager to do well in combat. We trained constantly in the Deep South, then in England, always training to be one of the army's first-class units. We trained from August 1942 until we jumped into France twenty-two months later. We received far more training than the average soldier. As a unit we were together almost two years before entering combat via parachute."

Running up Currahee at Toccoa was just the start of Easy Company's adventures. In the years to come, they would sweat and struggle and live and bleed together. Some men's war ended on June 6, 1944, during the jump into Normandy. Others met their fate in Operation Market Garden, September to November 1944, the Allies' failed attempt to liberate

Holland and force an early end to the war. The men huddled together in foxholes in Belgium, December 1944 to January 1945, during one of the coldest winters on record. They lobbed shells at the enemy across the river in Hagenau, fought their way through France and Germany, liberated concentration camps, and drank a toast to victory in April 1945 at Berchtesgaden, Hitler's posh hideout in the Alps.

The group developed its cohesiveness in stages. Not all Easy Company men were present at Toccoa in early 1942. Replacements and transfers joined the company throughout the war. A Pennsylvania wildcat named Ed Joint joined the company at Camp Mackall, North Carolina. Joint caught the vision for being a paratrooper right away and carried it fearlessly through the war. "Our job was to jump out of a plane and hit the ground ready to fight," Joint says. "We were used to being surrounded by the enemy. That didn't bother us none."

An engineering student from Marquette University named Herb Suerth Jr. joined the unit at Bastogne. He had initially signed on with a company of engineers but soon applied to the paratroopers, completed training, and joined Easy Company. Bastogne is where he saw firsthand the result of his decision to transfer to the 101st: "On my first day going up to the line at Bastogne," Suerth says, "we got out of the truck, it was just getting light. As we climbed out, all of a sudden everyone fell into combat intervals, columns of two by the side of the road. Guys went out in the woods to scout. All this happened with no commands—it just happened automatically. The men very suddenly turned themselves into combat machines. I saw this and said to myself, 'Whoa, this is a real combat outfit. They know what they're doing.' That's when I knew why I wanted to be with Easy Company and not with a bunch of deadbeats who wanted to shoot themselves in the foot."

It's been noted that soldiers in premodern eras sometimes went unnamed. A man was more efficient, so it was thought, if he was simply known as *soldier*—one of the many. But modern soldiers have names. Although the men of Easy Company functioned as a group during the war, all were individuals. They grew up in various places all over America. They had brothers and sisters, fathers and mothers. They had jobs, loved women, and dreamed of careers if and when they returned from battle. To help us start to get to know these men, two chapters near the beginning of the book are devoted to the individual histories of the men of Easy Company.

The action picks up again starting with Pearl Harbor—the day when everything changed. Then it's nonstop throttle forward to the end of the war. By the end of the book, as readers, we will feel we know these men, the survivors, on a deeper level. It's in tribute that we read about the lives they led after combat, how difficult it was for many to sort through the horror they had seen, and how few emerged from combat unscathed despite being victors. That's all to come.

But at the start of the book, simply envision the men of Easy Company wrestling their way up Mount Currahee one humid morning in July 1942. Surviving the mountain was their first test. One after another they took the challenge with resolution, each man developing the seed of an unconquerable spirit that followed him through the challenges to come.

In the words of Dewitt Lowrey, who ran Currahee that morning in 1942, "We were all young, carefree, ten feet tall, and bulletproof."

PERSPECTIVE

5,800

men volunteered to become paratroopers with the original 2d Battalion of the 506th PIR at Camp Toccoa, Georgia, 1942, an elite experimental fighting unit of World War II.

1,948

of the 5,800 made the cut. The rest washed out of training and were sent to other branches of the military.

140

men from the 1,948 formed the original Easy Company in Toccoa. Easy Company, along with Dog, Fox, and Battalion companies, comprised the 2d Battalion.

366

men are listed as belonging to Easy Company, 506th PIR, by war's end due to transfers and (mostly) replacements. Their names are listed in tribute in the appendix section of this book.

49

Easy Company men were killed in action. Their names are listed in tribute in the appendix section of this book. The majority of Easy Company men were wounded, many more than once. The company took some 150 percent casualties.

40

of the 366 Easy Company veterans were known to be alive at the beginning of the research and writing of this book, fall 2007, according to the Men of Easy Company Association roster. Other survivors may be alive today but are not accounted for.

3

of the 40 died before research on the book was completed in spring 2008. Men of valor, they are listed here in tribute: Jim Alley, Max Clark, Roy Pickel Sr.

5

Easy Company veterans were not approached for this book due to previously published memoirs. Men of valor, they are listed here in tribute: Buck Compton, Babe Heffron, Bill Guarnere, Don Malarkey, Dick Winters.

12

of the 32 remaining men declined to participate in this book, some due to health reasons, some because of a desire to remain out of the public eye, some for reasons unspoken, a few could not be contacted, some because they are contributing to another project solely about the 3rd Platoon. Men of valor, they are listed here in tribute: James Benton, Ed Bernat, James Coombs, Jack Foley, Bradford Freeman, Father Leo Matz, Bill Maynard, Philip Perugini, Paul Rogers, Ed Shames, J. B. Stokes, Rod Strohl.

20

of the 32 remaining men of Easy Company agreed to participate in this book. These are their stories.

Sources: Stephen Ambrose, *Band of Brothers.* Dick Winters and Cole Kingseed, *Beyond Band of Brothers,* (Toccoa statistics compiled by Major General Salve Matheson), the Men of Easy Company Association.

Always let the men speak for themselves.

—Stephen Ambrose

WE WHO ARE
ALIVE AND REMAIN

CHAPTER ONE

A Future That Nobody Could Prepare Us For

Bill Wingett

The first time I killed a man was out of desperation.

Ed Pepping

After I jumped in Normandy, I tried for some time to get back to my unit. I saw some horrible things along the way. It was typical to see a man lying on the ground with his chest split open. In one place there was one dead American paratrooper surrounded by nineteen dead Germans. In another place an American was found—the SS had hung him upside down, cut his throat, and stuck his testicles in his mouth. You sort of blank those things out.

Clancy Lyall

As we rushed around with the grenades, I ran around a corner in Carentan and was stopped flat by a German. I plowed straight into his bayonet. His weapon stuck fast in my gut. We were both frozen, still standing up—I think he was as scared as I was. I shot first. As he fell backward he pulled his bayonet out of my stomach.

Earl McClung

Under heavy fire you don't know whether you're mad or scared. You can't fight artillery. Small-arms fire—it doesn't bother you at all, you can fight back. But when you get in an artillery barrage, you can't. Me, I get more angry than scared. I can't do anything about it. There's nothing to fight.

Don Bond

I went out of the plane, checked my chute, and heard somebody hollering above me. I looked up and there's old Blaine knee-deep in my silk. He was looking down at me through the apex of my chute, screaming and hollering. I told him to get the hell off me. He had jumped and came down right on top of my chute. When he did that, his chute collapsed because there was no weight on it anymore. I knew we couldn't land like that. Even if all went fine, Blaine would fall the length of my chute, about thirty feet, as soon as I hit the ground. I kept hollering for him to step off.

Forrest Guth

A crossroads was identified as Dead Man's Corner. An American tank had been disabled there. Some of the crew were climbing out, and a man was shot. He hung over the edge of the tank for days. We couldn't get in to retrieve the body. So if someone was sent out on a scouting mission, you'd say, "Well, you go up to Dead Man's Corner and take a left," or whatever.

Ed Tipper

I was standing in the doorway when this blast hit me. It knocked me back. I didn't feel any pain, though my right eye had been destroyed by the concussion and both my legs had been broken. Strangely enough,

I was still standing and didn't drop my weapon. Joe Leibgott ran across the street. "You've just been hit by a mortar shell," he said. "Sit down." I reached up. My helmet had been blown off. My head felt like a watermelon, swollen and mushy, and blood was everywhere. I was in shock and my muscles had all tensed—that's the reason I was still able to stand and control everything. I sat. Several of the guys had seen the hit and thought I was dead. Eight or ten months later I visited Floyd Talbert's parents back in the States. They wrote to Floyd and said that Ed Tipper had come by to visit them. He wrote back, saying, "That's impossible. He was killed. I saw it. Whoever's claiming to be Tipper is someone else." He couldn't believe I was still alive.

Shifty Powers

There'd be about six or seven of us sitting around in one of those old barns in Mourmelon, playing poker. Now, when you're playing poker, you've got to concentrate. One of the guys took a hand grenade, screwed the top off, and poured the powder out. He put the grenade back together and loosened the pin. While we were playing poker, the guy came in and worked the pin so the grenade popped off his vest and fell on the floor. "Live grenade!" he hollered. Everybody in there dove anywhere he could. Money and cards flew everywhere. The guy who dropped the grenade ran off. It was all a big joke.

Joe Lesniewski

Heading up to Bastogne in the middle of the coldest winter in thirty years, I didn't have any boots. The old shoes I had wouldn't work—I couldn't run in those. I took them off and threw them away. I had some heavy wool socks, so I put them on, then wrapped some burlap sacks around my feet with some leather shoelaces I had. That's what I wore in Bastogne.

Henry Zimmerman

Buck Taylor and I came across the body of a dead German soldier in the snow. He appeared to be about twelve or thirteen years old. Buck and I buried the boy.

Herb Suerth Jr.

Coming home on the *Queen Elizabeth* I was on the promenade deck flat on my back with both legs in a plaster cast from my ribs down. Only my toes were sticking out. I thought, They ain't going to get me in a lifeboat if we get torpedoed. But by then you figure you've made it out alive, so you aren't worried about much of anything.

Frank Soboleski

As we got closer, we saw the open side of some of the sheds. Stacks of bodies were piled there, probably waiting to be burned to render out the fat. We approached cautiously. We smelled another odor now: horrible, sickening, sweet, putrid—it was burning flesh. What we saw then was the most unbelievable sight I have ever witnessed: human beings, some standing like mummies, most lying on shelves in buildings, live bodies mixed with dead bodies, all together on shallow shelves so hundreds of them would fit in the buildings. There were also piles of bodies burning. The constant sounds of low moaning and crying could be heard. The sound made you want to plug your ears to get away from it. I became sick to my stomach, as did many of us.

Roy Gates

We found out where the general was. He had been a commandant in a concentration camp and had some SS troops with him. Some of our sharpshooters took care of the troops. After a little firefight, we captured the general, still alive. We got him up behind a tree. That's where we shot him by firing squad. That was the first time I saw the back of somebody's head fly off. The war was technically over at this point, but I'm eighty-six years old as I tell this, so if they want to do something about it they better hurry.

CHAPTER TWO

Young Lions, East

Shifty Powers

I'll start with this:

I was born and raised in a coal mining camp. My father worked for the coal mines. I went to school in Clinchco, Virginia, the town owned by the Clinchco Coal Company. There were seven in my family. Dad made a hundred dollars a month. We ate on a dollar a day.

My dad was an extraordinary rifle and pistol shot. He taught me how to shoot. It took a quarter to buy a box of .22 rifle shorts. On weekends I shined shoes to get enough money to buy shells.

Squirrel season was two weeks each year. I hunted every day in squirrel season. It not only helped my shooting, it helped me be aware of things in the woods, valuable in combat situations. You think of squirrel hunting as just walking through the woods looking for squirrels to shoot, but there's a whole lot more to it. You learn to recognize every noise, every sound. If you see a limb shake you learn whether it's a bird or a squirrel. That's where I learned most of my shooting. I got to the point where I could throw a coin in the air and hit it with a rifle.

Once I was telling Earl McClung [another great shot] about how I learned how to do this. I started with a silver dollar and shot that. I moved down to a quarter and shot that. I took a nickel and shot that. But I tried and tried with a dime and never was able to hit that.

"Shit," McClung said, "if you can't hit a dime, you can't shoot a lick."

Dewitt Lowrey

I was born April 22, 1922, near Atmore, Alabama. Living on the farm meant lots of hard work for everybody, but it was a good way to grow up.

Our farm was far out in the country. My granddaddy had settled us out there. He owned a lot of land. The nearest neighbor was twenty-five miles. We had a radio but that was about it. We didn't get electricity until my early teens.

I have two brothers, one older, one younger, so I was the middle. I caught all the trouble. What kind of trouble? [laughs] Anything that came up, I was the one that did it—you know how that goes.

My family was pretty close. I don't reckon we could have had a better mother. But she also had a temper and knew how to use a switch. With Mama, you didn't cuss at all. Every once in a while I'd let slip with one of those words. So that meant a switch. Sometimes she just knew I needed one and gave it to me anyway. We were Methodists, and went to the church in a wagon. We didn't have a car. So we hooked the wagon up and away we went.

For first, second, and third grade, I had to walk 2½ miles to school each way. You got used to it. After that the county sent a bus to pick us up and we changed schools. I guess I was an average student. I was not a bright student by any means. But I did all right.

Daddy ran the farm when we were younger. When my brothers and I got old enough we took over the farm and Daddy worked at outside businesses: carpentry, as a guard at Atmore Prison, then in town at a grocery store's butcher shop. He had killed so many hogs and cows on the farm he knew how to cut them up and all. I liked farming. You were your own boss up to a point. You got up at 4:00 A.M. before daylight and fed the animals and milked the cows, then you got your breakfast and went to the fields. Everybody around where we lived did the same thing.

During the Depression we always had enough to eat. Daddy grew it and Mama put stuff up during the summer. We never lacked for food.

In fact, Daddy gave food away to people who didn't have enough to get by on.

Hunting and fishing—those were my favorite things to do. I liked to shoot doves and quail. I never had a bird dog when I was young, but I never needed one because I always knew where the quail roosted and where they fed. So any time Mama asked for some I went out and got us dove or quail for dinner.

I was in my early teens when I got my first deer. That was a big thrill for a country boy. Deer never came onto our farm, as big as it was, so we had to go to the swamp to get deer. There was always a group that went deer hunting together. You had a post where you were put so nobody got shot. It wasn't just boys who went, it was older men, too. When you got your first deer they bloodied your face. You didn't have a choice in it. They caught you and did it. I washed it off as best as I could in the creek before I went home. I was pretty proud still.

I've had knives all my life. I was pretty good with throwing a knife when I was a kid. We had this game called Mama Pig. You took an old Barlow knife with three blades and put the littlest blade in the ground. You tried to flip it to make it stick up on the big blade. It would be too dull for kids to play today. We didn't have the things they have now. But it took a lot of skill with a knife. I liked throwing a knife even better. It wasn't a contest—most of the time I was down by myself in the swamp, throwing it against a tree.

Buck Taylor

I've had my nickname, Buck, for as long as I can remember. I don't know where I got it. As a kid, I liked my real name okay—Amos—but Buck just seemed to fit me better.

Dad was with a bank in Philadelphia until all the banks closed during the Depression. He sold insurance after that, which he didn't like but had to do it to make ends meet. I don't know how Dad made out sometimes but we always seemed to manage. I guess you could say we were middle class, although no one had much during the Depression. We always seemed to have enough money for food. Dad enjoyed traveling so we did that a lot, even during the Depression.

I was always an outdoor type. There were four boys in our family. I'm the oldest. We were a close family, but I felt like the odd one out because I was always off in the woods somewhere, out on my own. I was in the Boy Scouts and made it to Eagle Scout. I loved being out in the wild. We lived on the edge of Northwest Philadelphia, near a beautiful valley with a creek flowing through it. I spent a lot of time exploring that.

By the time I got to high school I was camping out quite a bit. I don't think my mother knew where I was half the time. Once on Washington's Birthday, a three-day weekend, I got a couple of friends together to go camping in the mountains. Only problem was that it had just snowed like the dickens. Down below, traffic wasn't even moving on the side roads—it would be hard to even reach the mountains. Well, one of my friend's dads was a policeman. In those days a lot of coal trucks were on the road, and this guy's father stopped a coal truck for us and asked the driver to take us to the top of Hawk Mountain. That solved the problem of how to reach the mountains—his truck could make it through. So we hopped in, not realizing how crazy the plan was. From the highway, we got off the coal truck and trudged along railway tracks up into the mountains. We hiked far out into the snow, pushing our way through the drifts. I think we had only some canned food with us. We could have frozen to death—or starved if we had got lost. But it all worked out in the end. That's the type of kids we were—the type who went camping no matter how high the snow was.

After I graduated I took an office job with SKF Bearings in Philadelphia and worked there a couple of years. The war was just breaking out then. I went down to Baldwin Locomotives, who were making Sherman tanks now, and no longer locomotives, and got a job with Baldwin machining turret tops. I worked there until June 1942.

Frank Perconte

I was born March 10, 1917. I'm the oldest living member of Easy Company today. I'm ninety-one years old. My memory's not so good anymore, but I'll see what I can do here.

From as far back as I can remember I've always lived in Joliet, Illinois. My father ran a saloon. When I was nine or ten I used to go hang around with my dad. They had a pool table in there. Did I drink then? No. Not at all.

When I was twelve years old my dad died. It was 1929 and we went to live with my grandfolks across town in Joliet. There were four of us kids in the family, so it was a little tight. What did Dad die of? Well, he ran a tavern, so that's about all I can tell you. That's all I *want* to tell you. It was okay living with my grandparents. It meant living in a new neighborhood. I went to a different school and got to meet new friends. It wasn't bad at all. I really met most of the friends I have today down there. That's right—those are some good friends.

I was a fair student. We were Catholics and so we went to parochial schools. I graduated from high school in 1935. I was always sport-minded and played baseball for school. I played third base. My nephew, Jack Perconte, played with the Los Angeles Dodgers.

Jobs were scarce. Those were Depression days. But after high school I got a job. A couple of buddies and me went over to Gary, Indiana, and worked in a steel mill. We commuted out there and back every day. I ran a crane. I enjoyed the work. It was outdoors. It was a good job.

Ed Tipper

I was born in Detroit, Michigan, in 1921. My parents were both Irish immigrants. Dad came from Dublin. He had about a year or two of elementary school education only. When he was a young man he owned and operated his own pub, quite an accomplishment for his age and educational background.

My mother grew up in rural Ireland. She had more education than Dad, about nine or ten years. Mom and Dad came to the States, met, married, and had three children. One died within the first year. Then I came along. My other brother, John, a year younger than I, was born with a slight mental retardation. He died fairly young, at age forty-one.

When I was three my parents decided to move back to Ireland. We settled in Toomebridge, County Antrim, a small rural village in Northern Ireland, where we lived for the next two years. That part of Ireland was a paradise for a kid. It was completely safe. Every morning Mom opened our front door and said, "Go outside and play." All the kids' mothers did.

We played outside all day long. For lunch we ran to whichever house was closest and the mother there fed us. During the day we explored the countryside looking for bees' nests and honey. We chased butterflies. A favorite game was to trick another kid into bending over and holding that posture, then to coax a billy goat into bumping the kid from behind. We returned home from our play after dark. I was very fortunate to experience such an idyllic upbringing.

Dad was kind but very tough. He taught me how to box when I was small. Once I punched him in the face and knocked out two of his teeth. The dentist said he needed to have a couple more out. Dad said, "Naw, just pull them all out now and be done with it." The dentist pulled all his upper teeth, and Dad went home. Later that day at dinnertime he started chomping a regular meal just like that with his bloody gums. People like that don't exist anymore.

My father had an incredible work ethic. When we moved back to Ireland Dad ran a small general store and a coal yard. Everybody thinks the Irish burned nothing but peat, but if people ever got a little money they burned coal. When we returned to Michigan my father worked for the Hudson Motor Car Company. He ran a freight elevator and did general maintenance in the factory. It was humble work but it sustained us throughout the Depression. He had automatic retirement at sixty-five, but he fought the policy and won. He worked there until the day he died, at age seventy-four.

As a teenager, I know I gave my parents a lot of worries. I misbehaved in school and lost credit, which I had to make up on Saturdays. School officials let me walk through graduation ceremonies but even on the day of graduation I wasn't sure if I was going to get a real diploma or a blank. When they handed me my diploma I peeked inside. Fortunately, it was real. I graduated in 1939 from an inner city school in Detroit. They said the neighborhood was blighted, even back then, but we didn't think it was that bad.

Right after I graduated I worked for a major department store in Detroit, doing parcel and furniture delivery. The job had a hierarchy: the parcel delivery guys were at the bottom, the appliance delivery guys were at the top. I worked my way up and wound up delivering pianos and extra-heavy appliances such as walk-in refrigerators.

It took quite a while for me to realize and appreciate my parents' accomplishments—emigrating from a foreign country, then losing one child and having another child with special needs. They overcame these challenges and were able to give me a strong start. I think one of the most important lessons I learned from them was persistence, something my dad and mom both had. Persistence serves you well. Even if you don't have major skills or education, if you keep at your goal and don't swerve from that focus, you will succeed. Persistence is a tremendous quality, underestimated by most people, I would say.

Norman Neitzke

I was born February 12, 1926, in Milwaukee, Wisconsin. I had one brother, who died at birth, so I was basically an only child. My parents were both from Milwaukee. My grandparents were from Germany.

My father worked as a Milwaukee City firefighter, so he always had a steady paycheck, even through the Depression. He had fought for the American army and been wounded in World War I, gassed, and had been in the hospital for a while because of that. I know he was at Château-Thierry in France, an area that the 506th PIR went through in 1945, twenty-seven years later. I don't know much more about him in that capacity—he didn't say too much about the war. Not many men do.

Henry Zimmerman

My given name is Henry, though I go by either Henry or Hank. I was born March 26, 1925, in Larksville, Pennsylvania. There were seven boys in my family: me and two brothers, then I have four half brothers. Back then they had big families. I'm the oldest.

Dad worked in a coal mine. He wanted me to go to work, so he got me a job in the coal mines with him. I didn't have much schooling. I had to quit school, which I hated. I didn't want to quit, but my old man told me I had to go out and get a job. My old man was a tyrant. I was about fifteen when I quit school, maybe younger, I don't quite remember. This was just after the Depression, and times were rough. Luckily we always had enough to eat, but I wouldn't say we were loaded. We lived from day to day.

My brothers and I fought a lot but mostly good-naturedly. Everything was physical. Once for fun I climbed to the top of a big tree like Tarzan and yelled to my brothers below to cut it down. They did, so I rode the tree all the way down to the ground.

Well, I worked for two months in the coal mine, then one day Dad came home and said, "We're going to move to New Jersey and get a job down there." I was never so glad in my life. Just walking through those coal mines looking at the ceilings—a lot of guys were killed in cave-ins in those mines. I had a cousin killed in a cave-in. I hated the coal mines and wanted nothing to do with them, but my father was a very dominant man. In New Jersey he worked at Phelps Dodge Copper products. I got a job down there, too, making cables.

About that time I wanted a change. I was sixteen and I lied about my age to go into a CCC [Civilian Conservation Corps] camp [you had to be eighteen], and went back to Pennsylvania for this. It was mostly forestry work and building roads. I stayed with the CCC for two years, the maximum time allowed. When my time there was up I had to leave, but I wanted to stay so bad, I felt like crying. I loved it in the camp. And I learned a lot of things there. I slung a sledgehammer breaking rocks. I used a two-man saw and learned how to fall trees. I really loved it.

Frank Soboleski

My father was born in Poland and my mother in Austria. All of their children are first-generation Americans. I was born June 18, 1925, into a family of fourteen children, number eight from the top. I had eight sisters and five brothers, all of us born and raised on our farm in International Falls, Minnesota, so there were plenty of chores to keep us busy and strong. When I got my chores done, I liked to spend my time outdoors hunting, trapping, fishing, swimming, riding horses, and climbing trees. It didn't matter what season it was, I was always outdoors. I grew acclimated to all the seasons.

When I was thirteen I trapped a bobcat. Earlier I had found a moose carcass that was missing the hindquarters and had placed my trap near it. After school one evening I skied up to my trap and discovered the cat. I approached it, not knowing he had backed way up on the chain because he was trying to get away from me. Suddenly he sprang on me, claws out, stripping off my stag pants like corn off a cob. I fell sideways, grabbed one of my skis (still strapped on), and beat off my attacker. Then I loaded him up and took him back to the farm to skin him and collect a bounty.

Roy Gates

I was born (of all places) in New York City, July 25, 1921. My dad was a human resources type of guy. When I was quite young he went to Atlanta and became head of the Community Chest (now the United Way), so when I was ages four to eight, we lived in Georgia. Then he went to New York and was in the movie business. He made films like *The Silent Enemy* and *The Vikings*. My father did well financially in his earlier years, even through the Depression. In the movie business he associated with the Whitneys and the Vanderbilts, what they called old money. But he also had a little problem with alcohol, as did his son later on, so he pretty much blew it in later years and wasn't affluent after that.

I was only fifteen when I graduated from high school. They thought that because I had lived in France when I was a kid that I was smarter than I actually am, so they skipped me a couple grades. Dad had made a picture called *Through the Centuries*, which was all about the history of the Catholic Church, so Dad went back and forth in France working on that movie and getting permission from the pope. My mother and I stayed over there in 1930 and 1931, when I was nine and ten years old. I went to school near Versailles right outside of Paris. I learned how to speak French, which was a great help during the war because many people in Europe speak two or three languages, one of which is usually French. Some of the German prisoners, if they didn't speak English could speak French, so that was a good thing to know.

Later Dad started Marine Studios here in Florida, where I live today. He made underwater movies. He was with the studio until they opened in 1937 and was then bought out. So we went and lived in Key West on a boat. Here, I'll name-drop for you—Ernest Hemingway. I went to school with his son Jack when we lived outside of Versailles. (Jack was nicknamed "Bumby." He was the father of the models Mariel and the late Margaux Hemingway.) The Hemingways had a pool, and Bumby and I swam together as kids. He was a couple years younger than me, but since there were only a few Americans in the school in France we tended to stick together. Then later they moved over to Key West, so I knew Jack Hemingway in both places—Key West and France.

Did I get into many fights as a kid? Yeah—that's my middle name: fights. That's the reason I stayed a second lieutenant. When I went to the 10th Armored Division I roomed with a guy who was just out of West Point. I was just out of Texas A&M, and we partied and drank together. The next thing I knew he became my battalion commander. He decided that I knew too much about him and got on my case (this is just my side of the story, of course). At a private party he kept following me around telling me my rifle was dirty at inspection. Finally I had had too much of it and hit him. He wanted to court-martial me. But my commander said no because it happened at a private party. So the guy put an "S" on my efficiency report, the lowest score, which meant you couldn't get a promotion even if General Patton wanted to promote you. So I was a longtime second lieutenant.

To back up, I didn't enter university immediately after high school. After I graduated I figured I needed to grow up a little before college, so I got a gravy train job with the road department. My father had done some politicking in Tallahassee and knew the commissioner of the state road department. So I spent some time on an engineering crew. I didn't have any experience. The job was really handed to me. I entered university when I was eighteen and majored in economics and history.

Joe Lesniewski

I was born in Erie, Pennsylvania, on August 29, 1920. Dad worked at Griswold Manufacturing Company, making cast iron cookware. He spoke seven languages, and the FBI kept on bothering him because they wanted him to work with them, but Dad had a hard time speaking English. So over the years, I took it upon myself to teach him. All the kids in the neighborhood could speak English, so that's how I learned. I spoke fluent Polish as well.

As a kid, Dad had been sweet on a girl—they had both grown up in the same town in Poland. Unknownst to him, his family came to the

United States on the same boat as her family did. They met again in the States. They were still in love, so they got married. That was my mom and dad.

In the early 1920s and '30s, everybody was poor in Erie. Everybody looked for money and food. Nobody had much. You saw maybe two or three cars on the streets. You saw an airplane maybe once every two or three years. We had a place in one of the city's parks with a big building in it. The people who didn't have anything to eat went there—morning, afternoon, and evening, and could eat. It went on like that until the late 1930s.

From the time I was about thirteen years old onward, I did a lot of running. I ran from my home to Presque Isle Bay and back home again— ten miles round trip. I did that three to four times a week. Most of the kids in the neighborhood ran like that. We were very conscious of our physiques. In summers we went swimming across the channel, about four hundred to five hundred feet wide. We were all in pretty good shape.

I graduated from Erie Technological High School in 1939. You could study a lot of trades there: printing, drafting, woodworking, electrical engineering. I studied electricity and ran all the machines. I was taught to run any machine we had in our school building. For a year after graduation I worked in a CCC [Civilian Conservation Corps] camp on Bull Hill in Sheffield, Pennsylvania. They trained us in the CCC camps just like in the army. Each morning we got up early and ran five miles. We trained in close order drills with wooden rifles. They really put us through it. That helped put me in a good position to go into the service. I was able to get right to work after the CCC camps with General Electric, where I was a tool and dye maker for a year. Then I decided to volunteer for the army.

Ed Joint

I was born in Erie, Pennsylvania, in 1923. Yeah, I know Joe Lesniewski pretty well [also from Erie]—he followed me all around the war [laughs].

My father delivered coal. In those days they didn't have furnaces, they had coal stoves. As a little kid the truck used to come and dump it by a chute down in the cellar. It was a pretty dirty job. It was during the

Depression when I grew up, hardly anybody was working. You didn't see cars on the road or big stores or anything. Everybody I knew was poor.

We lived in the middle of the city—in those days Erie wasn't as big as it is today. My family was very poor. Yes, we always ate, but they had a food bank and we used to go up and get food for free. It was tough. You just didn't have stuff. You couldn't get a job. In my family there were eleven children. I was third from the last, nearly the baby. Rough as it was, we all got along pretty well. We made up our own games—kick the can, we always seemed to have a football around, maybe a baseball. We usually made our own baseballs.

We were Catholic and all grew up going to St. Patrick's Church and School. We had a nun for a teacher. You had better do your work or she'd crack you over the head or hit you on the shoulders with a stick for talking or fooling around. She'd crack you really good. Everybody was scared of her. I played a lot of sandlot football and a little bit of basketball—never in school, though. I liked sports and always played as much as I could. In high school I was about 5½ feet, maybe 130 pounds.

I used to help my father delivering ice. You picked up 25 pounds of ice with these prongs. If he had to go someplace he always called me to help. He sold the ice for 50 cents. He cut the ice up. That was the refrigerator—you had a big box in the house and you'd put the ice on top. Near the lake they had a little shack, two or three blocks from the ice. The ice didn't come off the lake. You had to get it at the place that made all the ice. Everybody would buy it. I delivered newspapers for a while, if you call that a job, but there just wasn't no places to work.

I had one other brother who went into the service. He made it through the war. Afterward he got married and lived pretty far away, but I managed to see him quite a bit. His name was Charlie, but we called him Chubby. I don't know why we called him that—he wasn't chubby. I had another brother, Gerald, and we called him Softy. I asked him, "Why do they call you Softy?" He worked in a coal place, so he said, "because of soft coal." I couldn't connect that, but that's what they called him anyway. I had another brother, Robert, and we called him Bibs. How the hell did he ever get that? Another brother, James, we called him Pep—I don't know why they called him that either. I was the only boy in the family who didn't get a nickname.

Al Mampre

I grew up in Oak Park, Illinois. Our family is Armenian. Dad was a carpenter early on but switched to Oriental rug repairing, which he did most of his life. My father managed to keep us going during the Depression. He worked hard day and night to keep us afloat. My mother was a housewife. During the war she participated in the Gray Ladies (Red Cross). There were two boys in our family, my brother and I. He was with Jimmy Stewart's air force [General James L. Stewart] as a teletype man.

As a boy, I had no idea I wanted to be a medic later on. I was a Boy Scout and took first-aid classes with them. My family is Episcopalian, so when I graduated from high school I thought I might want to go into the ministry. I went to a Methodist school first, Ohio Northern University, then a Baptist school, Hardin-Simmons, in Texas.

At Ohio Northern I joined a fraternity. I was the only fraternity boy who was a member of the Timothy Club, for preministerial students. My fraternity brothers could hardly wait until I became a preacher so they could sit in the front row and heckle me. They called me the PPP. One time at a fraternity dance somebody called me that and a girl wanted to know what it meant. I didn't want to tell her it meant *piss-poor preacher.*

Faith became more personal for me as the years went on, nothing I wanted to impose on anybody else. I also thought it would be unfair of me to go into the ministry and get married—in those days it was assumed that your wife would go into the ministry with you. So I didn't want to impose that on a wife who maybe didn't want to choose that sort of life. I went into psychology after the war.

Herb Suerth Jr.

My name is Herbert J. Suerth Jr. My dad was Herbert J. Suerth Sr., that's how I ended up with the nickname Junior in the outfit. My dad sold insurance for a living and also had a couple other jobs. In the Depression you did about anything and everything you could. He ended up being a model maker in a furniture manufacturing business. Dad was of German descent. Our last name traces back a thousand years from Cologne (sometimes spelled Köln), Germany. Our last name used to have an umlaut over the u, but it was dropped before World War I because of the anti-German feeling that existed in those days, and even worse as we approached World War II. My grandparents were both born in the United States.

I was born in Chicago, Illinois, on October 28, 1924, an only child. My dad did not speak English until he went to grammar school, but I never knew that until years later because he never spoke with an accent. I learned a little German from him but not enough to get me a drink of water in Berlin. We were middle-class. Dad inherited a few thousand dollars in 1937 and he and Mom bought a house in a nice middle-class neighborhood. They lived in that house until they moved in with me and my wife in 1956.

I grew up in Chicago. I'm a product of a very Christian/Catholic family. I went to a Catholic grammar school, then spent most of my high school experiences at a Catholic school, DePaul Academy, a high school attached to DePaul University.

Out of ninety graduates from DePaul, four or five were already in the service by the time we graduated. I enrolled in Marquette University in mechanical engineering the summer of 1942, then went to university that September. Before the semester was out, Congress lowered the draft to include all eighteen-year-olds (the upper limit was age thirty-seven), and we knew that we would all be drafted if we didn't enlist. I chose to enlist. I stayed in university until the end of the semester; then, rather than start another semester, I dropped out and worked for a couple months. This proved to be a good decision, because all the guys that I was in class with were all on the same train going to Fort Belvoir, Virginia, a few months later.

When I dropped out of university to work for a few months, I had no job skills to speak of, but you could get a job just about anywhere right then because the country was revving up for the war. My mother worked in the accounting department of a foundry, so I got a job there, working in a factory that made metal castings. Everybody on the crew was Hispanic. No one spoke English. I worked there to get myself toughened up. I worked a different shift than my mother, so we didn't commute together. Every morning I rode an hour and fifteen minutes on a streetcar to be at work by 6:30 A.M. I worked manually all day. When I came into the service it was really a breeze for a while. Getting up early didn't mean a thing to me, and most of the physical training early on was not that difficult.

My call came up in March 1943. By that time some of the classmates who had dropped out of the school when the war started were already overseas. Those early draftees got yanked into combat early. One of the reasons I had enlisted when I did was so I could select my branch of service. I figured since I had studied mechanical engineering I should go into the Army Corps of Engineers, so that's where I went at first. I shortly found out that it didn't involve much mechanical engineering and was mostly construction, deactivating mines, building bridges and roads, not what I wanted.

Forrest Guth

We grew up near Allentown, in rural Pennsylvania. During the Depression we didn't have much money, but we had good parents who always provided for us. In his earlier years my father was a teacher in a one-room schoolhouse. Then he worked as a station agent for the Redding Railroad. They closed during the Depression, and he worked in a cement mill. Then he went back on the railroad. My mother worked in a clothing factory. They were hardworking people, Pennsylvania Germans. We had four children in my family, three boys and a girl. One of my brothers went into the navy. My sister was a nurse. My other brother was the smart one and became superintendent of a cement firm—it was a defense industry position, and he didn't go to war.

My parents never gave us kids money to buy things. If you wanted something, you had to work for it and save up. I worked for other farmers harvesting potatoes and earned enough money to buy a bicycle. Being poor was actually a good experience because it taught me how to improvise. I learned how to make things and be mechanically inclined. If I needed a part for my bike I couldn't go to a hardware store and pick it up. But we had a dump close by so I'd go there and look around. We found enough wood at the dump to build a little boat. It was helpful to learn all that. Later on in the service I became the armorer for the guys. I could repair and modify weapons. When we came back to England from Normandy I altered a few carbines for the guys. Sometimes I fixed their rifles. In combat you didn't have much to do because there are always lots of weapons around that aren't being used anymore. So it's easy to resupply then.

Out in the country our school went up to eighth grade. But for high school, we had to go by bus to the city. I graduated from high school and went to work with Bethlehem Steel, making armor plates for battleships. The job was in the defense industry, which meant I was exempt from military service. But I had two crazy friends, Rod Strohl and Carl Fenstermaker, who talked us all into going into the paratroops. The three of us enlisted in August 1942 and stayed together through most of the war. All of us were in the hospital at one time together. All three of us came back after the war.

CHAPTER THREE

Young Lions, West

Earl McClung

I was born April 27, 1923, on the Colville Indian Reservation, up in northeastern Washington State. I'm three-eighths Indian. My mother was half Indian, my father was a quarter.

During the Depression we were poor but we always had enough to eat. There was always wild game. We always raised a garden. My mother always canned. Eating was never a problem, but sometimes it got awfully cold in the winter because the building we lived in wasn't that good.

Hunting and fishing—that's what I loved to do as a kid—anything outdoors. I trapped beavers, muskrats, coyotes. Once in a while I got a mink. I killed my first deer when I was eight years old. I was with my father. We were on horses, quite a ways up in the mountain. There was snow on the ground. He spotted it and handed me his rifle. He said, "Here, you want to shoot a deer?" I sat down and shot it. We dressed it up and brought it home. It was really something—it sure was to me, anyway—I was beside myself. Ammunition was hard to get for one thing, and I was amazed that he let me shoot his gun. That's why I knew I better not miss. His gun was an old World War I 30–40 Krag. I had a .22 that

I carried all the time and I was pretty good with that. I had killed grouse before but never a deer.

On an Indian reservation, you more or less learned to fight before you learned to walk. If you don't learn to fight, you wouldn't get on your feet long enough to learn to walk. It guess it was tough growing up, but I never really thought about it. I thought that's what everybody did. I never noticed alcohol while growing up, but some of the kids did. I never drank until I got in the service. After the war it got to be a bigger problem.

I went to school in a little town called Inchelium, Washington. There was one teacher and eight grades, maybe only fifteen kids total. I never did really good in high school. We had a lot of work to do around the home, and I missed a lot of school. They drafted me in February 1943, which didn't matter to me—I knew I was going in anyway. I wouldn't have graduated until June of that year, but they graduated me early.

Ed Pepping

I was born in Alhambra, California, on Independence Day 1922. Growing up, we always had big family celebrations on the Fourth of July. Mom made a birthday cake in a huge dishpan. Everybody came over, and we had enough people in my extended family to make two softball teams.

Dad used to work twelve to fourteen hours a day. During the Depression he worked for Ralph's Grocery Company in Los Angeles, but the store he worked for was destroyed during the big earthquake of 1933, so Dad was let go. After that my dad and uncle painted houses for thirty-five cents an hour, doing whatever they could to make ends meet. We grew vegetables in our backyard and ate healthy foods. We did all right.

During the Depression we had nothing but we had everything—we had each other. We didn't need to have television to entertain ourselves. Many times we kids just sat on the lawn in a circle and played games or talked. Everybody in the neighborhood had a lot of friends. We played kick the can, rode bicycles, and roller-skated. Everybody had roller skates. We took the skates apart for the steel wheels and made box scooters out of wooden boxes and old two-by-fours.

Our neighborhood was a combination of Latino and Caucasian families. All the kids played together. If the weather was bad we invited kids to our house. We had a pool table and a huge dining room with a fire-place. As many as twenty-five kids came to our house for games, sleeping on the floor of our dining room overnight. As long as the kids acted right they were welcome, but if anyone caused problems he was sent home. Being banished from the other kids was considered a horrible punishment.

You could drive in town when you were twelve years old. I got my license at thirteen. Our family had an old 1926 Buick. Alhambra had streetcars then and tracks going down the streets. You could put your car in the streetcar track at one end of town, start driving and not touch the wheel, and go all the way through town on the tracks. We packed up to nine kids in the car, with everybody hanging out the window beating on the side and went to football games that way. The kids all played bumper tag with their cars. Somebody would be "it." Everybody else parked some-place around town and hid. The person went to look for them. When he found a car he'd bump it with the bumper. Then that person was "it." Nobody really got out of line. The police knew everybody. Anybody who touched liquor or drugs—they were considered outlaw kids.

I was just barely thirteen when I went into high school in Alhambra. We had a wonderful school music teacher, and I joined the orchestra and played kettle drums. When I was fourteen I played in the Pasadena Symphony. The San Gabriel Valley Opera Company recruited in our school, and I learned how to sing opera in two different languages, Italian and French. Half the time I didn't know what I was singing, but it was a very good school experience. I don't think kids had as many distractions then as they do today. We made our own toys and got old bicycles and recon-structed them. We had a marvelous library in town and always read books.

I had no idea what I wanted to be when I grew up. I never considered medicine, though later I became a medic in the paratroops. I spent many years in Boy Scouts and took first-aid classes, but that was about it. A medic needs to have a certain amount of compassion, but he's also got to have strength. Looking back now, I think what helped develop these qualities in me was a creed that a buddy and I adopted as our own. As kids we were fascinated with the stories of the Knights of the Round Table—King Arthur, Sir Lancelot, Sir Ector—extraordinary warriors who lived with service, honor, and valor: that's what impressed us. We made wooden swords and dashed around. The knights were our heroes as young boys. They were all we hoped to become.

Clancy Lyall

I was born October 14, 1925, in Orange, Texas. My father and grandfather were from Scotland. How did our family get to Texas from Scotland? Well, in those days these old steam vessels came across the Atlantic up the Gulf of Mexico over to Texas and picked up barrels of oil, then returned to Scotland—that's what my dad did for work. On one trip to America—1921, I think—my father landed in Texas and went inland to see the Native Americans. He wound up in Oklahoma, where he met a girl and fell in love. On his next trip over, they got married. My mother was a full-blooded Cherokee.

Mom and Dad bought a farm in Texas, where I spent my childhood. The farm was about 120 acres, 20 of which we tilled. We also had chickens and cows. My father made some money from his work on the tanker but it wasn't much, so during the Depression we used to barter stuff we raised on the farm. We might barter a dozen eggs to get a sack of flour. Then Mom might use the flour sack to make us clothes. We weren't rich by any means, but we got along okay. With Dad's job we only saw him about every three months whenever he returned from the trips. I was an only child, so it was just Mom and me working the farm. As soon as I learned how to walk, I learned how to follow a mule out in a field.

Then there was wood. It was an everyday job for me. The only heat we had in the house came from a huge wood cooking stove in the kitchen. It never snowed in Texas, but it got down to twenty degrees in winter. By the end of fall, if you didn't have all your wood in, you were hurting.

I chopped thirteen cords for the year and kept four cords on the front porch and half a cord in the kitchen. The kitchen floor was just dirt, but Mom kept it clean. I soon figured out how to saw up wood an easier way. After I chopped down the trees, I hitched up our mule and drug the trees up to our house. We had an old Model T Ford. I jacked the Ford up and put a belt on it attached to a table saw. It worked. That's how it went. A lot of kids around that area did the same type of work I did.

In school I was an average student. We had a one-room schoolhouse

with maybe fifteen students in it at any one time. Sure, I got in a lot of
fights at school—you know: *half-breed, your mother's a squaw*—I heard
stuff like that a lot. Also, you have to realize in that part of Texas everybody
is named Jake or Big John—and my mother named me Clarence. That got
me into a lot of fights, too. I always wondered why in the hell she named
me that—there were no Clarences in my family. I asked her once. She said,
"Don't you know what Clarence means in Latin? Illustrious one." I thought,
Oh, shit [laughs]. I grew up defending myself, that's for sure.

I hunted a little as a kid, but not much—mostly squirrels, snakes,
small stuff. When I was about nine or ten the cattle people paid ten dollars apiece for a cougar. My friends and I went out with Winchesters and
didn't come back in until we got at least two cougars each. Then each fall
we went over to the swamps in Louisiana and picked moss to sell for mattresses. I think we got ten cents a load. We thought we were rich.

About that time, I was maybe nine, my father taught me how to swim.
The Sabine River in Texas divides Texas and Louisiana. Swimming in
that nasty-ass river are water moccasins, copperheads, little crocodiles.
Dad threw me right in. I doggied out of that place like you never saw. But
I always knew if I had a problem, he'd jump in after me. Years later he
was on a merchant marine ship and got torpedoed while crossing the Atlantic. I was joking with him about the experience:

"Good thing you can swim," I said.

"Swim?" he said. "Hell, I can't swim."

Was Dad hard on me? Nah. He taught me that you can do anything
if you put your mind to it and don't be afraid of it. I carried this all
through my time in the war—I still carry it today: what's going to happen
is going to happen. Forget about yesterday, don't think about tomorrow,
get through today—that's how we worked.

I laugh about it now—Dad had this old bagpipe brought over from
Scotland. He couldn't really play it but he liked to make a lot of noise.
Whenever he came home he sat on the back porch with it. All the animals
would take off.

In 1939, when I was thirteen, we moved up to Pennsylvania, where
my father started working for an oil company. We were able to see him
more there, about once every fourteen days. That's where I gave myself
the nickname Clancy. Life went better for me after that.

Don Bond

I'm probably the baby of the Band of Brothers. I was born January 29, 1926, didn't join Easy Company until Hagenau, and I had my nineteenth birthday on the boat ride over to Europe. One guy my age was Johnny Martin, although he was a three-mission man. Johnny went in the service when he was fifteen, or something like that. His folks let him fib about his age to get in. By the time I got in he was already a sergeant. Some of the guys like Leo Boyle—I think he was fourteen years older than Martin and me.

After I was born we lived in Baker City, over in eastern Oregon. Mom and Dad had come out there when they were little kids in the 1890s. My grandmother taught school in a mining town called Granite, Oregon. It's a ghost town now, but back then it was bigger than LeGrand is today.

When I was six months old, Dad went to work in timber, so we moved over to Bend, then we moved back to Nampa, Idaho. I went to all of grade school and my first two years of high school in Boise. In many ways Boise feels like home to me, even though we live in Oregon today.

My family, we were working people, but during the 1930s I don't think there was anybody very rich. Fortunately, my dad had a pretty good job during the Depression. He made a hundred dollars a month driving a truck for a wholesale grocery company. Every other night he was home. We didn't hurt for anything. We had plenty of clothes and a decent house, five milk cows, and a well. Every morning I pumped water for the cows and milked five cows every morning and night.

I left high school at the end of my sophomore year and was going to go into the navy. But I'm color-blind, so they wouldn't take me. So I worked for a roofing company making paper and shingles in Portland. It burned down one night in a huge fire. Then I worked for a sand and gravel outfit driving a truck for just a little bit. I had a girlfriend from high school and her dad was the superintendent of the company out on Ross Island there in Portland. I had to go to work on a tugboat to get out there.

The next January I turned eighteen and they drafted me a few months later, in May. The draft didn't surprise me at all. I wanted to go and had tried to get in. When I came home from the service I was going to finish high school, but they did some tests and gave me a GED instead. They did that with a lot of GIs who didn't finish high school.

Bill Wingett

I was born in July 1922. My dad was an auto mechanic and a truck driver. He worked for P. F. Johnson and Son in Richmond, California. During the Depression, P. F. Johnson kept busy, so we never had down times, like so many people had. We never went hungry. Dad hauled a lot of produce. When it was watermelon season, we ate watermelon preserves till they were coming out of our ears. When it was apple time, we ate apple pies. The hardest thing was that Dad drove that truck such long hours. He used to haul bathtubs from Richmond to Los Angeles—five days on the road at forty-five miles per hour in those old trucks. We saw him on weekends; that was it. There were no such thing as forklifts, either—whatever Dad carried, it was all by muscle. That was Dad—muscle from top to bottom.

After five days on the road, Dad came home tired. He wanted to get some rest. Mom always complained to him about whatever me or my brothers did when he was gone. I had a half brother and three other brothers. So whenever Dad came through the front door, he just lined up the five of us boys and started at the top with a heater hose. He figured we needed a licking for one thing or another. But then it was over.

I had a good childhood, but when I got into junior high I became a little unruly. I never did anything really bad. It's hard to know exactly what the hell turned old Principal Schellenberger against me. I didn't hate him. I sure didn't like him, though. I got thrown out of school and went to the California Junior Republic, a vocational high school for boys. I ended up doing pretty well at my new school. When I graduated I got the state bankers' award and the FFA award. I studied farming and animal husbandry. In my junior year, old Pop Forester, one of the teachers, thought I was about the best thing that come down the road as far as a farmhand was concerned. I guess I'm bragging. But that's not all—the last few years I've participated in county fairs. I got to drive the Budweiser Clydesdale team, twice. These are heavy draft horses. It's not everybody who gets to do that. But I did.

Rod Bain

My father was a cook when he enlisted into the U.S. Army in order to fight the Germans in World War I. He and his brothers and sister had immigrated to the United States from northern Scotland around 1900 and settled in Portland, Oregon. My dad decided to volunteer into an infantry company, as he felt he wasn't really doing much to end the war as a cook. No sooner had he joined the infantry when he was seriously wounded during a German shelling. He was hospitalized in the States for a long period of time while healing.

My mother's family also emigrated from northern Scotland around 1900. It wasn't long before the two met and were married. My dad owned and operated restaurants in the Portland area for quite some time. Disaster struck my family as the Depression overcame the economy, and at this time my mother died, leaving my sister and I motherless.

It didn't take long for my dad to find another mate. She had two children and was having a hard time of it, as she was divorced and living hand to mouth. Once again we were a family, this time with two boys and two girls.

We moved from Portland and bought a large house in Long Beach, Washington, a summer resort area that drew many visitors. Most people burned wood for heat and cooking, and my father, seeing an opportunity, bought a truck and began hauling scrap lumber pieces from a lumber yard some thirty miles away. It was profitable, and we four kids finished high school at Ilwaco High School in Washington.

My stepbrother was killed while taking flight training in Texas. I received the news while stationed in Aldbourne, just before the invasion of Normandy.

CHAPTER FOUR

The Day Everything Changed

Joe Lesniewski

I remember it so well. I had graduated high school and was working as a tool and dye maker for GE. I had saved enough money to buy a brand-new car, a 1941 Oldsmobile. There were four buddies of mine from the neighborhood. We got together one day and started talking about taking a trip to Canada. So we decided to go to Buffalo and then cross into Canada. We crossed the border and went to a souvenir place. As we walked in, this guy was standing there with a weird stare in his eyes. He said, "You guys got your guns?"

And we're like, "What's he talking about?"

Then he said, "You got your uniforms?"

We said no.

"Well," he said, "the Japanese just bombed Pearl Harbor."

Everybody got so still. Right when we heard that, we turned around, got in our car, and went back to Erie. From the time we left Canada until we got back to Erie, nobody spoke a word. We knew what was happening. This meant war. Then, when we found out how bad it was—how many people had got killed and how many of our ships had got sunk—we were really mad.

Years later I met a guy who was on one of the battleships moored at Pearl Harbor when the Japanese planes came in one after another. They dropped eight torpedoes on the ship he was on. He was on one side of the boat by himself. There were about eighty or ninety guys on the other side of the boat. When the first torpedo hit, he got blown into the air about a hundred feet and went into the water. He was one of the few who survived. Those guys on those boats that were sunk—I would not have wanted to be there when that happened for anything.

Frank Perconte

I was here at home in Joliet. It was on a Sunday, and we heard it on the radio. What was my reaction? Well, a war with another country, my God. We were all surprised.

The draft was on, and we were about to be drafted. So we enlisted instead. That way we knew when we were going. I was twenty-six when I joined. We went to a theater and saw a show about paratroopers. When they said they were paying paratroopers extra money, well, that was that. Why else would we jump out of a perfectly good airplane?

Clancy Lyall

I was at home. We had an old Selco radio and used to listen to the soaps. It was Sunday when the news broke. Within about two months most everybody was lying about their age to get into the service.

Did I lie? Sure. Mom let me go. She knew I was going to enlist anyway. I didn't have a birth certificate because a midwife delivered me, so there was no way to prove how old I was. At 16 I was big for my age, 5 foot 11, about 160 pounds. So me and another couple fellows reported to the draft board and told them we were 18.

"Hell," the man said, "you want to go in now or in two weeks?"

"We're ready now," we answered. They didn't care how old we were.

What was our motivation for signing up? Everybody was real patriotic back then. Everybody helped everybody else. I didn't know where Pearl Harbor was, but our navy was there, and the enemy had killed our people. So that was enough for me.

You've got to think that enlisting was an adventure, too. We had all grown up watching cowboy and Indian movies. They never shot back. So we were going to go over there and the enemy was going to run away—just like in the movies.

Well, they sure didn't do that in real life.

Ed Joint

I was downtown in a park. There was a kid selling papers saying, "Extra! Extra!" I was with a couple other kids. We didn't know what he was talking about. We hollered, "What's going on?"

He said, "There's a war. They bombed Pearl Harbor."

We weren't impressed. One guy said, "Aw, we'll send a couple ships down and they'll snake 'em. That war will take a week and they'll be over with it."

I enlisted that same month. I was kinda young when I went in—not yet 18. It was getting so everybody was going in the service. A lot of them were being drafted and had no choice. I saw that going on, so figured I might as well join up when I could decide what I wanted to do. All the guys I knew were enlisting. None of them were staying home.

I had just finished high school when I enlisted. They let me finish early. Usually you had to be eighteen to join the service, but somehow they passed me right through, they were probably hurting for people. I think they just turned their heads. I didn't lie about my age, no one ever asked.

Bill Wingett

I was at an all-night party in Crockett, California, with a girl named Virginia Russell. Her dad had been a truck driver at the same place as my dad. Then her dad had taken a job at a brickyard where they lived. That's where the party was. I stayed overnight. When we got up next morning, someone turned on the radio. Every time the music stopped, someone flipped it to another station, so it wasn't until noon, December 7, 1941, before any of us learned about Pearl Harbor. I got right in the car and went home. The next day early in the morning I drove to San Francisco and joined up. The feeling was a little different then—I think every one of us had it. The country needed us. We needed to do what needed to be done—I like to say that the country needed it, my family needed it, and I needed it—it was that simple.

You can understand, there was an awful lot of confusion in the system all at once. So they signed me up in the army and sent me home, saying as soon as we've got some place to send you, we'll be in touch. That was December 8.

Well, on December 9, I got into an automobile wreck. I went to the big army hospital in Frisco—Letterman General. The car had rolled over on me. I had been driving with my mother and another fellow. (Dad had gone back into the army when they called up the National Guard, and my mother divorced him then.) I had a broken collarbone, broken pelvis, broken arm, and was smashed on the side of the head. I was all screwed up. I was in the hospital until May 1, 1942. When I got out, the army said they couldn't use me anymore because of the accident. So I was no longer a soldier.

I went back to my job as an apprentice carpenter. I worked for a guy with one arm, digging ditches for foundations, doing the crapwork, really low. I hated the job. I had always lived around a lot of construction—that's how I got the job. You follow the flow, that's how it goes.

On August 19, 1942, I didn't go to work. I went back to the recruiting office and enlisted again, only this time I didn't mention the car accident. I passed their physical. I don't know if they lost my first records or what. It wasn't like today, where they go to the computer. I don't even remember having discharge papers the first time.

Everett Gray, Bill Dukeman, Pat Christenson, Dick Garrod, and I [five men who would become part of Easy Company] all joined the army in San Francisco on the same day. We met in the recruiting office. We weren't from the same hometown or anything. Christenson and I were both from California, but I was from Richmond, while Christenson came from Oakland. The other two guys came from Keenesburg, Colorado. I don't know where Garrod was from. Dukeman and Gray had been touring around on motorcycles, seeing the country. Their motorcycle broke down somewhere near San Francisco, so they decided to sell their motorbike and join the army.

They put us up in a hotel that first night with a bunch of other enlisted men. The next morning we all went back to the recruiting office. That's where we found out about the Airborne. We were all interested. What were we thinking? Who knows? None of us knew anything about the Airborne, but hey, we were all strapping young guys, full of piss and vinegar, and—why not join the paratroopers?—this is something new! Could be the adventure of our lives! There was a General Wingate in the British army in Burma, related to me distantly—hell, we might end up there! I don't think any of us four in the group thought we'd end up in Europe. We all thought *Jap*. Hell, we were all West Coast. We weren't even thinking about Europe.

Herb Suerth Jr.

Pearl Harbor happened when I was still in high school. I was seventeen in December 1941. I played football the last two years of high school. Football season was over for the year by December, but we had a neighborhood scrimmage organized in a park. On that Sunday, it was probably one or two in the afternoon, I came home from playing football. My dad's mother lived with us at the time, and when I came inside the front door, Grandma stood at top of stairs and said, "We're at war." I knew what she meant right away. The way she said it, very flatly, she was upset. She had had three sons in World War I.

As the radio reports came in, we found out more. I don't think it dawned on me at that point—I was going to be eighteen in less than a year. I guess I realized I was going to be involved in the war sooner or later, but didn't think too much about it.

Pearl Harbor pretty much rattled through our neighborhood. One of my aunt's close friends had a son killed on the USS *Arizona*. Goslin was his last name. His name is on the monument there today. He was a young guy, very wealthy family, just out of Annapolis Naval Academy.

Forrest Guth

It was a Sunday afternoon, and I was on my way to work at Bethlehem Steel, where I was on the swing shift. When we heard the news we were all shocked. In those days we had no idea where Pearl Harbor was, the same way we had no idea where Normandy was. I guess we were peeved, too. We were burned up that we could be invaded. It was a new idea to us—that we could be brought down if the enemy tried hard enough.

Rod Strohl and Carl Fenstermaker (two other Easy Company members) and I had grown up together. We went through grade school and always hung around. I didn't have to go to war because my job at the foundry meant I was exempt. But we just figured . . . well, if you go, I'll go—that type of thing. We talked ourselves into it. I'm glad we did it.

As kids we didn't have clubs to go to. You made your own entertainment then. We all seemed to get a car quite early—as soon as we turned sixteen. You could buy a fairly good car for seventy-five dollars back then. My first car was an old 1929 Whippet, rather small, a four-door, nothing fancy. Rod's father was a car dealer, so he had it made. Carl's father was a farmer and worked for a dairy as a truck driver. Carl and Rod and I went to a lot of parks and picnics and ran around with the girls. There were great musical programs that we went to, mostly Western hillbilly music. We enjoyed that a lot. It was a good, wholesome growing up.

When I enlisted, there was no opposition from my parents. They weren't overjoyed about me going to war, of course, but they were very patriotic people. We enlisted early on, in 1942, so there wasn't much reporting on deaths yet or anything. I'm sure they weren't aware of what was coming. My parents and I always kept in touch during the war as best we could. Mail was slow. It took a week or two to get a letter, even longer to get a package. So it was hard to keep in touch, but we all tried hard.

Rod and Carl and I took a streetcar from Allentown to Philadelphia and were sworn in. We had our examination and got our clothing, then went on a steam train to a camp near Harrisburg. Along the way we picked up a few guys. Walter Gordon was one we met on the train. He lived in Mississippi. They had turned him down in Mississippi because of flat feet, so he came to Pennsylvania to enlist. He was a very good soldier. Traveling from Pennsylvania to Georgia, it was summertime, and we were in this dirty old train, quite small. A mainline train came through and we had to get off on a sideline somewhere to wait for it to pass.

Rod Bain

I was minding my own business as a student at the University of Washington when suddenly we were in a world war with no apparent limitations. December 1941, the Japanese bombed Pearl Harbor. Many students quit university and signed up for various military branches. We faced the task of defeating Germany and Japan, the two powers who wanted to rule our world.

I was nineteen and decided to finish the school year. I was a member of the U.S. Army Reserve, so I figured I'd be going soon enough. In the Reserves we learned short-order drills, listened to lectures by old-time sergeants of the regular army, and marched. After graduation from college we were to become part of the army as officers.

July 1942, I volunteered anyway, although I wasn't done with college yet. The sergeant in charge of the recruitment office told me to come back in a month. I went to see my parents at our home at Long Beach, Washington, a seaside resort town of beauty and calm. It was the last calm I saw for quite a while.

Vacation over, the recruiting sergeant sent me by truck to Fort Lewis, Washington. If felt strange to me—my father had enlisted at Fort Lewis for World War I.

On my first day in the army, they placed me on KP. The next day, the assembled draftees took an IQ test. After the test, an announcement was made asking the assembled soldiers if they would like to volunteer for an Airborne unit. If you qualified as a jumper, an extra fifty dollars per month was assured. I was the only volunteer out of probably two hundred, and many a strange look came my way.

The next day, my second as a member of the U.S. Army, I was again placed on KP.

Day three, they outfitted us in army uniforms, with shoes and overalls and everything.

Day four, I was on my way by train to the great state of Georgia, where Airborne men gathered. Never having been out of the states of Oregon or Washington, I enjoyed the cross-country travel—the Rockies, the plains, then finally the Deep South.

Ed Pepping

You've probably never heard this from a paratrooper, but when Pearl Harbor happened, I was recording the Metropolitan Opera. The Metropolitan just happened to be a favorite of mine—I forget which opera they were performing. We had a recording machine where you recorded music from the radio with a stylus. President Roosevelt came on and announced the bombing of Pearl Harbor. I recorded the announcement but lost it over the years. Boy, I wish I had that today.

At nineteen I worked in an electroplating plant. I was already the foreman. That's not as glorious as it sounds—all the guys were going into the service, and I had become foreman only by elimination. We plated all the tools for Wright Air Force Base.

Right away my dad and I became air raid wardens in our neighborhood. Everybody just did what they could. I worked at the plant until I was almost twenty, but staying at home got to be too much. Everybody was going into the service. The attitude was that this was our country, and we had to go. I really wish that you could have felt the aura of that time. It was indescribable. The whole country was united. I just felt I had to enlist. My mother signed for me because Dad was at work.

Two buddies and I went to sign up in LA. As I walked down a hallway to join the air force as an aerial gunner, I noticed a table with all these sharp-looking guys around it with parachutes on their caps. A sign read, "Do you dare?" That was as far as we got. My buddies and I signed up for the paratroopers. In a short time we were headed down to Fort MacArthur.

Shifty Powers

After I graduated high school, some of us guys went down and enrolled in a vocational school in Norfolk. I took a machinist course. That's where I first met Popeye Wynn.

Popeye and I finished the course and went to work in the shipyards in Portsmouth. We found out they were going to freeze everybody to their jobs on account of the war effort (we had just started in on Germany). I said to Popeye, "Now, we don't want to get left out of this war. If we're going to get into it, we'd better do it now." So we both went over and signed up for the army paratroopers. When we came back to the shipyards and quit, the guy in charge really jumped on us. We were supposed to stay there and work on those ships, he said. He called a recruiter who said, "There ain't nothing you can do about it. They signed the papers. They're in the army now."

So we left there together—Popeye and I. We went to a little camp in Virginia, where we got our uniforms and all our shots. We were there for a week. Then they sent us to Toccoa.

Al Mampre

I graduated from high school in 1940, so I was in college in 1941. I was home in December and watching a football game when the bombing of Pearl Harbor was announced.

That February I left Ohio Northern and transferred to Hardin-Simmons. It was ten degrees below when I left Ohio. I wore a big old horse blanket around me when I left. When I got to Texas they were all in short-sleeved shirts.

Later that spring (1942) I enlisted, wanting to be a paratrooper. I enlisted in Dallas at the Mineral Springs Induction Center and was shipped to Toccoa, where they were just forming the 506th.

Henry Zimmerman

I was in Elizabeth, New Jersey, then, when they attacked Pearl Harbor. I got in line to enlist. I wanted to get over there and fight. There was a long line of young guys looking to enlist. But they told me I was too young, so I had to wait.

Several times I tried to enlist, but they kept rejecting me, saying I had too much sugar in my urine. Around the third time they rejected me I said, "What in the hell do I need to do to get into the army?!"

The guy said, "You want to go that bad?"

I said, "Why in the hell do you think I keep coming here?!"

I had to wait until they finally drafted me. I went in December 31, 1943. I was eighteen. They came down the line pointing to us saying army, navy, army, navy, and that's where we went. I wound up in the army.

Don Bond

We were living in Boise then. I was about fifteen at the time. I had a sister about ten years older than me who had two boys; the oldest was about seven. My folks and I were over at her house for dinner. I had taken my nephew over on my bike to Gowen Field to see the planes; it was only about a mile away. For some reason that day the B-26s were really flying around, lots more than usual—just taking off and landing. We headed home and heard the news about Pearl Harbor on the radio.

My brother, Lou, was seven years older than me. Everyone was worried about him having to go into the service. Nobody ever thought I'd have to go. My brother went into the air force. He went over to Spokane, then to Douglas, Arizona. In four years he never went anywhere except those two places. I was in the service for 20½ months and was in 9 foreign countries and a bunch of states. I really saw the world.

Roy Gates

I think everybody remembers Pearl Harbor. I was a sophomore at A&M and had been to a movie that Sunday. When I came back the radios were all on, telling about Pearl Harbor. My first thought was that we were into it up to our necks. My second thought was Wow, well, here we go.

A&M was an ROTC college, so we were technically already in the army upon enrollment as university students. For the first two years you were required to be in the corps. Then you got a contract with the government to get a commission the last two years. Because of the extra training, we went to school year-round.

When we graduated they sent us to Camp Beauregard in Louisiana, then to Fort Sill for thirteen weeks of field artillery, where I went through OCS school to become an officer. From there I went to the 10th Armored Division.

What was my initial goal in the military? To get out! [laughs]. After it was explained to me what an S meant on my report (the poor grade I received for fighting with my battalion commander at A&M), I knew I wasn't going to go anywhere in the service. So it was a matter of putting in time. But I was gung ho to get overseas and get into the fighting.

Dewitt Lowrey

I finished the eleventh grade, then got a job loading boats in the ship-yards. I was making big money. I had every intention of returning to school, but by then all my buddies had gone to the service.

I tried to get into the navy with my cousin. They turned me down because they said I was color-blind. About two weeks later I went down to the post office and saw Uncle Sam pointing his finger at me saying, "I need you." A paratrooper sign was over on the left and I said, "Now, that sounds exciting."

So I went over to the recruiting sergeant and said, "I'll join, but I don't want the regular army, I want the paratroops, nothing else."

He said, "That, I can't assure you."

I said, "If I don't make it, I want to get back out and join the air force as a bombardier."

He said, "I think that can be arranged."

I joined up right there. I think it was after dinner. They carried me out to the country for Mama to sign my papers so I could get in. Then they shipped me out that night. I went to Fort McPherson, then over to Toccoa.

As it turned out, I made the paratroopers all right, and everything went smooth from then on.

Why did I volunteer for the paratroopers? Well, I had never done anything like that before, and it sounded like fun. In fact, it *was* fun—until they sent us overseas.

Fortunately, I didn't get the same test for color-blindness that I had in the navy. With the navy, they gave me a page full of colored dots and I had to say which number was on it. I got one of those wrong, so that was it for the navy. Now, I don't think I'm even color-blind. I can tell all the different blues and greens and yellows. But that particular number I couldn't pick out of those dots. They didn't give me that test for the para-troopers. I never had any trouble with the paratroopers.

Norman Neitzke

I was a sophomore in high school. It was a Sunday, a nice, sunny afternoon. I was home studying and heard about it on radio. We were just shocked. None of us knew where Pearl Harbor was. After that, we learned quickly. When we came back to school on Monday they had the radio on at school. President Roosevelt gave his declaration of war. We thought it was terrible that somebody would do that to our country. Everybody about my age group or just a little older volunteered for the service right away. I was fifteen, so I waited a bit.

Frank Soboleski

My mother and father were from Austria and Poland, and in the months before Pearl Harbor we heard in the news how the egomaniacs in Europe had gobbled up country after country. That intensified the situation for us. On December 7, 1941, we had the radio on at home and heard the news that Japan had bombed Pearl Harbor. I knew right then that I wanted to join the army. I had almost completed the enlistment process when the recruiter demanded to see my birth certificate. Earlier I had told him I was eighteen, but I was only sixteen. When I couldn't produce a birth certificate, he told me to go home and grow up. That ended my army career for the time being.

I had so much I wanted to do in life, and with the war on I felt like I was wasting my time in high school, so I quit. (Later in life I regretted not graduating, even though after the war I took classes and got my GED.) Early in 1942 I and two friends of mine took a bus to the Twin Cities in Minnesota to try to get a job in a defense plant. We wanted to do something to help the war effort. They wouldn't hire us in a defense plant; underage again. But the Armours meat-packing plant in South St. Paul was desperate for help, so we got hired there. That's where I got well acquainted with blood and guts. When summer 1942 came I decided to try something different so I hopped a freight train to Tulsa, Oklahoma, and got hired to drive a truck hauling beans during the harvest. With the harvest over I heard the railroad was hiring men, so I signed on there. We rode a day coach to Needles, California, where the workers were needed.

I was awestruck at what I saw in California. You could just reach up to a tree and eat your fill of oranges and grapefruit, or sleep outside and be comfortable. But after working for the railroad for a while the heat became unbearable, so I hitchhiked to the ocean and looked for another type of work. I found a refrigerator box under a roller coaster in Long Beach and camped out. That was my home for a while.

One day I stopped by a movie set where they were filming a Western. Being used to horses, I asked if they needed someone to ride them. They said they could use me as an extra, so I signed on. I was a good-looking kid, blond, blue-eyed, well built. They asked for my phone number so they could call me in again. Unfortunately I didn't have a phone at the refrigerator box, so that ended my movie career. Whenever I see a John Wayne movie, I think he probably got my job.

I had always dreamed of flying a plane, so I hitchhiked to San Diego to enroll in a vocational school that taught flying. I had seen P-38s at a military airport and decided I wanted to fly one in the service of my country. I attended classes so I'd be ready when the air force was ready for me, and got a job as a soda jerk in a Waffle House on Market Street to feed myself. I could eat all the waffles, banana split sundaes, malts, and sodas I wanted. With all the free fruit off the trees, I was well fed. I found a small house to rent in Ocean Beach that I shared with three other men who worked in a defense plant. I commuted to school on a bus for ten cents each way.

Five or six months after enrolling in the vo-tech school they tested my eyes and found that I was partially color-blind and had poor depth perception. They told me then that I would never be able to be a pilot. That took the wind out of my sails, so I decided to head home to see my folks. I stuck out my thumb and made it back.

In International Falls I worked on the farm, logged, hunted, and fished until I turned eighteen. On my birthday I hightailed it down to the recruiting office and signed up for the army. This time they took me right in. It was 1943. I rode a bus to Fort Snelling for induction and right on to Fort McClellan, Alabama, for basic training.

Ed Tipper

A football buddy and I were out at Dearborn Village, a museum featuring the life and accomplishments of Henry Ford. We were riding a bus from one location to another when somebody stopped the bus and said the United States had just been attacked. The bus driver turned on the radio news, where we heard the details. A few women started crying. I didn't know where Pearl Harbor was; I thought it might have been some remote U.S. military installation, but started joking with my buddy that if we lost the war we'd all be eating fish heads and rice soon.

Here's a story that relates to Pearl Harbor—back when I was about 6, just before the Depression hit, I had what they called a wild tooth. My father took me to the dentist, who said I needed braces. My father said, "Pull the tooth." The dentist argued, saying that pulling that tooth would be the worst thing for me and that my teeth would be crooked my whole life unless I got braces. Dad said, "You pull that tooth out or I'll take him home and yank it out myself with a pair of pliers." That was the way he was. The dentist pulled it. I didn't know it then, but that small act would affect my whole life.

When Pearl Harbor happened, thousands of American kids my age immediately joined the military. I was the same way. Now, when it came to enlisting, the important thing for me was the quality of the soldiers I was going to be with. I wanted to be in the absolute highest-quality group where I would not hesitate to have my life depend on others' performance. I signed up for the marines because I thought they were the best, but the doctor there said they couldn't pass me because my teeth wouldn't bite together. He said, "Come back and enlist in a couple of weeks. They're going to relax the standards then."

I was furious. It was just my teeth; the rest of me was in great shape. I said, "I'm not coming back, then—or ever! I'll find something better than the damn marines. I don't know what, but I'll find it."

Here's the twist: if I had joined the marines then, I would have been in one of the very earliest groups to go overseas and invade the Pacific islands. My chances of survival would have been very slim.

When the marines wouldn't take me I checked around. The rangers and the paratroopers were two other high-quality groups. I liked the idea of the paratroopers more, so I enlisted there. I ended up going to Toccoa with one of the first groups of paratroopers—all thanks to a wild tooth.

Buck Taylor

A bunch of friends used to hang out and eat ice cream in a little coffee shop on Ridge Avenue. That's where we were when we heard the Japanese had attacked Pearl Harbor. We thought, Hoo boy, what a mistake they made. The Japanese—we can just walk right over there. That was our first impression, anyway. Boy, were we ever wrong. Back then we thought Japan was not much of a country to be reckoned with. It was so small. The truth is that they were better prepared to face war than we were at the time.

It didn't matter who you talked to—pretty soon all my friends knew we were going to be drafted. None of us doubted it. So I put on my thinking cap and figured out what would be the best thing to do. In school we had studied the history of World War I. It was all trench warfare, guys getting shot as they went over the top, and I thought, Boy, that's not for me. But the paratroopers—you jump out of a plane and you're on your own. If you survive, it's to your own initiative. Fine, then; the paratroopers it would be.

In July 1942 I signed up. At the swearing-in ceremony I met four guys who would all become part of Easy Company: Forrest Guth, Rod Strohl, Carl Fenstermaker, and Walter Gordon, who was from Mississippi but for some reason had enlisted in Philadelphia. The four of us were eventually put in 3rd Platoon, so we were able to stay close through the war. We joined in Philadelphia, then went to Indiantown Gap for a couple of days where we got our group together. Then they put us on a train down to Toccoa.

CHAPTER FIVE

Cutting Teeth at Toccoa

Ed Tipper

In July and August 1942, young men from all parts of the United States gathered at Camp Toccoa, Georgia, where the 506th Parachute Infantry Regiment was activated.

I was surprised at the intensity of physical training at Toccoa. There was a reason to the intensity, and it didn't take long to figure it out: they wanted the best. If a guy couldn't do something, he was gone. Just like that.

I played high school football and considered myself in great shape. Boy, was I in for a surprise. The first day at Toccoa I suited up in the assigned trunks, T-shirt and boots, looked up, and saw Mount Currahee— 3½ miles up, 3½ miles back. I thought, Well, we're going to be here for four months of training; probably by the end of that time we'll climb to the top of that mountain. The same afternoon somebody blew a whistle and they ran us up to the top and back. A lot of guys dropped out right then.

The reason I made it that first day? Ahead of me was a guy I considered very old. He was probably twenty-five or twenty-six. He'd been out drinking the night before, and the alcohol fumes were coming off him.

I thought, Well, if that old guy can make it, I can, too. He went all the way to the top and back. I did, too. That was Jack Ginn, from Oklahoma.

After the first day, running Currahee became an everyday thing for us. Captain Herbert Sobel, our company commander, led the group in the runs. People always talk about Sobel's incompetence, but he could run with the best of them. The guys all complained about Currahee, but it soon began to stand for something. Currahee separated the troops. Sometimes the guys would have a couple of beers at night and someone would say, "Let's go and run the mountain." So guys ran Currahee just for the hell of it. We wanted to be the best.

You have to realize that most guys who tried out for the paratroopers were all highly motivated, physically fit young guys to begin with. Being a paratrooper was voluntary. At Toccoa you could drop out anytime. If a guy dropped out he usually went to a regular infantry outfit. Guys regularly came in for a day or two, tried the training, and were gone by day two or three.

When I initially joined, I wondered if I could make it. But soon I knew I would. It was an issue of pride. I looked around and knew I was as good as any of the guys there. I knew I could do this. It came back to that persistence thing I learned as a kid.

Everything at Toccoa was extremely physical. One time we had a bunch of telephone poles. Ten or twelve guys lay on their backs and worked together to do bench presses with the poles. These were huge logs, mind you—it's a wonder one of them didn't slip and crush a man.

I think I was fairly immature at this stage of my life. At Toccoa we had a no-nonsense drill sergeant named Harvey Moorehead. He was tough as nails and played a strong role in having me grow up. One time we were standing at attention and I made some comment to the guy next to me. Sergeant Moorehead barked out a command: "You men are at attention. There is no talking in ranks. And Private Tipper"—he spoke the next phrase very deliberately—"one more word from you and you are out!" I knew he meant it. I chose to shape up right then.

At the end of our time at Toccoa we went to Atlanta, where we boarded a train for Fort Benning, Georgia. At Benning we made our five jumps and became qualified paratroopers. How did we get from Toccoa to Atlanta? We marched—all 118 miles. I don't think that will ever be equaled. It started out as a rumor that went around camp. Colonel Sink read a magazine article where the Japanese Army had marched 88 miles in three days, so he wanted to outdo that. He said, "My men can do a hell of a lot better than that."

When we heard we were actually going to make the hike, the reaction from the guys was pretty good. "Hell, we can do that," someone said. We believed we could do anything. So we marched the distance in three days, carrying full equipment. You think of Georgia as having good weather all the time, but when we marched it was in freezing rain. The temperatures dipped so low that our boots froze at night. We toughed it out. My feet are still not the same today; I've got one foot where I can't walk on concrete for long thanks to that hike. It was difficult, but I'm glad we had that experience.

When we finally arrived in Atlanta the next day, we had a fifteen-mile parade in Class A uniforms from Oglethorpe University to the train station. We were in a foul mood when we started the parade but got into the spirit of it as we went along.

Here's a story about the hike: Company E had a sergeant, Sherman Irish, sort of a golden boy who smiled all the time. He was a favorite of Captain Sobel's, or certainly didn't have a conflict with him, like others did. Irish was competent; everybody loved the guy.

Well, when the time for the big hike came along, Irish went to Sobel and said, "You have a car, I'd like to make the hike, but somebody needs to take your car to Benning, and I'd rather help you with your car." Sobel had a newer-model Ford and agreed. Irish further volunteered to pack along any of the other officers' valuables in the car. Other officers obliged.

The day of the hike came. Irish got in Sobel's car. The rest of us started walking. We arrived in Benning, but Sobel's car was nowhere to be seen. Sobel received a telegram saying the car's transmission had broken down in Atlanta and that Irish needed a hundred dollars to get it fixed. Sobel sent the money, but the car still never arrived. Nor did Sherman Irish.

Months later, they caught him. He had sold all the officers' items, including the wheels off Sobel's car. Irish was court-martialed but was represented by some strong legal counsel evidently, because he was found not guilty on all charges. Irish came back to the outfit. I was there when he knocked on the company orderly room door (Sobel's office). I think Sobel almost had an apoplexy. Sobel had him transferred out the same day.

After the parade in Atlanta we got on the trains to go to Fort Benning for parachute training, then to Camp Mackall, then to Fort Bragg for refitting. We still didn't know where our destination was. When we went to Camp Shanks, New York, we had a pretty good idea we were going to Europe.

Forrest Guth

In my estimation, Captain Sobel was good for us. He was tough and very much a disciplinarian. As far as I'm concerned, Sobel was the one who made E Company tough.

You could get out of paratroopers anytime you wanted, or if they didn't like you, they sent you out in a hurry. I never wanted to quit or even thought about quitting. I said, "If this guy can do it, then I can do it." Some of these guys were city boys and not used to rough work, but we had been brought up with not the best living condition so we didn't expect a heck of a lot more out of the army.

Everything was very competitive: between the companies, between the platoons, and definitely with the Japanese—that's the reason we marched to Atlanta.

After jump training at Benning we went across the river to Camp Mackall, North Carolina. We did the same thing—lots of marches and runs, and more jumps, at least one a week. It was summer, hot and miserable. We had jiggers to contend with, the little bugs, but we still horsed around and were never too serious about anything. That's what I remember most about the service: the good times, the camaraderie with the fellows. We'd pick on guys. One guy didn't like creepy-crawly stuff, snakes, spiders or lizards, so we put lizards in his trunk and ammunition bag—always something like that. Floyd Talbert was often a target. Walter Gordon was brilliant and could think of more ways to tease a guy—he was usually one of the ringleaders. Paul Rogers was always making up songs about guys. If a fellow had a weakness, you wrote a song or a poem about him. The whole company seemed to blend together; it didn't matter if you were the target of a joke or the one who made up the joke.

Dewitt Lowrey

The first night at Toccoa I was put in a tent with another boy. They were still building Camp Toccoa then. Rain was pouring down, and water came right down through our tent, filling the floor. I said, "C'mon, let's go into town. We'll come back in the morning."

He had been in ROTC in school and said, "No, we can't do it. That would be AWOL."

So we put all our stuff up on our cots and sat on the piles all night. We never did get any sleep.

The next day we started running Currahee. It didn't bother me. On the first run—I'll never forget it—they had ambulances waiting for you. If you couldn't make it they picked you up, carried you down the hill, and you were discharged. That was the deal: you had to have the stamina to stay in and run it. Either that or find something else to do.

Once, we were on a forced march going up a hill. James Alley and I were marching together. He said, "Let's sit down on this log, wait here, and catch the company as they come back down."

That sounded like a good idea to me. (It's a wonder we weren't washed out for doing this.) We were sitting there just having a good old time when along comes Major William Boyle (of the 517th). He said, "What are you boys doing sitting over there?" We shrugged and tried to answer the best we knew how. He said, "Nothing doing. Fall in behind me!"

We fell in behind Boyle. He took off up the hill faster than I've ever seen—boy, he was really putting us to it. We weren't marching now, we were running. On the way up the hill we passed our company coming down. We got some funny looks, that's for sure. We went to the top of the hill, turned around, and ran back down. We passed through the company and kept running straight by. We kept running and ran up another hill. Then another. Finally we looped around and joined up with the end of our company. The major said, "You boys can fall out now, but don't let me ever catch you doing that again."

Later, Lieutenant Dick Winters asked us why we were running behind Major Boyle. We told him. Winters sort of smiled and said, "I bet you boys didn't know Major Boyle was a cross-country runner."

On the march to Atlanta a little dog started following us. He had no collar or identification and must have been a stray, for he kept up with us for several miles. Finally we noticed he was limping. I picked him up and saw that his toenails were worn to the quick and the pads on his paws were sore. I told my buddies, "If y'all will take the stuff in my backpack, I'll put that dog in my backpack and carry him." So they did. The dog rode to Atlanta on my back and on to Fort Benning. We named him Draftee. He became our mascot. He was a pretty cute old thing. At Benning, a bunch of nurses had just transferred in. They took one look at him and said, "We'll take care of him." So we gave Draftee to the nurses.

Along with the dog, I carried my machine gun for the whole march. Some guys traded off the heavier weapons, but I figured I had been issued that weapon and might have to use it someday. So I needed to keep my hand on it.

At Benning we had four day jumps and one night jump. On the first round of jumps, the pilot turned on the green light for us to jump, but the jumpmaster wouldn't let us jump. We wanted to know why. He said, "Well, if you jump now you'll land in the Chattahoochee River." We had to make another circle, come around, and line up for the drop zone again.

One man ahead of me got in the door and froze. I had my foot on his butt but couldn't push him out, he was wedged against the door so tight. Other guys tried to push him out. Finally the jumpmaster pushed him out of the way and I jumped. The man went back to Benning, but I don't think he ever made paratrooper.

A lot of guys didn't make the training. When I jumped I was scared. I don't know about everybody else, but I was scared every time I jumped. I had never been in an airplane before that. Down on the farm, I had no reason to go anywhere on a plane. So I was always on the leery side of that. I figured the good Lord was taking care of me, so I let it go.

Al Mampre

A large group of tents had been set up called W Company. We called it Cow Company. That was one area you didn't want to be in. Sometimes guys went there for a few days before training, but mostly W Company was for the guys who couldn't make it. The W stood for "washed out."

Right away, one guy did something wrong—I don't know what, maybe blew his nose the wrong way—and they put him in front of the whole regiment with his barracks bag. Drums rolled and they stripped the stuff off his uniform. It was real shameful. A lot of guys got kicked out from then on—it wasn't always as public as that. Guys washed out for not being able to do the physical training, for breaking rules, or if they just flat-out quit.

I should mention that the first day at Toccoa I met Ed Pepping, who also became a medic. He's proven to be a great friend over the years. That first day, Ed and I and a couple other guys decided to jump off those thirty-four-foot training towers, just to see if we could do it. We didn't want to be chicken the next day if they asked us to jump. So we jumped. We didn't have harnesses or anything. That was a long way down. It's a wonder we didn't get hurt.

It's true, as a company we were pretty high-charge guys. We finished training at Toccoa and went to Benning. The first week of Benning was supposed to be all physical training. But we had had so much of that already, it was all duck soup for us. Right away the training sergeant told us to run five miles. I was on point, leading the group, and I stepped up the pace, which meant the sergeant had to step it up, too. We ran for some time. Then I said, "Aw, this is too slow," and took it up another notch. All the guys just laughed. We could see the sergeant starting to fume. Then I yelled, "About face!" and we all ran backward for a while. Boy, did that infuriate the sergeant.

"Two more miles for that!" he called.

That was just what we wanted, 'cause he had to run two more miles with us. A seven-mile run was nothing to us. Hey, a run on flat ground [laughs]—that was practically like going to sleep for us. We could run on flat ground all day.

One medic, Phil Campezi, was a bodybuilder who hated to run because he thought it slimmed his physique too much. But Phil could do push-ups forever. During the first week at Benning a sergeant told Phil to crank out a hundred push-ups, which was pretty standard. Phil said, "You'll have to be more specific."

The sergeant snapped, "What do you mean, *more specific*?"

"Well, do you want me to do them with my left hand or my right hand?" Phil said.

"All right, wiseguy," said the sergeant. "Do a hundred with each."

Phil cranked them out—a hundred one-arm pushups with his left, then a hundred one-arm pushups with his right. When he was done, he turned to me. "Al, get on my back," he said. Phil did a hundred more pushups with me on his back. I bet he could have done a thousand.

Phil's arms got broken in a glider accident in Holland. That was the last time I saw him. He was a great guy.

It's true, medics were a bit of a breed of their own. One time we were at a party. When I came back it was late evening. I walked into the dispensary and saw two medics—Captains Shifty Filer and Buck Ryan. Ryan was sitting in a dental chair. "What's going on?" I said. "Why are you pulling his tooth at this time of night?"

Shifty, the regimental dentist, answered, "Well, we have this deal. I'm going to pull one of Buck's teeth and he gets to pull one of mine." They had both been drinking pretty heavily. Buck nodded. (There was nothing wrong with their teeth.) I convinced them they might want to wait until morning.

A guy found a bobcat and brought it to camp, planning to put paratrooper boots on him. Some guys built a chicken-wire cage for the bobcat, big enough to get a couple of guys in it. Well, they called some medics over to give ether to the cat to put him to sleep so they could get the boots on. The cat looked pretty calm, the guys were talking to him all nicely, so me and a couple guys went into the cage. Boy, suddenly that cat came to life—claws all over the place. The other two guys slipped out quick but for some reason I had more difficulty reaching the door. I swear—there were nine cats in there with me all at once.

We were able to get that cat calmed down and put boots on him. Later we made a jump with him. That wasn't uncommon; we made jumps with a lot of things—bobcats, stray dogs, souvenirs. Once a Red Cross girl made a jump with us. I don't know how she slipped in there.

We created a makeshift operating center out of tent material and headlights. It was all enclosed. The idea was to simulate the medical conditions we'd encounter under combat. Different men were designated as casualties and given various wounds for us to treat. Captain Gross was a big, burly guy with a mustache. We put him under, put his arm in a cast, and shaved off half his mustache. Well, he was going to get married that same afternoon. Boy, you talk about one mad guy when he came to. He wasn't putting up with any of this. He pounded his arm on a truck, trying to break the cast. But his fiancée was tickled pink because he needed to shave the rest of his mustache off. She had never liked it much to begin with.

It wasn't all crazy stuff. We did some good, too. The Deep South—that was tough country in the 1940s. You got outside of the base and were able to observe families who lived in the area. The kids were cute as all get-out but the parents all looked much older than they really were. One of my jobs was to make medical checks in the community, checking to see if the water was safe to drink.

The war was right around the corner. Once while making a training jump, my musette bag came loose, smacked my head, and knocked me out cold. The bag had all my medical equipment in it—it was pretty heavy. I came to as I hit the ground. The sunlight was just catching the white silk of my chute, and some tall grass was brushing my face. In that instant I thought I was in heaven.

Ed Pepping

I signed up in LA and was sent to Fort MacArthur in California, then got on an old coal-burning train cross-country to Georgia. From the moment we signed up as paratroopers we considered ourselves elite.

I met Al Mampre one of the first days at Toccoa. He was a real sharp guy with a good sense of humor. We were instant friends and have been friends ever since. We both became medics.

We ran Currahee more than a hundred times—sometimes just for fun. We ran Currahee in 110-degree heat. Sometimes it was so cold there was frost on the rocks. Rain exposed the rocks on the dirt trail and made it very difficult to run. We had guys who fell and broke an arm or leg. We hopped over them and kept going. Course, that guy was washed out.

We were so gung ho to jump—one of our early jobs was to put mattresses on all the beds. A warehouse nearby had beams across the ceiling. We piled the mattresses on the floor, climbed to the top of the beams, and jumped off into the pile of mattresses. I used to be six-foot-one, but I think all those jumps shorted me up. I'm about five-foot-ten now.

I can't believe some of the ridiculous things we did for fun. Down in the South they have these trees about six inches in diameter. We limbed the trees, then bent them back and tied them off with ropes. We put a pad on the top of a tree, a guy would sit on the pad, and we cut the rope. Instant catapult. We had to stop doing it after a while because guys were getting hurt.

Why did I decide to become a medic? Well, I wasn't sure if I could actually shoot somebody. I knew I could defend myself; I knew that if I had to shoot somebody I would. They gave us all these tests, and through these tests they picked guys for different things. It was really an honor to be picked as a medic.

As medics we didn't go from W Company straight to Easy. We were put into a medical detachment, one medic was assigned to each platoon plus regimental headquarters. During the war there were 142 medics with the 506th, counting replacements. As a medical attachment we trained by ourselves. We decided right from the start we were going to be the best unit in the regiment. Using one-inch tape, we put crosses on our helmets. We had some of the best shots in the regiment. We had the team record for running up Mount Currahee and the team record on the obstacle course. We were known for our close-order drill—people used to come and watch us drill. The other guys started making fun of us. They called us pill rollers and chancre mechanics [pronounced *shanker*, a chancre is an open sore you get from VD]. But that was only in camp. If anybody ever said anything bad about the medics outside of camp, he got decked.

After a while we were assigned companies. I was assigned Easy Company, 3rd Platoon, under Lieutenant Fred "Moose" Heyliger.

Bill Wingett

They shipped us to Toccoa, Georgia, on the train. This is different—I, and the guys I was with at first, were never in W Company. Almost everybody who arrived at Toccoa hung out in W Company for several days until taking a physical. But we got off the train and took the truck straight out to Toccoa to a medical dispensary to have our physicals. That same night we arrived we were in E Company. We were all in the

1st Platoon of E Company. Christenson and Dukeman were in the first squad. Gray and I were in the second squad. We may have been some of the very first men in E Company.

Gray and I ended up a machine gun team. We were that way until we got to England. Being a machine gunner wasn't something I picked. I had picked being in the airborne, but I certainly didn't get to choose what I was going to do or who was going to be my partner. If Gray and I had arrived a day apart we would have never been partners on the machine gun.

A machine gun squad was made up of four men: a gunner, an assistant gunner, and two ammo carriers. The two ammo carriers were just plain foot soldiers. The gunner and the assistant gunner were trained as gunners and traded off. When you had a list in the squad, somebody had to be first. On paper Gray was the gunner of the second squad. The gunner, in theory, carried the gun. The assistant carried the tripod and a rifle. But you all traded off, including the ammo carriers—everybody took turns carrying the gun.

When we went out on the machine gun range, ground squirrels stood out there on the fields. I was a great one for shooting those with a machine gun. That made my target scores pretty low sometimes. No credit for varmints.

Have you ever been to Toccoa? If you do, don't pay a lot of attention to the road up Currahee road now—it's sand and it's graded all the time. In those days it wasn't graded at all. Somebody had run a bulldozer up and down the thing a few times to get the brush and trees out of the way. A rain gulley ran right down the middle of it. The rest of it was rocks, and if you're in formation, and your part of the formation runs over the rocks, you do, too. Some of those rocks were marbles and some were baseballs. It was damn hard not to fall. Your foot rolled on the rocks. You stubbed your toes. We wore boots when we ran. They were nothing like today's running shoes. It was just a leather boot. I'm not certain when we got our taller jump boots. We must have had them when we went to Fort Benning. But I know we started out with what amounted to a nine-inch boot. Somewhere along the line they gave us a combat boot, which had leather on the lower part and straps that buckled. We couldn't wear those jumping because the static lines got tangled in the straps too easily. I think we wore those at Camp Mackall.

Sure, I was a Toccoa guy, but one thing that gripes me about some of these Toccoa guys is that we feel we're a breed alone. We trained under a tough guy, Captain Sobel, but that isn't any credit to us, except that we happened to be there.

Here's what I've got to say about Sobel: One day Sobel called me into his office and asked me why I was having some trouble in training. I told him about the car accident—there wasn't much choice; they were going to find out anyway as soon as they took X-rays. Sobel had the opportunity to flush me right there. All he had to do was write a note, send me to the dispensary, and I'd have been down the road like the rest of those guys. But he didn't do it. He simply said, "Well tough it out." So I toughed it out. It's pretty goddam hard for me not to respect the guy who did that. I'll argue hands down with anybody who says Sobel was the SOB they often say he was. He was tough, yes, he was as tough as anybody you'll ever know. But he was not a bastard. There are incidents that they talk about in the book and show in the movie, [*Band of Brothers*] like Dukeman and his loose collar getting chewed out by Sobel. I don't remember that, and I stood in ranks right behind Bill Dukeman every damn formation we had at Toccoa. I don't know why anybody made that up, but somebody sure as hell did. I think Sobel was as fair a guy as anybody who came down the road.

Another thing about Sobel—people gave him a hard time about his map-reading skills. I can't think of anybody I know who doesn't lack in some skill or another. Any damn fool who's been in the army knows that if you're company commander you depend on the sergeants for that bullshit. I wasn't very good at map reading either, and I know a lot of other guys who weren't.

I'll tell you something else. You've heard of General Sal Mattheson. Long before he was a general he was our first platoon leader at Toccoa— the first one I remember, anyway. Well, when we were in Paris with HBO, for whatever reason, his wife, Colonel Robert Strayer's wife, and my wife, Peg, simply hit it off. So that put me, Colonel Strayer, and General Mattheson palling around together. We went to a nursery or something where they grow fancy roses. The three of us were sitting out front on a bench while our wives went inside, and Strayer turns to me and says, "You know, what they did to Sobel was not right." [Sobel was removed from command in Aldbourne.] I says, "Well, you must have been listening in to some of my disagreements with other people." Mattheson broke in and said, "That was the wrong thing for them to do." Strayer was battalion commander. If it was the right thing to do, he would have known it. Certainly Mattheson was a good officer. If he thought it was wrong, that justifies my thinking.

As soon as we got our wings, we were authorized to blouse our pants. It was an issue of pride for a paratrooper. I can remember [Sergeant Bill] Evans telling us that if we got to town and saw anybody who wasn't a paratrooper with bloused boots to knock him on his ass and take his boots away.

Now, there was a guy I didn't like: Evans. I hold him responsible for having me transferred out of Easy Company to Headquarters Company. He didn't like me, and I didn't like him. When I went in to Headquarters Company [2nd Battalion], we were just getting ready to jump into combat. It was three days before D-day. And all of a sudden I'm a replacement among a whole bunch of guys I don't even know. All thanks to Evans. I went to see my friends from E Company and cussed like hell as I packed my barracks bag. I can't remember the name of one person out of Headquarters Company, not even the commander. I went ahead and fought the war with Headquarters as a machine gunner. For a while when I was at Bastogne I was attached to I Company.

My friend Everett Gray (we were a machine gun team before I was transferred to Headquarters) was killed on D-day plus two. I believe that if he and I had been together, it might not have happened. We lost him awfully soon. No one knows quite how he died. He was all alone.

I think Evans thought I was a favorite of Sobel's. Now, because I wasn't afraid of Sobel, I never hesitated to walk up to Sobel and ask him questions, which some guys wouldn't do. If fact, I'm sure sometimes I went up to him and asked him questions in order to keep Sobel from asking me questions. So I don't know why Evans transferred me. Of course, he was no favorite of mine, either.

I remember only three guys who ever voluntarily transferred out of

Easy Company. One was Dick Garrod, the guy I met the day I enlisted back in Frisco. Another was a guy named Cowboy Grant. We used to kid him about having a stump ranch because he was from Oregon and everything there is trees. Cowboy Grant was six foot, two inches tall, rawboned as hell. If he hit you just playfully it was like a goddam mule kicking you, his knuckles were so hard. The third guy who transferred was named Cox; I'll tell you about him in a minute.

When we were at Fort Benning, the army decided we should all learn to ride a horse. So they assigned some horses to the 506th. They put Cowboy Grant in charge of the horses. I had some horse experience, so Grant asked me to help him. We went over to the horses at night and went for rides—he and I and Garrod and Robert Van Klinken and somebody else, can't think of who.

So we saddled up the horses and grabbed a handful of cherry bombs. (We used cherry bombs in training for simulated artillery.) We were all smoking cigars. All the buildings around there are built on stilts because of heavy rains. Every time we came around one of those Holy Roller churches we lit a cherry bomb and chucked it under the building. We rode back away and watched the people boil out of the windows and doors. It's not something I'm particularly proud of nowadays, but we thought that was great sport back then.

The third transfer—Cox—he and I didn't get along. He was a burly corporal, very athletic, a Golden Gloves something or other from New York State. We had an inspection every Saturday morning, and one Saturday we were all dressed up, cleaning our rifles, getting ready. I was sitting on my cot doing the final touches on the rifle—you had to get every speck of dust out of there or you were afraid Sobel would see it. Somebody passed a T-shirt down—a wonderfully clean T-shirt—to get the final oil and dust out of the guns. So I'm using the T-shirt, and along came Corporal Cox and grabbed the goddam T-shirt. It hooked on my rifle and it went flying. He said, "What the hell are you doing with my T-shirt?" Now, I don't know why his T-shirt came down there. Gordy Carson or someone at the head of the barracks picked it up and started it down the line. Everyone was using it. So I mouthed off to Cox, and he mouthed off back, "Right after inspection, I'll meet you behind the latrine," he said. "We'll settle it—I won't be wearing my stripes."

That put me on the spot. I was not fond of the idea. He was a boxer and I didn't know anything about boxing. I figured he'd clean my clock. But it had to happen. And it did. I don't remember how it ended up except that I wasn't whipped. He got his meal. But I got my sandwich. I'll say this: I must have stood my ground okay against Cox because no one ever challenged me after that.

This is a real mystery to me—in my memory, there was an Indian in E Company named Quick Bear, in 1st Platoon. I don't know if that was his nickname or his last name. He was a great big fellow, as big as Bull Randleman. I came in the barracks at night to go to bed and this man was sitting at the table writing a letter. I said to him, "Sending a smoke signal to the squaw?" He didn't bat an eye, just said, "Yep, got to do it once in a while." In my mind it was just a good-natured remark. I certainly didn't have any aggravation with the Indians. I woke up later on. Gray, and I think it was Albert Blithe, were struggling with Quick Bear. He had a trench knife and was going to kill me for having said that. In years since, I have not found anybody who remembers Quick Bear. I haven't asked everybody. But I cannot accept that I dreamed that up, or even the name.

Sergeant Gordy Carson was a good friend of mine. He was a real ladies' man. He went with some real nice-looking ladies. I was more shy with the girls; I never chased them much. One time we had finished maneuvers in Tennessee and were waiting orders to go back to Camp Mackall. We got a pass and went into town at Evansville, Indiana. Carson and I hadn't gone to town together, but we met on the street in Evansville. The truck that was supposed to pick us up was gone. There was a Ford V-8 sitting at the curb with the motor running. I said, "Gordy—jump in." So we jumped in and took off. I knew the way out of town. Thank God a cop didn't come along—we'd have been in hot water for sure.

Carson and I got out on the highway. There were no lights on this damn car—no headlights, no dash lights; it was completely dark. So I tucked in behind this big truck. That son of a gun was going like hell. We got to this one place where we went through a big cut in a hill. Two or three cars were coming the other way. I could see them edging over. I knew the second car was going to pass the first. Sure enough, it did. He could see the truck but couldn't see me. The car came right at us. I drove up on the bank and did a big half circle and kicked in back behind the truck—all at full speed. About a quarter mile from the camp gates we dropped off the car there and walked back. The first time I saw Carson after the war was in San Diego in 1984. That was the first thing Carson talked to me about—taking that car back to Mackall.

Another time at Mackall I made a jump and I landed one leg on a tree stump, so I was assigned to sick quarters. On Saturday four of us decided to go out to town. I didn't have a pass but went anyway, so I was AWOL. We went to Rockingham and met these girls. I was supposed to have a date with one, but she didn't show up. So I tried the others. I was hot to trot but didn't get anywhere with them. I was too backward to get anywhere, I guess.

Rockingham was a dry town; you couldn't buy booze. We found a cabdriver who had some. Boy, the stuff he gave us was right out of a stone. Man, it was rocky stuff. I wanted to drown my sorrows because my date didn't show up, so I got drunk. It was the only time in my life I ever got drunk like that. I don't remember going back to camp. I don't know today how the hell I got back. I probably got in *because* I was so drunk—or else they would have found out I didn't have a pass.

But I got caught anyway. It happened like this. On the morning the four of us had decided to go to town, they had taken roll. Now, they usually called the companies in order. But that day they called the companies out of order and called E Company last. I had gotten tired waiting because I was supposed to have this date with that girl. So I just took off and went and wasn't there when they called my name.

The next morning somebody shook me and said, "Captain Sobel wants to see you in his office." I got up, and oh, man, I wasn't even in the right bunk. I was in Gray's bunk. He had a lower bunk. I had a higher bunk. I had to run to the end of the building. I went out the door and got off of the porch just far enough to puke on a tree. I must have killed that tree with the stuff that came out of me—green it was, I can almost see it today. I went down to the headquarters and stood in front of Captain Sobel's desk. I couldn't even stand up on my own. I had to lean against the desk to keep myself from falling over. I managed to salute him. I remember Sobel looking at me for the longest time. Then he says, "One of the best soldiers in the goddam company, and look at you—just look at you." I didn't want anybody to look at me. He shamed me. He just flat shamed me. That may have been one of the reasons I never got that way again.

Shifty Powers

Captain Sobel, our company commander—I'm sure you've heard a lot about him. Real hard training there. The thought was that if we went to war with Captain Sobel, he was going to get a lot of us killed because he just didn't know that much about tactics. But over the years I've thought about Sobel more and I've realized that he's responsible for making Easy Company such a good company. He trained us well. Anything he'd ask you to do, he'd do it—I always admired that about him.

Here's a story about Popeye: While we were in Toccoa, Captain Sobel told us, "Anybody who makes expert rifleman gets a three-day pass." Me and one other guy, Buck Taylor, made expert. Well, Toccoa, Georgia, is three states away from Virginia, where I lived. Popeye and I were good friends by then. He asked, "You going home, Shifty?"

"Nah," I said, "I don't have enough money."

"I'll take care of that," Popeye said. He got one of those steel helmets and walked through the barracks giving a big talk: "Shifty's got three days off and doesn't have enough money to get home. Everybody chip in a bit. Here—I'm going to start it with five dollars." He placed a bill in the helmet. Everybody else threw in a dollar or fifty cents, whatever they had. Popeye handed it to me to count. "How much money you got in there, Shifty? You got enough?"

"Yeah," I said. "In fact, I've got a little bit left over."

Popeye grinned. "Then give me my damn five dollars back."

So I gave him back his five dollars [laughs].

Buck Taylor

Toccoa was tough. Captain Sobel wanted his boys to be the best. He really drove us to do a good job. Sobel was disliked by some of the enlisted men for that reason, but I never had a problem with him for pushing us hard. I appreciate it now.

It's true, one time at Fort Benning I got very annoyed with Captain Sobel. To explain: Back in early 1942, before I enlisted, I had gone to a sorority club meeting one evening to pick up a girl I had a date with. Instead of one girl meeting me, three or four girls jumped in my car—none of whom was my date. That was fine with me because one of the girls who jumped in, Elaine, was a gorgeous brunette and I thought, Boy, she's better than the one I was going to meet. So I took all the girls home and Elaine was the last one I dropped off. That was the start of it all. She was in high school still; I had just graduated. We dated pretty heavily from then on.

Anyway, when I was at Benning we had all been given three-day passes after our jumps. I had made arrangements with Elaine to spend time with her that weekend. She worked in Philadelphia but was able to get a train ticket to meet me down in Jacksonville. Everything was set. But on Saturday morning something irked Sobel and all passes were canceled. I thought, Gee, what am I going to do? Here's a young girl on the train all by herself coming down to Jacksonville with nobody to meet her. There was no way of getting word to the bus station to explain what had happened.

So I started figuring out a plan. I had already gotten my pass earlier on Saturday morning before Sobel canceled them. I thought, Heck, the worst thing they can do is bust me. So I went AWOL and took the bus to Jacksonville anyway, met Elaine, and we had a great weekend together. Carwood Lipton was married, his wife was in North Carolina, and he had made similar arrangements to spend the three days with her. I think Carwood skipped out of camp same as me.

We never heard a word from Sobel.

Elaine and I were married right after the war. That was the first important thing I did Stateside—marry Elaine. She's the best thing that has ever happened to me. We're still married today, more than sixty-three years later.

You have to understand that I never hated Sobel. But this is also true: Sobel could be quite unfair sometimes, and it went much farther than just the incident with the passes. Some of the men downright hated him even to the point where Sobel's life was in danger. As NCOs, we had all heard comments from the other enlisted men such as, "Boy, if I ever get

Sobel in my sites he's a goner"—stuff like that. You never know if those comments are actually going to be played out, but there was a strong feeling among the men that Sobel couldn't be trusted in a combat situation. If the bullets were flying it could have been easy for someone to catch Sobel in the crosshairs.

I was involved in the meeting that the NCOs had in England [to all turn in their stripes as noncommissioned officers in E Company, thereby casting a nonconfidence vote for Sobel in hopes that Colonel Sink would remove Sobel as company commander]. Mostly I just listened during the meeting. Sergeants Mike Ranney and Salty Harris ran the meeting. It happened about eight o'clock one night. They called together some of the NCOs; not everyone was there. We all knew the troops were unhappy with Sobel, and the big question was, "What can we do about it?" We all knew Sobel wasn't cut out for combat. We knew that if he made the wrong decision it would cost some of the fellows their lives. So we decided that something should be done—that was how it was left at the end of the meeting. I assumed (though I never had confirmation on this) that Ranney or Harris went to Captain Winters—I don't know who else they could have gone to who would have understood the situation. Anyway, within about two weeks Sobel was moved down to a training assignment. Ranney and Harris were both busted. Harris was shipped out to another company. Ranney was busted down to private.

As I've thought about that incident over the years, here's my conclusion: Captain Sobel was a good training officer, strict, he wanted his men to be the best. I admire him for that. But you could not trust his judgment in a battle situation. For the good of the outfit, I think what we did was right.

In 2002, at the Easy Company reunion in Phoenix, I was sitting by the pool at the hotel one afternoon, taking life easy. This young man came over to me and said, "Mr. Taylor?"

I said, "Yes."

He said, "I'm Herbert Sobel's son. Could you please tell me why you fellows did what you did to my father?"

His comment nearly knocked me off the chair. Why did he talk to me? I think because when he came to the group and introduced himself someone said, "Hey, why don't you go over and see Taylor." I think that was the case. Otherwise why would he have come to me?

I explained to him that we did what we did for the good of the company—in fact, it was for Sobel's own benefit, too. I think his son understood that. I certainly mean him no harm in telling this story. Sobel's sister was invited to our reunion in Valley Forge several years ago. She came with a small speech prepared. She said, "I understand exactly how you felt about my brother. He was a little strange sometimes." So I think her saying that has sort of smoothed things over.

CHAPTER SIX

How the Rest of Us Trained

Earl McClung

I never went through Toccoa. I went to camp in Utah and took tests, then they sent me to Fort Walters, Texas, for basic training. Basic training didn't bother me. I thought it was pretty easy, kind of fun. The city kids didn't care much for it, though. I always liked to be outside rather than inside. During basic you were outside a lot and did a lot of walking. You learned something new, something you had never heard of. For an Indian kid that was altogether a different life.

There was no ridicule in the service for being an Indian—it was more or less the other way around. The other guys thought that was pretty great. If they found out you had Indian blood, well, you were made first scout. I was a good shot, too, on the rifle range, so I was popular with the infield.

After we finished basic training they put us in a big hall and asked where we wanted to go from there. Most of us had taken infantry basic. Somebody said something about a new outfit being formed, the paratroopers, where you jumped out of airplanes. I remember a couple of guys saying, "Well, who in the heck would want to do something like that?" Then another guy says, "Well, it pays fifty bucks a month extra." So about five of our hands went up. I did it for the fifty bucks a month [laughs]. That was a lot of money in those days.

For parachute training we were sent to Fort Benning, Georgia. I think it took five weeks. Training at Benning was harder than the infantry training. First week was strictly running, tumbling, climbing ropes, doing push-ups eight to ten hours a day all day long. You never walked anywhere, you ran, all in the Georgia heat. The heat was miserable. I was in shape, so the training never bothered me, but a lot of guys washed out.

When the time came for my first jump, I just went out the door. When the chute opened, I thought, Hey, this is fun. You're scared the first four or five jumps, but I never had any problems jumping.

From Georgia I went to a repo depo [replacement depot]. Whenever somebody was short of people they'd call in and you'd go from there. So I joined the 506th E Company in Fort Bragg, North Carolina, after they had finished jump school.

We were outsiders in E Company. They had all been together for over a year and knew each other really well. Some would talk to you, some wouldn't. They were looking at us seeing if we were going to last. You were an outsider until you got in combat; then things changed. I came in with a bunch of guys with the last name M—Mellett, McMahon, Mayer. I don't remember them all. Some of them didn't last too long.

Clancy Lyall

After I enlisted I went to basic training at Camp Blanding in Florida. At Blanding the mosquitoes were bigger than goddamn B-17s. We did a lot of work in the swamps there, escape, evasion, and survival training. It was okay. I already knew how to eat the animals found in a swamp and navigate at night—I had learned that back in Louisiana.

Then I went over to Fort Benning, Georgia, for airborne training—the frying pan area, they called it. It was across the river from the main post. The first three or four weeks of training there were pretty horrific. The easiest jump I ever made was my first because I didn't know what I was in for. The hardest was your second—then I wondered what the hell I was doing up there.

It helped to have a lot of preparation for the first jump. We learned how to exit the door, how to land, how to guide our chutes. To train, we jumped off thirty-four-foot towers. But it was a little different when we got up about nine hundred feet in a damn C-47. Then it was shake, rattle, and roll. I couldn't look down or I'd never jump. When I looked down I saw ants, and that was a shock. So I always looked straight ahead. One time I looked down just as I was jumping and damn near couldn't jump. I had to haul myself out the door.

In those days the chutes opened up and you felt like a tassel on a whip. Bang! It didn't break your back but it damn sure pulled you around. When you're jumping out of an airplane, you're never not afraid. I don't care who says they're not. You always have that little fear that says your chute won't open. But after a while you settle in and it all becomes second nature.

On a few jumps I experienced what they call a Mae West. That's where your suspension lines go over the parachute and your parachute looks like two bosoms. It was my fault. When I jumped I twisted, and the lines went that way. I was always able to shake off the Mae Wests and be okay. A few other times I got blown panels in my chute. Those old T-5 chutes were crazy. As soon as the chute opened up you had a hell of a snap. Then with blown panels you whistled down a lot faster. I had two incidences of that.

From Benning, I got my wings, then went home on furlough. Then I was sent to England, to Chilton-Foliat Jump School. Chilton was the place for all the guys who weren't paratroopers but were going into Normandy (such as doctors and priests) to learn how to jump. I got there the last part of February 1944 and was assigned to 2nd Battalion, 506th. Me and a couple other guys were picked to train these guys at Chilton. Then we went back to our respective companies last of May in Upottery. Of course, on June 6 we jumped into Normandy. That's where I got hit. After I got out of the hospital I was reassigned to Easy Company. That's where I stayed. That was August 1944.

Frank Soboleski

I went to boot camp at Fort McClellan. It was a lot warmer weather in Alabama than I had grown up with in Minnesota. One day I was just itching to go for a swim, even though somebody with stripes had said, "Do not go into the water under any condition." I couldn't figure out why they were so strict about that. I peeled off my duds and dove into a creek that ran behind the barracks. Well, it didn't take long for me to figure out why they were so strict. When I came up from the dive I peered at two water moccasins swimming right at me. Right then I figured if Jesus could do it, it was time for me to try. I swear I was walking on water getting the hell out of there. From then on I decided to listen to those guys with stripes on their sleeves.

I noticed in boot camp that a lot of guys appeared like they didn't want to be there. They weren't serious about learning how to be good soldiers or watching another guy's back in combat. All they were interested in was drinking, smoking, barroom fighting, and women. I grew nervous with the idea of being sent to fight with a bunch of chicken-shit soldiers and figured I was taking a bigger chance of getting killed if sent to combat with them.

So the first time I saw a poster wanting men to sign up to be paratroopers and heard how hard it would be to make it in, I knew that was for me. I wanted an elite group of soldiers around me.

I was sent to Fort Benning, Georgia, for paratrooper training. We never walked anywhere. It was run all the time without stopping. I never smoked or drank, and I was in good shape, so what they were showing us to do wasn't beyond my abilities. It was something to be proud of.

From there, I was sent to Fort Bragg, North Carolina, for training in heavy equipment operation and demolition school.

After Fort Bragg we were sent to Fort Meade, Maryland, for assembly. That's the first time I got to go home, but not on a furlough, just a seven-day delay en route. I visited my family and went right from there to Camp Shanks, New York.

Henry Zimmerman

They sent us to Camp Croft in South Carolina for basic training. One day they came around and wanted volunteers for the paratroopers. I was always one for excitement, so I said, "Yeah, I'll go." I had never flown in a plane before, but it sounded good.

They sent us to Fort Benning to train as paratroopers. The physical training was pretty rough. But I did 'em. I had to run ten miles every morning. For practice jumps we had to jump from the top of two-hundred-foot towers with chutes that guided us to the ground. After that it was the real thing from a plane.

I was a little leery about jumping out on the first jump. But when the guy ahead of me went I said to myself, Well, if he can go, I can go. I went out right after him. And I got to like it. I enjoyed it.

Herb Suerth Jr.

I went through twelve weeks of basic training at Fort Belvoir, Virginia, in May 1943. It was a real mix of guys there. Half the guys were from the Tex-Mex border, and many didn't speak English. The guy bunking next to me had a bullet hole healing right next to the heart—he had been shot in a barroom brawl. The rest of us had a semester of college. It was quite an interesting group. Fort Belvoir was a good post. It wasn't out in the middle of nowhere, only thirty miles out of Washington, D.C., so we were able to get there a few times.

When I finished basic training, they separated all the guys into two groups mostly. A lot of us went into the Army Specialized Training Program, which was basically going back to school. The rest went into advanced training and soon made the invasion of North Africa. I was sent to the University of Pennsylvania. At the end of my first semester they closed that program, and we went back to basic training in the Corps of Engineers because they had lengthened the program by then by another four weeks to emphasize more infantry training. When I finished that, they pulled a lot of guys out and we went to electricians' school in New York. I was stationed in downtown New York City for three months. Boy, that was tough duty [laughs].

Joe Lesniewski

Right after Pearl Harbor I quit working at GE and volunteered for the army. They put me in the air force instead. They sent me from Pennsylvania to California. I was in seven different camps in six weeks. I was bounced around from Mather Field, to McClellan Air Force Base, to San Bruno, California, to two camps in Stockton, then to an interment camp at Tanforan. I was upset about this.

Living conditions were terrible at Tanforan. It was a Japanese interment camp, though there were no Japanese there at the time with us that I knew of. They supplied us with a cot, a blanket, a pillow with straw in it, then another blanket to cover us, and a pair of galoshes.

Why the galoshes? The foundation of the barracks was built level with the ground. We got a lot of rain in the San Francisco area, and the water washed right into our cabins. So it was hell if you went to sleep and you took your galoshes off before you got to bed. Up to three inches of water would be on the floor. A lot of our men got sick—it was so damn cold in there. A couple men caught pneumonia. I knew a couple who died from it.

As long as I stayed in California, we had no kind of training whatsoever. We weren't doing anything—just sitting around looking at the sky. It was six weeks of doing absolutely nothing. This was happening all over. They were sending so many people to the military camps that they couldn't handle it. There were so many people enlisting it was overwhelming.

I went to Camp Stockton and volunteered for the camp's boxing team; that's when things started to turn around for me. I had boxed in Erie when I was a kid. We used to fool around every couple of weeks; we had oversized gloves and nobody would get hurt. We used to work out that way, nothing else to do, you know. Sometimes it would be at the Boys' Club, but other times we boxed right in the neighborhood. When we did, everybody was warned to not get mad or hurt anyone. It was just about learning how to box. Some older guys would train us. We got pretty good.

Boxing came easily to me. I hardly ever drank or smoked, and I was in good shape. What did I look like as a young man? To tell the truth— very handsome. Did you ever see Paul Newman? You send me your address and I'll send you a picture of me looking like Paul Newman. You think I'm kidding you?

The boxing team was part of the Diamond Belt Tournament. You fought four rounds of two minutes each. On the East Coast it was three rounds of three minutes each, so it was a bit different on the West Coast than what I knew back home. In the tournament were both military men and civilians. A couple of the guys I fought were civilians. The rest were military. I joined as a representative of the military.

The man who trained us was Max Baer, a former world heavyweight champion. If you ever saw the old TV show *Beverly Hillbillies*, the part of Jethro Bodine was played by his son, Max Baer Jr. Everybody who boxed wanted to win. I didn't get to the top, but I did beat the hell out of a lot of guys. I fought in featherweight division. I weighed about 112 to 114 pounds back then. I got much bigger after that.

Boxing was fun, but I wanted to go somewhere where I could learn something in the military besides boxing. So I asked for a transfer from California to Chanute Field, Illinois. There, they taught us how to repair planes that had been shot down or crippled up. I was there about a month, maybe longer.

Then I talked to the captain and asked him about cadet training to be able to fly a plane. I took a test and ended up with the highest mark of anybody at Chanute Field. With my score on that exam, it meant they were going to send me to Nashville, Tennessee, to learn how to fly a P-51 Mustang, the American long-range single-seat fighter aircraft. These were the fast, highly durable fighter planes that soon helped America achieve air superiority in World War II. I had first seen that plane in 1941—as soon as I saw them I knew that's what I wanted to do.

I couldn't wait to begin flying. But the military lost my exam records. I hung around another month while they tried to find them. They couldn't. So they sent me to Detroit to the U.S. Rubber Company and taught me how to repair self-sealing fuel tanks. This wasn't what I had in mind at all. I wanted to learn how to fly or at least be around planes, so I asked for a transfer—any airfield except in California. They sent me to Hunter Field at Savannah, Georgia, where I lay around for about a month. They had us stationed at an airfield with big planes coming in and out, very dusty all the time. We were in big tents that held about twelve guys. Every day we had to go to an area and wash our clothes to get all the dust off. I was upset about that, so one day I went down to the captain's office and volunteered for paratroopers.

"When do you want to leave?" he said.

"Right away," I said.

That's how I got into the airborne. Incidentally, they found my records to be a pilot about seven months later, but by that time I was in the airborne, ready to go overseas. I still have those records today.

Ed Joint

For basic training they sent me down to Camp Walters in Texas. Nobody I knew had heard of the base. It was mostly older guys there. Most of them couldn't speak English or write their own names. Whenever they got mail from home they asked me to read it for them. I didn't know what the hell the service was going to do with them. I couldn't wait to get out of there. I wanted to be there, but not *there*—it was just me and all these older guys who couldn't write their names.

One guy at Walters was nice, an officer. He found out I wanted to go to the paratroopers, and he wanted to go, too. A real nice guy, can't remember his name. We weren't at Walters very long. He got shipped someplace else. Then I remet him at Fort Bragg, where we got fitted up to go overseas. Then I saw him again at Camp Shanks in New York when we shipped out. I checked up on him after D-day. They told me he had died in Normandy. It kind of shook me up. He was a real nice guy.

From Walters I went to Fort Benning for paratrooper training and did my five jumps. I enjoyed jumping out of an airplane. I liked seeing the sky and the landscapes. Course, when they start putting all that equipment on you, that changes. And when the bullets start flying, it's not too nice then. Every day at Benning we went out and ran and ran and ran. It was a lot of physical training, cleaning weapons, learning how to do things, we were all young kids—none of us knew much of anything.

I joined Easy Company when they were at Camp Mackall. I was put in the 2nd Platoon. It was a bit hard to break in at first. I wasn't at Toccoa, where they had formed up. But I didn't have no trouble with the guys. Some of the Toccoa guys are hard—they still are—but they're good men. I don't want to say nothing bad about them.

Roy Gates

In my battery in the 10th, there was a kid named Peterson from Kansas, a cross-country and track man, who kept saying we ought to stop going on maneuvers and go fight a war. So when a man came around looking for volunteers for the paratroopers, we signed up. You made extra money for jumping out of an airplane. That sounded pretty good to me. Peterson and I both signed up.

A-stage at Fort Benning was all physical. They ran you until you couldn't run anymore. If I was lagging, Peterson would put his arm under mine and keep me going. He did great on the running part. But in the end he flunked out. After five jumps you had to jump another two jumps on your own, a day jump and a night jump. Whenever Peterson got pushed out of the plane he did okay, but couldn't muster the guts to jump if forced to step out by himself, so he wasn't able to do the last two jumps. I never knew what happened to him.

Jumping came easily to me. My adventuresome father had run a flying circus in Atlanta where they did wing walking. I never wing-walked but I had been in airplanes quite a bit as a kid. Some of these poor kids at Benning had never even been in an airplane, much less jump out of one. Jumping felt like swimming underwater to me—once your chute opened it was a very calm situation. Of course, with the chutes today you land like a feather. In those days if it was a windy day you could oscillate quite a bit if you weren't in the right position and hit the ground pretty hard.

Here's a story about jumping. When we came back to France from Germany we had to make one jump to stay on pay status. Ed Shames, my platoon leader, was a high points man, and just before he left to go home to the States he called me over and told me about a sergeant who sweat his jumps pretty badly. Out of concern for the guy, Shames told me to make a bet with the guy so he wouldn't worry—you know, just to take his mind off the jump. So I bet the guy he couldn't tackle me while going out the door of the plane. That was a bad move.

It turns out that yes, you can. I went out first. The sergeant was right behind me. He won the bet. We tangled up and started to come down like a bullet, passing other jumpers who had jumped before us. It could have been worse—we could have had a streamer, where the chute doesn't inflate at all. But we came down on about a half a panel, about one quarter of one of our chutes had inflated.

I don't remember exactly what we yelled to each other. He was pretty panicky. We had jumped from about fourteen hundred feet, a higher jump, so we had some time. We started to unwind from each other, but he fought it and we got more tangled. I was calmer, I was involved in trying to get him to take it easy and help us unwind that I didn't even think. Luckily it was a windy day, and right before we landed the wind popped us away from each other. Then we hit. Boy, we plowed up some ground. Good thing it was a freshly dug field. We dug it a lot deeper.

Afterward we had a few beers together to calm our nerves.

Norman Neitzke

I signed up in March 1944 during my senior year of high school and went into the service in May 1944, just before D-day. I had two weeks to go before high school graduation, but I left school early. Some friends and I signed up together. I was eighteen.

A few weeks before I enlisted, one of my best friends had enlisted and ended up at Fort Hood in Texas for basic. Next month I was down there and wound up in a row of barracks, with my bunk next to his.

We went through thirteen weeks of basic training. We learned discipline and how to fight. When we graduated from basic we all had decisions to make as far as any special services to go into.

The thought of jumping out of airplanes didn't bother me all that much. You're always a little concerned when you jump, but it sounded exciting. I had done a fair amount of flying with the Civil Air Patrol before I went into the service.

I went to Fort Benning for airborne school. This was more advanced training than basic, a lot of PT [physical training], very grueling courses. Sometimes you wondered if you wanted to stay in this thing. But it turned out I made the right decision. After five jumps I got my wings. I was very proud.

We continued on through advanced airborne training. That December I got my first furlough. When I came back, the Battle of the Bulge was happening and the Allies were really hurting for men. (We found this out later.) Instead of ten to twelve men to a squad, the troops over there were down to four or five men per squad. The army rushed people out as fast as they could, so away we went. We knew we were heading to Europe, but we didn't know where we'd end up or why they were fast-tracking us through.

Right after New Year's Day we shipped out. It was a cold, cold day in January 1945. We went across the Atlantic on the *Aquitania*, a sister ship to the *Queen Mary*. The trip took eight days, which was considered fast. We had no convoy with us because our ship could outrun subs. We had a couple of big guns on board, too.

We embarked in Glasgow, Scotland, then went by rail through London and ended up in Portsmouth, southern England. We were in Portsmouth for a day or so, then took a ferry to Le Havre, France, where we were put on trains again. We traveled across France up to Alsace, on the eastern border of France. We ended up in Hagenau, on the Moder River, where Easy Company was on the line. They had just returned from Bastogne, and the ranks were really thin.

Don Bond

I mentioned I had tried to join the navy but couldn't because I was color-blind. Well, you couldn't be color-blind in the paratroops, either. When they drafted me I went into the regular infantry and took basic training down at Camp Roberts in California. When I finished basic they gave a talk there, looking for volunteers to go into the paratroopers. Me and another guy in my platoon volunteered. He never did make it; he got blisters on his feet from all the running and couldn't get through A-stage. He went back several times to start over and try to get through A-stage, but I don't think he ever made it. That wasn't uncommon. In the class I trained with, we started with 1,250 men and graduated with 550.

We trained at Fort Benning, four hours every morning and four hours every afternoon. If you quit they had a big red brick wall there, maybe ten feet high. Written on it in big white letters were the words "I am a quitter." Anytime you wanted, you could go stand against that wall with your nose and knees touching it and you were through. Boy, a lot of guys stood against that wall. And boy, the drill sergeants did everything they could to try to make you quit.

So how did I get in the paratroopers if I was color-blind? Well, when we volunteered back at Camp Roberts we all went to take the physical. We were all stripped off stark naked going from one place to another. For one test they had all these colored balls of yarn in a box. This guy in front of me stepped around the screen and I heard them telling them to pick out a red ball. (Now, I can see larger colors like that anyway. I just can't see the colors on those charts.) It didn't matter anyway, because I was looking right at the guy when he lay down the yarn ball and I saw where he put it. I came in, they said the same thing to me, and I picked up the same ball. That was all it took. I was in, and I never told them different.

I never had any trouble with my color-blindness all the way through. When you jump you have to watch for different-colored lights, but I could always distinguish those. I just could never see those eye charts. Even today it says I'm color-blind on my driver's license, but I have no problem telling which traffic light is which.

The training I got at Benning was a real henhouse, just like those guys at Toccoa went through. We got off the train and boy, we were all gung ho to be paratroopers. Then we saw those 250-foot towers that they dropped you off of, and our mouths gaped. They had us line up and the drill sergeants told us how it was going to be. One says, "We have a deal around here. We say, 'Knock out twenty-five.' And you do them. We'll show you what we mean." One of the other noncoms drops down and doubles it. He does fifty push-ups, just bang, bang, bang, bang. Then it was time for roll call. The sergeant tells us to say our first name and middle initial. He gets to the third guy, and his voice is sort of soft. The sergeant says, "You son of a bitch—sound off like you've got a pair of balls. Drop and give me fifty." That's the way it was from that day on. It was all push-ups and running and calisthenics. If you were in your barracks and had to go to the latrine you ran there and back. If they caught you walking, you did fifty push-ups. They had guys out there watching for you.

Training involved four stages. A-stage was all calisthenics. B-stage was jumping out of a mock-up of an airplane and half a day of calisthenics. C-stage was jumping off the high tower and calisthenics. D-stage was five jumps, one a day for five days, and calisthenics whenever you weren't doing that.

During B-stage the second week we jumped out of 34-foot-high towers. You climbed up stairs, they hit you on the butt, and said, "Go!" You were wearing parachute harnesses with lines hooked on the back. When you jumped, the cable caught and snapped you so you felt an opening shock. You bounced up and down hanging there, then you hit the ground and they moved you around like the wind was blowing you.

Well, a big, burly guy in the barracks next to me could do all the physical training during A-stage; no problem. One of the noncoms called him the best soldier in the battalion. But during B-stage he got up to one of those 34-foot mock-ups and he wouldn't jump. He put his hands on the sides of the fuselage and wouldn't go for nothing. They tried shoving him, but he fought back. He wasn't moving. Finally this big, burly guy started crying. They let him off the towers and he went and stood against the quit wall.

During C-stage they raised you up a 250-foot tower. You took a piece of paper with you. They yelled on a loudspeaker to let the paper go so they could see for sure which way the wind was blowing. If the paper blew away from the tower in any of three directions, they let you go, but if the wind was blowing into the tower, they wouldn't drop you. When they dropped you from that height, you came down fast.

I remember each of my five jumps during D-stage. You stand up, hook up, and check the equipment of the guy ahead of you in the aisle. You crowd up together, and the jumpmaster says, "Stand in the door." The first guy pivots on his right foot and puts his hands on the edge of the door. The other eleven guys are pushing on him. Pretty soon the green light comes on, the jumpmaster hits him on the rump, and hollers, "Go!" Boy, it's just one right after the other out of that plane.

I made one jump where the third guy out slipped on the metal flooring and fell down. Everybody went right over the top of him. We didn't even stop. He was the last guy in the plane. There's a bar above there, and the jumpmaster swung on that and kicked him hard with both feet. Out he went. You need to go out all as a group like that. If you don't, you're strung out all over the place when you land.

You don't have any sensation of falling. You make a pivot on your right foot, put your left foot right on the edge of the door, and kick with your right leg. The airplane's going about 120 miles per hour, and the prop blast from the engine on the side hits you. You don't jump out, really; it blows you out of the edge of the door. Then you're counting, one thousand, two thousand, three thousand. If you get to three thousand and don't feel the shock of your chute, you pull the reserve. We made some low jumps, too, and I don't think the reserve chute would have even had time to open on those jumps.

How's it feel when the chute opens? Good [laughs]. First thing you do is check the canopy to see if any of the panels are blown out. You've got twenty-eight panels in those old chutes. You can blow one or two, I've had that happen, but you don't want many more blown than that. You look around you to see if you're falling about the same rate as everybody else. Too fast and you've got too many blown panels.

I was in one of the last classes who ever trained to make a night jump. I went through jump school in September and October 1944. D-day had been the previous June. It was a night jump and it had been such a mess that they soon stopped doing night jumps altogether.

Night jumps are hairier all around. You're floating in blackness. You can't tell whether you're drifting backward or forward. Our drop zone that night was about three miles long and a mile wide, with low timber all around. I was drifting backward and missed our drop zone but landed in a little cut-out space at the edge of the timber. When I got up I could just make out a huge tree stump a few feet away. If I had hit that I would have broken my back for sure. Boy, I didn't like jumping at night. I never had to do it after that.

I knew an Indian kid named Blaine, every day he had something bad happen to him. He was always right behind me in the plane. On his second jump he got his chin strap hooked under one of his risers. It skinned the hell out of the bottom of his chin. It about half hung him.

About the third day we jumped, I went out of the plane, checked my chute, and heard somebody hollering above me. I looked up and there's old Blaine knee-deep in my silk. He was looking down at me through the apex of my chute, screaming and hollering. I told him to get the hell off me. He had jumped and came down right on top of my chute. When he did that, his chute collapsed because there was no weight on it anymore.

I knew we couldn't land like that. Even if all went fine, Blaine would fall the length of my chute, about thirty feet, as soon as I hit the ground. I kept hollering for him to step off. Flying through the air as we were, he was able to walk himself to the edge of my chute, where his chute filled out again and he could jump off.

On his last jump Blaine was really nervous. I was standing right next to him in flight. By mistake he pulled his reserve chute while he was still in the plane. They wouldn't make him jump without a reserve, so he didn't jump. When the plane landed, they went and got him and made him take off his jump boots. There was a gravel road about a mile long that led from the field back to the camp. They made him run back to camp barefooted on that road. The next day he was shipped out.

There were two Indians in our group. They'd come in together. Just before Blaine left, the other Indian found out that Blaine washed out. He said, "You son of a bitch. We joined together and now you've done and quit." Boy, he was burned. He took Blaine out back and beat the hell out of him. Paratroopers were a breed all by themselves, particularly when it came to fighting.

After all four stages, we graduated. When we graduated a cadre come along, shook hands with us, and said, "Congratulations, paratrooper." That was a proud moment, brief as it was. From then on we wore jump boots and got to blouse our pants. We went over to Phenix City, Alabama, a lot and saw regular infantry guys blousing their pants. That was an instant fight. We figured we were the only ones with the right to blouse our pants.

After training at Fort Benning I got a twenty-one-day furlough and went home to Portland. When I got back we had advanced training until December. We made a few more training jumps then.

One more story that happened during training—this happened while traveling by train from Camp Roberts over to Fort Benning. There was a good-looking Mexican kid on the train with us, Armando C. Caballero, who lived in Tucson. He was married and had a couple kids. He hadn't seen his kids for five months at least. He knew it would be a long time before he saw them again.

Well, the train we were on went through Tucson, and the tracks went right by his house. His home was only about two blocks from the depot.

That train stopped, and Armando could see his two kids from the train window. They were out playing in his backyard. But they couldn't see him, and the kids didn't know their dad was on the train. Armando wanted to see his kids so bad.

Now, they had told us before we got on the train that if anyone ever got off for any reason it was desertion. They didn't beat around the bush about that one. Finally Armando decided he was going to get off the train and go see his kids, just for a minute. He was a good soldier and we knew that if the train started going he would never be able to catch it. Everyone held him down. He fought us but we didn't let up. Everybody felt really sorry for him. That's tough for a guy.

CHAPTER SEVEN

Aboard the *Samaria*, Toccoa Men

Ed Joint

In September 1943 our regiment went from Camp Shanks to the docks at New York. We rode across on an old ship called the *Samaria*. It was a little ship, not too big. An English ship. We didn't like the English ships. The bunks were six foot high. I got sicker than hell and went out on the deck to stay. I guess there were a couple subs hanging out around our ship. But we didn't see them. I didn't sleep at all. It was bouncing around so much.

Frank Perconte

How was the Atlantic crossing? The food was horrible. I think all I ate was Hershey bars.

Dewitt Lowrey

On the ship, most of the guys spent their time playing poker, shooting craps, just enjoying life. We didn't know what it held for us on the other side, when we landed.

Buck Taylor

We crossed the Atlantic in a convoy. All the ships with us had antiaircraft gun crews up on the deck, so everything was uneventful.

Carwood Lipton and I decided to not sleep belowdeck because it was so hot and smelly down there. We staked out positions with the British crew at the stern of the ship. The food on board was pretty bad—I don't think I ate anything other than candy bars on the trip over. In fact, I don't remember going to eat at the mess facilities at all. The fellows who did all said it was just awful.

Salty Harris was with us on the trip. Here's a story that involves him, one that's never been publicized as far as I know—I don't know if Captain Winters even knew about it. One afternoon we were up on deck. It was foggy and you couldn't see very far. Before becoming a paratrooper, Salty had had two years at the Naval Academy in Annapolis. So he looked over the side of the ship and saw a little thing being dragged on a line through the water. It was spraying water up about four feet. Salty knew it shouldn't be there. He alerted the British crew right away and they adjusted the course of the *Samaria*. It could have been disastrous.

What Salty had spotted in the water is a standard navy device—there's a name for it, but I can't remember what. When weather conditions in a convoy were like that they put this device on a line behind the ship so that the ship behind it could keep a safe distance from the one ahead of it. What Salty spotted was a signal that we were bearing down on the ship ahead. None of the crew on the *Samaria* had spotted it. I think there were only a couple hundred feet between our ship and the next before they got things squared away and we altered course. I would say that Salty saved the day.

Forrest Guth

The *Samaria* was dirty, hot, and uncomfortable. We had some escorts with us and never traveled in a straight line—you had to continually zigzag so the German subs couldn't zero in. I remember eating fish chowder for breakfast. We did some calisthenics on board and worked a bit. Guys gambled and made and lost money. We had bunks down in the ship, but it was hot and miserable down below. I took blankets upstairs and slept on the deck.

Earl McClung

I joined Easy Company at Fort Bragg, so I rode over on the *Samaria* with them. The ride wasn't too bad. It wasn't as bad as the one coming back. On the way over I didn't get sick, but I did coming back.

Going over, I was up on the deck. They had a hold down below but the smell was too bad for me. So I grabbed a blanket and lay on the deck. Down below, guys were sick. I went below to take showers but then got the heck out of there. It wasn't cold up on the deck. You leaned up against the bulkheads to stay warm. We ate some kind of "sausages," they called them. I think they were made of sawdust.

Ed Tipper

Back at Camp Shanks while we had been getting ready to leave the United States, we were ordered to remove all parachute insignia the day before we left. We cut off our shoulder patches with razor blades and pulled our pants out over our boots so we looked like regular soldiers. When we landed in Liverpool, England, and left the ship, we were put on railway cars with windows boarded up so we couldn't see out. We went directly to our billets in Wiltshire, England.

When we got to our billets somebody said, "Lord Haw Haw's on the radio." So we all gathered around. Lord Haw Haw was the nickname given to an English-speaking traitor on German radio. It was a propaganda show meant to demoralize the Allies. We heard Lord Haw Haw say, "To the 101st Airborne, welcome to England. We were watching you at Camp Shanks when you cut off your insignia. We were watching you as you landed in Liverpool. And we were watching you when you boarded the blacked-out trains. And when you come to Europe, we will be waiting for you."

Now, that was unsettling. Someone said, "How in the hell did they know that—they must have spies everywhere." We weren't afraid, but it made us mad to think that people were spying on us. Our thought was, We'll show them.

Four or five years after the war I found out what had happened. Unknownst to the Nazis, every German agent who entered England during World War II had been caught by English Intelligence and offered the choice between cooperation or execution. Plenty of German spies agreed to cooperate. Throughout the rest of the war, English Intelligence controlled and transmitted harmless bits of information to the Germans, such as the arrival of the 101st. It wasn't vital news, but it gave the impression the German spies were still in control. So that's what we had heard from Lord Haw Haw that day—something that had been leaked on purpose. It was all part of the Allied strategy.

CHAPTER EIGHT

Atlantic Crossings, Replacements

Joe Lesniewski

We headed across the Atlantic in a naval convoy—the ships stretched as far as the eye could see. Conditions on our ship were pretty good. Whoever the captain was made sure we were treated right and that we had plenty of food, clean quarters, and good showers. I don't know of any other ships that were like that. My bunk was first deck below the top, not down below, in the hold. Those boats didn't have windows, or if they did, they were painted over. I wasn't seasick at all—hey, I was born on the Great Lakes. Being on the water didn't bother me whatsoever.

We had gone about a third of the way across the ocean when we got word from the boat captain to "hit the top" because there were U-boats in the area. So all the guys got up on deck. There were about three thousand people on our boat, it was a smaller civilian vessel, part of the Cunard–White Star line, not the *Queen E.* From the deck we saw a sight that I never forgot—we saw a flash of light from a ship about five miles away. On the ocean, it's not hard to see that distance. Two of our boats were being torpedoed. One sunk in three minutes; we heard we lost a lot of people on that one. The other was hit in the stern and didn't sink right away. It took about two hours, we heard, so our guys were able to save everybody who didn't get killed by the blast. The first one, I don't think they were able to save more than ten lives. Our boat was too far to be involved in the rescue operation. There were other ships in the area that were closer. The boats were carrying troopers. We heard that one of the boats had a lot of ladies on it, nurses, but that's just a rumor.

After we crossed the Atlantic, we landed in Northern Ireland. One of the officers came to the billets, asking if anyone could speak Polish. I could, along with five other guys. They sent the five of us to London—we wondered what for.

We were taken to No. 10 Downing Street, the residence of Prime Minister Churchill and the headquarters of Britain's government. They introduced us to General Vladislovas Anders, head of the Polish Armed Forces. Anders had been imprisoned when the Soviets invaded Poland in 1939. But when Germany declared war on Russia, Anders had been freed and told to re-create the Polish Army, whose initial task was to fight alongside the Red Army.

We met General Anders and talked with him. He was pleased with our command of the Polish language, so we were sent about thirty miles away from London, to a training area. We were there for three weeks for specialized training. In one exercise, they blindfolded us and taught us to take apart and reassemble German and Russian machine guns. We did it over and over again. Our stated mission was to train the Polish underground to fight the enemy, yet exactly *which* enemy became clear over time: it was the Russians.

The Russians were trying to get as much territory as possible. At the same time they were pursuing the Germans, they were trying to kill as many Americans as possible. You need to know that even though Stalin was our ally, he was never in love with us. Stalin had raped Poland. He hated the Americans. You don't hear too much about that nowadays.

For this mission, the five of us were made members of the Office of Strategic Services (OSS), the wartime intelligence agency that eventually became the CIA. All the time we were in training, we were told we were going to make a jump into Poland to help the Polish resistance. Then General Anders told us he was canceling the operation. The Russians had overrun our jump area, so we were sent back to Northern Ireland.

We must have done something right, because one of the officers asked the five of us where we wanted to be stationed. We were given the opportunity to go anywhere in the world. I had heard about the 506th Regiment of the 101st Airborne. They had a very solid reputation. I told the captain that there was an outfit I'd like to join. He said no problem. So after a couple days I joined Company E.

Frank Soboleski

We were assembled with more troops and loaded to be shipped overseas on the *Queen Mary* to England. When we sailed out of the harbor, all the lights of New York were out for a total blackout, including the Statue of Liberty. All we saw was her silhouette.

What a hellish trip that was. The majority of the men figured they wouldn't be coming back, so they smoked, drank, played poker, and shot dice around the clock. It was rough all the way over, and everybody got seasick. I couldn't stand the sloshing of vomit on the floor in the sleeping quarters down below, so I found an empty covered lifeboat on deck. That's where I camped out for the rest of the trip.

It took the *Queen Mary* seven days to get to England. She shut down every time we spotted a submarine. After the war was over, we were brought back home on the *Queen Mary* from Le Havre, France, and the trip only took three days because there were no submarines to stop for. On the way back we had German prisoners cooking and serving us. They couldn't do enough for us. We had steaks, ice cream, almost anything we wanted.

Roy Gates

We were at the POE [point of embarkation] to get on a victory ship to cross the Atlantic. I was escorting a platoon of rejects, guys who had been in the guardhouse. They were being sent overseas as regular infantry. A fellow second lieutenant says to me, "Boy, you're really going to have some trip with these guys on the way across." Well, they hadn't fed these kids for about twenty-four hours after letting them out of the guardhouse. They were all hungry. As we lined up to get on the ship I saw a Red Cross wagon where the ladies were giving out doughnuts. I thought,

I'll make friends with these guys by getting them something to eat. So I jumped over a rope and asked the lady about the doughnuts, but she said no, that she couldn't give them to prisoners. So we got in an argument, and in the end I guess I won because I was able to get doughnuts for the guys. This made me a hero down in the belly of the ship. I didn't have any trouble with the guys the whole trip.

We landed at Le Havre, France, got packed up in trucks, and wound up in Mourmelon, in a replacement depot. Once there, I delivered the men I was escorting over. They went one way, I went another.

Herb Suerth Jr.

I was sent overseas the last part of June 1944. D-day had already happened. We went over on the *Queen Mary*. My bunk was just below waterline in the bow of the boat. It was a section cut off by a destroyer in the early 1940s. We could see the weld marks in the hull. We landed in Greenock, Scotland, then got on a train and rode the full length of Scotland in daylight. It was a beautiful summer day. We were sent to a replacement depot in southern England. Thousands of guys were at the depot, to be processed and shipped out every day. But for some time we just sat there and sat there. I was an engineer replacement in the Corps of Engineers, probably slated for a service company, where we would do light electrical work, such as wiring up barracks or hospitals. At that point I had no idea I'd see combat.

The replacement depot was a base camp. While we were there, guys who had been wounded were coming back and in the barracks with us. A good friend of mine was also with me at the depot, Elly Chase. We had hooked up in the second basic training and went all the way through electrical training in New York together. Elly and I were with a lot of older guys, tradesmen, draftees. The older guys talked about how if they ever got into combat they would get out by shooting their toe off or trying to get pneumonia. Elly and I were nineteen and thinking, Holy man alive, we don't want to be with these guys. So one day Elly said to me, "Herb, if we go to combat with these guys we're going to be the only ones fighting. I saw where the 101st and 82nd are looking for replacements." And I said, "Let's do it." The next day we went to the commanding officer to see if we could transfer. He told us we couldn't transfer because as engineers we were part of the service forces, similar to the medical corps, and we couldn't transfer from service forces to ground forces. So we hunched our shoulders and figured the regular army had stopped our way.

It couldn't have been more than ten days later, a colonel or a major got up at this big formation with a couple thousand guys, I don't remember who it was. He said, "Congratulations, guys, you are all now all in the infantry." So Elly and I went back to our captain and asked about a transfer again. This time he said, "Yep, go and good luck." Elly went to the 82nd as a combat engineer and went to Berlin. He never got a scratch. I went to the 101st and began training under the famous Captain Sobel, then in charge of the 506th jump school.

I had a pretty good idea of what it meant to join the paratroopers. One of my mother's friends had a son who was a paratrooper who had talked about it quite a bit. He was later killed in Holland. He was standing next to an ammunition truck when it blew up. They were lucky if they found his dog tags.

Transferring to the 101st meant I was joining one of the best divisions around. I'd do it all over again today—to have been where I was and serve with the outfit I was with. I lucked out.

I went through parachute training in England, the same type of training the company received back at Fort Benning, Georgia. I knew nothing about Captain Sobel at the time. I saw him only once, in parachute school. He had been relieved of his command of Easy Company by then and was in command of the parachute school. His reputation had been buried. I never heard any of that stuff until early reunions after the war.

We were between our third and fourth jumps in parachute school when Easy Company was sent to Holland on September 17. We finished our jump training the next week and got our wings and 101st patch, but just sat there waiting until the company was relieved in Holland and sent to Mourmelon, France, at the end of November.

As soon as we got off the plane, we dragged our bags to battalion headquarters and lined up. The officers were all there sizing us up like they were picking players for a baseball team. We reported our name, rank, and serial number. One platoon leader says, "I'll take this one."

Another, "I'll take that one." Lieutenant Ed Shames walked up to me and said, "I'll take this one. Your name is Junior from now on." That's the way it went. So I went to 3rd Platoon, where Ed was the leader. Ed had received the first battlefield commission in the 506th at the end of Normandy. He was an excellent map reader; it had been a hobby of his since he was a kid. He had been an operations sergeant in the 3rd Platoon and built all the sand tables for the regiment for D-day before he got his commission. He's still in the service today.

On my first evening with the 101st I asked some guys where I could find a latrine. They showed me where. It was kind of dark in there and all I could see was two holes in the floor and a set of footprints next to it. I had never seen anything like it and had no idea what it was. Next to it was some kind of a basin that I figured was the urinal, so I relieved myself in that. I had just buttoned my pants when another guy came in and started to wash his face in the same basin. Thank God he didn't see me! I'm sure I would have ended up dead.

Easy Company had come off the line from Holland on a Wednesday or a Thursday in late November. Everyone celebrated Thanksgiving the day after that. Within a day or two of that we had a full retreat parade—ODs [olive drabs, uniforms], boots shined—the guys didn't have half the stuff they needed. I was in good shape for the retreat, gearwise. I had a good pair of boots, not too hard to polish, not too much wear yet. I still had my ODs, so I was pretty well ready. But some of the other guys definitely had other thoughts about the parade. The way some guys talked, I thought there was going to be a mutiny.

Earl McClung's bunk was next to mine. He wasn't moving. Just before the parade, somebody came to Mac and said, "Hey Mac, gimme your boots." Mac handed them over and the guy started shining them for him. I wondered what was going on. Another guy came up and said, "Hey Mac, gimme your pants. He started pressing them for Mac, and so on till Mac was completely ready for the retreat. They were polishing McClung's boots and pressing his pants for him! They knew he wouldn't, and if everybody in the company didn't participate, then nobody would receive any passes.

Over the years I've had to ask myself if I remember that story correctly. Now, you have to realize Earl McClung was one hell of a combat soldier, one of the best that ever was. That's why the guys pressed his pants for him. Well, one night years after the war McClung and Shifty Powers and I were drinking Calvados together and McClung says, "Y'know, I wasn't a very good garrison soldier." I said, "Well Mac, my impression is that you were maybe the world's worst." He looked right at me and said, "You're right!"

After we did that retreat, the guys got their passes. I went back to the barracks. Mac came in, took off his pants, kicked them under his bed, took off his blouse, kicked it in a corner somewhere. As I was saying to him years later, "Mac, I bet they're still there to this day." He says, "I betcha they are, too."

Don Bond

The Battle of the Bulge began near the end of our advanced training at Benning. They split us up in three shipments to head overseas. I went in the first shipment. It was just after Christmas 1944. We went to Fort Meade, Maryland, then to Camp Shanks, New York, then went over on the RMS *Aquitania*, a Cunard ocean liner, run by the English.

The crossing took just over a week. About ten thousand of us were on the boat. Big as the ship was, everybody got seasick. The whole ship smelled like vomit. That was the first time I ever ate Brussels sprouts—you got your meal, then they threw a big bunch of boiled Brussels sprouts on top of your mess gear. I ain't never liked them since.

We landed in Scotland. You came off the gangplank and walked under this canvas deal right up to where you got on the train. People couldn't see who was getting off the ship. We went by train to Southampton in England. We thought we would be training in England for some time, but just a few days later I joined the 101st in Hagenau.

We went up there in semi-trailer trucks. There were maybe six or seven hundred guys who went to the 101st at this time. Signs were all along the road warning about mines. When we got there, Colonel Sink came out on the balcony of the regimental headquarters and gave us a pep talk. He wanted to know if anybody had questions. A guy raised his hand and asked when the 506th would go back on the line. Colonel Sink looked a bit flabbergasted. He said, "Trooper, the Germans are right over there about two hundred yards. You're *on* the line." That was the first time we realized how close we were to the enemy.

They peeled us off and sent me and about five other guys to company headquarters. I reported to Captain Ron Speirs, a stern-looking guy with dark, bushy eyebrows. He had come over to E Company from D Company, and there were all sorts of stories floating around about him shooting guys—both the Germans and his own guys if they goofed off. Speirs made me sit in a chair across the desk from him and asked me if I had ever been in combat. Now, when you're back at Fort Benning, all the paratroopers go over to the bars in Alabama and get in fights. So I said, "No, sir, only in Phenix City."

Speirs stared at me for a long time from under his bushy eyebrows, not saying a word, never cracking a smile. "That'll be all," he said at last. I worked closely with Speirs from then on.

One of the five new replacements went right on guard duty. He was hit in the neck within forty-five minutes. I don't know if he lived, but he never did come back. His war was pretty short.

CHAPTER NINE

Aldbourne: Calm Before the Storm

Ed Joint

Easy Company arrived in Aldbourne, England, in mid-September 1943 for more training. It was a nice place, not too bad. We were hardly ever there, actually; mostly we were out in the field. I was in a Quonset hut. I don't remember how big it was. A lot of guys slept in the hut.

Earl McClung

In Aldbourne we spent most of our time walking: ten- to twenty-five-mile hikes in the mud. That's what I remember. It was pretty cold, miserable. We did a lot of training there, but I've forgotten most of it.

Forrest Guth

Aldbourne was made up of lots of nice English people who treated us well. I don't know why—they were overrun by Americans. But they were very obliging. They did laundry for us or baking if we asked them. The English had a saying, "The Americans are oversexed, overpaid, and over here." Some of them felt that way anyway.

We spent time in pubs after hours and in fish and chips joints. They didn't have wax paper but wrapped the fish and chips in newspaper. Fish and chips was a mainstay.

Shifty Powers

Aldbourne was a small village in a rural area. I was told that the residents of Aldbourne were preparing to be invaded by the Germans. They had hidden some food out in the woods and were practicing to defend themselves against German soldiers. All they had to fight with were pitchforks, shovels, and hoes—no guns. After the war and what I had seen in combat I've thought about what a massacre that would have been. The Germans had burp guns, Mausers, and machine guns and would have wiped that village out. I think the people in Aldbourne felt a sense of safety to have the American soldiers there.

Ed Tipper

Most of the guys had never experienced surroundings like Aldbourne before, but it was not unusual for me because of my experiences in Ireland when I was a child.

The English in Aldbourne tended to live simple lives. Big excitement to them would be to go to a café and have a cup of tea. Our guys were quite a contrast to the English. We were loud. They were reserved. Sometimes our vocabulary proved offensive to them. Often we didn't understand them. For instance, "bum" meant "vagabond" to us, not "ass," as it did to them. Bloody in England (used as an adjective) was a horrible word, referring to menstrual blood. I was a bazooka man, but I learned to be careful in describing what I did—you couldn't say bazooka, because it was their slang word for penis.

We were told to be nice to our billets because we would be staying in Aldbourne for a long time. I had no problem there. Near my billets lived a tremendous family, the Mindenhalls. Sometimes I stole tea from the mess hall and brought it to them. All kinds of groceries were being rationed by then, so they were happy to get it. For at least fifty years after the war I kept in touch with the family. Today I'm still in contact with the last surviving member. We write two or three letters per year.

I enjoyed myself in Aldbourne, though the training was intense. We were looking forward to combat. We were ready and knew we were ready. Altogether, we had a year and nine months before we went into combat. In those days, a typical infantryman received about four months of training before going into combat. So we were receiving all this specialized training, including how to drive a train. Many of us expressed doubts that we'd ever need to know that. But one guy I knew, not in our outfit, was captured and then escaped. He got in a train and raced away from the town he was imprisoned in. So the specialized training paid off for at least one guy.

Sometimes they brought in English sergeants to train us. We couldn't understand them and they couldn't understand us. One sergeant's English was almost incomprehensible. His mouth came open and sounds came out but that was about it. The word he used consistently after he showed us something sounded like "appee." It was always a question: Appee? Appee? He said it all the time.

"Yeah, yeah, sure, sure," all the guys said, though we had no idea what "appee" meant. Finally one of us figured out it meant "happy"—like, "Are you happy with what I've said?" He was asking if we understood him. Sure, I guess so. We could figure out what he was showing us far better than we could by what he was telling us.

At one combat range targets popped up and we shot at them as we advanced through the range. It was probably February or March of 1944, and by then most of the men I knew were totally unhappy with our company commander, Captain Sobel. We worried about having him lead us into battle. Sobel sometimes wore a big sheepskin jacket with a lot of wool around the collar. Just before target practice one day he walked out on the range ahead of us. A few guys started shooting really close to where he stood. Pretty soon we were all shooting close to his head as he moved forward. It was live ammunition. Nobody was trying to hit him. We just thought he'd get the message. We were putting shots about a foot from his head. I'd say a dozen shots were aimed as close to Sobel as possible. He just sort of waved, his back facing us as he led us through the combat range.

Al Mampre

There were some Scotchmen in Aldbourne who went for drinks in a pub every morning about ten o'clock. Sometimes I went there, too. They argued back and forth in their Scotch dialect—just "barumpt armph bah"—I never did understand what they were saying. Every morning they argued. I couldn't understand a word. One morning I decided to join in. "Barumpt armph rut rut," I said. It was complete gibberish. One of them looked at me and said, "That's right, Yank," and kept right on with his conversation.

Ed Pepping

I met a girl in Aldbourne; she was sixteen, I was twenty. I like to say that she trapped me. One day I was walking up Oxford Street and heard piano music. She had her door open and was playing the piano. That was the start of a wonderful friendship. We went for long walks, to concerts, and to church. We danced together in her kitchen. She was a lovely girl, slim, with beautiful hair. She was very polite. We really matched each other well—we were both sort of polite, shy people. Her full name was Josephine, but everybody called her Jo. There was definite romantic attraction. It was very difficult to leave each other. She was in school when I left for the staging area, so we didn't have a chance to say good-bye. We wrote but lost contact after I was out of the hospital. For many years I had no idea what happened to her.

Well, in 1994 I went back to England. I was hesitant to try to contact her because I didn't know what her status was. At a party the tour organizers had for us they gave us a magazine that had been distributed in Aldbourne. When I got back to the States I wrote to the magazine distributor to ask if he knew Jo's family.

It turns out that Jo's sister-in-law worked for the distributor. He gave the sister-in-law the letter, she gave it to Jo, and we've been writing ever since. She had married a guy nineteen years older than her who apparently didn't treat her very well because she suffers from depression. My sending her cheery letters and cards has helped her a great deal and encouraged her to take her medicine regularly. She's gotten better and better. We talk on the phone about once a week.

Joe Lesniewski

I had wanted to join the 101st from the beginning. I joined them in Aldbourne, England. It was late 1943. When you're a new guy coming into an old outfit, there are a lot of guys who don't like you at first. That's what happened to me. I had a couple fights with them, and I knocked the hell out of a couple of 'em. I made short work of the guys—two of them, I ain't going to mention their names, both are deceased now, and that would be wrong of me. One was a real smart alec with everybody. I don't recall exactly what he said, but he pulled a gun on me once. I told him, "You better make sure you kill me, because if you don't, you're done." So the guys kept us away from each other.

After that most of us were real good friends. Finally, after about a month and a half, things started to look pretty good between us. I didn't have any more problems. Later on I had more friends than I ever expected to have. Alex Penkala and Skip Muck became great friends of mine.

One day we were sitting in this room in Aldbourne, this kid had a guitar, I can't think of his name, he was playing one of the songs I knew. Alex and Skip came over. When I was in the States, I had learned a lot of the Western songs, so I started teaching the guys the songs, and we started singing. We had a pretty good group there. We kept it to ourselves mostly. I'm not sure if the other guys enjoyed our voices. I had a book with some of the Western songs, so I could teach them the exact words. Our group didn't have a name. It was just for fun. I still have the song-book somewhere. It's been so long ago.

Alex and Skip didn't make it. They were killed in Bastogne. It's hard to talk about.

CHAPTER TEN

A Bad Day for a Lot of Young Men

Forrest Guth

At the end of May 1944 we went to the marshaling area in southern England and were quarantined—nobody in or out. That's where we learned our mission was to invade Normandy.

Everybody had some time to get prepared, so you sharpened weapons or wrote letters home. I was usually hungry and thought I might want to take some extra supplies with me, so I sewed a couple of pockets on the left sleeve of my jump jacket and on the back of a coattail. We got K rations and candy bars from home or from the PX. You could carry as many as you had space for, so I put food in my extra pockets. I was known as a chow hound, but it's just because I was hungry. I also carried extra ammunition.

Other guys sewed similar extra pockets. We found out in Normandy that if these pockets were not reinforced (and many weren't), then the pockets would rip and stuff would fly out. My pockets worked out okay and didn't tear.

Buck Taylor

The days and hours before the D-day invasion were filled with tension and nervousness. We knew this was it. We pored over maps and sand tables, studying the area. I think we knew every road and bridge in Normandy.

Al Mampre

I missed the jump on D-day. I was in the hospital with an infection on my neck. It was a cyst, a big lump. I don't know how I got it, but it just grew and grew. It felt disappointing to miss the jump after all the training we had had.

Ed Tipper

Upottery Airfield was circled with barbed wire. We knew we were going to invade Europe. On June 4 they gave us great food, wonderful food, ice cream, food we had never seen all the time we had been in England. We knew this was it.

We boarded the planes on June 4 in preparation for a June 5 jump. But Eisenhower decided the weather was too bad, so we disembarked and went the next night, June 6, instead. I felt like we were ready. I was totally confident in the men we had and in the training we had received. We were as good as we would ever be. I don't think anybody was particularly afraid.

The flight over the Channel was exactly how it was shown in the miniseries. Everything was calm, then the antiaircraft fire started up. It was violent and intense, beyond what we had imagined. Planes ran into a fogbank and started to break formation. The pilot of my plane went down low. Instead of slowing down, needed for a good jump, he gunned that damn plane as fast as it would go, then pushed the green light to get rid of us. We landed about nine kilometers away from our drop zone. We found out later this was fortunate, because the Germans had the area we were supposed to drop in well covered with machine-gun fire. We could have been badly cut up if we had dropped there.

Earl McClung

When we went over the Channel, I looked out and saw all these ships. I was just amazed at the number. When we got over the Normandy coast, the flak was heavy. You didn't pay attention to ships anymore, you just wanted to get out of the plane.

Dewitt Lowrey

So much has already been said about D-day, I'll put it like this: D-day was a bad day for a lot of young men.

Bill Wingett

I think I slept most of the way over in the plane. I don't remember being nervous. I was aggravated because the last thing before I got on the plane they handed me one of those leg bags to wear. I never knew what was in that leg bag. They didn't tell me—a truck came alongside of the plane, they dumped out a half dozen bags, and somebody said to put it on. It felt like a brick. They had to help you get in the plane because you couldn't walk, you were so heavy.

That leg bag almost cost me my life. I was one of the very few who actually landed with the damn thing. Most of them came off in flight, but mine stayed on. There's no way to know for sure how high we were when we jumped, but I know it wasn't very high because it was such a quick trip down. I could see tracers. Every one of them felt like it was coming right toward me.

When I landed I was in water over my head. I couldn't get the leg bag off me. It was like wearing an anchor. I've never been a swimmer. When I was seven years old my uncle was teaching me to swim and ducked me. That didn't make me fond of water. I'm still not fond of water today. (I like a good soak in the tub, but I always know where the bank is there.) So I tried to stay above the water but couldn't. There was too much weight. I was able to get my trench knife out. I got a breath of air, then went down and tried to saw the damn leg bag loose. When I came up for air, people were running past me. I hollered for someone to give me a hand. They just kept going. As soon as I got loose I found I was standing in a big ditch. The water was only about eighteen inches deep on the edges, but I had landed in the middle, over my head.

When I landed, I was still clutching my rifle but dropped it while trying to free myself. I wasn't able to find it in the water. I climbed out of the ditch. All I had left was my trench knife and a canteen. My pack was soaking wet, heavier than hell. I dumped all the contents out on the ground and walked away, everything except a silver flask full of brandy. It held about a half a pint. I kept that.

After I landed, I didn't know where I was. I don't think anybody did. Formations had broken up. We were all scattered about. When I finally got going, I met up with some guys from the 82nd Division. I stayed with them for just a little over three days. During that time the only people I saw who I knew were Pat Christenson and Colonel Sink. I gave Colonel Sink a shot of brandy. He says, "Well, a soldier who knows what equipment to carry."

CHAPTER ELEVEN

Fighting in Normandy

Rod Bain

It's all a nightmare.

Dewitt Lowrey

After the drop, I didn't hit the ground. I hit a tree and hung there. It was a big old tree with big leaves on it and I could see two machine guns in each corner of a field shooting at me. Those bullets just whizzed past me through those leaves and branches. It sounded like they were firing at a barn. I could see the tracers coming right at me.

My buddies took care of the machine guns. I must have been near a farmhouse or something because after that a big old Rottweiler came up and had me bayed up in that tree. Some lady came out in her nightgown and took the dog away.

I cut my ammo off my leg and let it drop, let my machine gun drop, then got myself out of the harness, and that's the way I came down. It was quite a distance from the drop zone and we had to get back to the unit.

When it comes to the war, that's all I talk about. The only person I ever talked to about what happened was my wife. She was the only person who needed to know.

Bill Wingett

I haven't revealed my first action to anybody, and I don't know if I really care to. I don't think of it as hidden. It's not very easy to kill a man. After you've done it, and after you've been shot at a few times, it becomes pretty easy. The first time I killed a man was out of desperation. The column that I fell in with was moving up this causeway, and somebody said, "Three men: out there." I went with a couple of other guys up this hill, more like a little rise. We saw some enemy soldiers and ducked down. Amazingly, these three Germans came within fifteen feet of us and started to set up a machine gun. I decided that I had to do something. The other two guys who were with me had rifles. I was hoping they'd shoot. They didn't. So I killed the first guy with the knife I had. I went up behind him and ran it right into his kidneys. He had a rifle in his hands. As I hit him, he went down shooting, wounding one of his companions and killing the other. One of the other guys who was with me shot the wounded German in the head. It couldn't have happened more than an hour after we jumped. That was when I got a rifle. I got it from the guy who shot the German in the head. It made him sick and he threw down his rifle. I picked it up. I never learned the names of the guys I was with. I don't know if I ever saw them again. Then we went down the hill.

I had sewn a knife into the top of my boot. On the jump, the leg bag drove the knife's tip into my ankle and it dug in. By the time the Battle of Carentan happened, I was back at Utah Beach with my foot all swelled up. About half an inch of the knife's tip had broken off in my ankle, stayed there, and festered. I had made the mistake of taking my boot off, and I couldn't put it back on.

On the beach I looked up and saw a German pilot strafing the beach. Two of our P-38s came out of nowhere and took him out. Bang. I saw where he landed in his parachute. He was dead. I took some pictures off him that were in his pocket and a scarf. I have those pictures in my scrapbook today.

Earl McClung

When I jumped I landed in the town square of Ste. Mère Église, about thirteen miles from where I was supposed to be. Flak was coming at us when we jumped. It was horrific. It looked like everything was coming right between your eyes. There were Germans all around. Machine gun rounds, small arms, tracers. I landed on the roof of a little shed behind the church. Underneath was water. There was a Nativity scene out in front of it. I'm not a religious man, I was baptized Catholic, but that's about it—so there was no significance to me landing next to the scene.

It was dark when I landed, no moonlight, dark. Some of the guys say there was moonlight, but not where I jumped. I found out later that was the case along the coast: that clouds come and go, so it could have been dark or not dark depending on when you jumped. As I came down, there were two Germans running down a walkway toward me, shooting at my parachute. It was no contest. I always jumped with my rifle in my hands, ready to go. The church was behind them, and I could see their silhouettes against the church, but they couldn't see me. I was only five feet from them when I shot them.

Bullets were coming from all around. The way the bullets were flying, I knew I had to get the hell out of town. So I crawled about two blocks to the edge of town. They had a cemetery there. I crawled out through the gravestones and got out in the woods. Did I think I would survive the war? Maybe you get those thoughts later, that you're going to die. But right then I thought I was invincible. I didn't think I could be killed. Probably when we got to Bastogne I started changing my mind about that. Sometimes hoping I would get killed [laughs].

In the woods, I ran into a guy from the 502nd. We stayed there until daylight. Then he got shot in the ankle the next day, so I went looking for medics for him. I ran into some guys from the 82nd, so I turned him over to them. They said they had some more guys from our outfit with them. So I went up to 82nd, and that's when I got with Paul Rogers and Jim Alley.

With the 82nd, about thirty of us tried to take Ste. Mère Église. We tried three times over the next several days. I slept during the days a little. At night was patrolling. I got to know that graveyard well because I crawled out of it three times over six days. We'd charge into town, but the firing would get so heavy. They'd start opening up on us with 88s, so we'd have to get the hell out of there. No one was leading the 82nd that I knew of. We were more or less on our own. We had a 101st officer lying face down in a trench hollering at us. I never did see him get out of the damn thing. But we weren't paying any attention to him anyway.

On my last patrol into Ste. Mère Église, I went around the town and came in from the back. I found nine tanks. I came back and told them they were crazy to think we'd ever take the town—there were a lot more Germans in it than we ever imagined. When I counted the nine tanks I got the hell out of there. A rifle doesn't do much good against tanks. Later we found out there were about three thousand Germans.

Somewhere around there is when I got my nickname. I had been on patrol all night and I came back and was lying there asleep and some second lieutenant came up and asked Alley and Rogers who the machine gunner was. They both pointed at me. I was sound asleep. So he just put the machine gun by me. I wasn't very happy about being made a machine gunner. As far as I know, that machine gun is still there. When I woke up there were some strong adjectives being thrown around. So Rogers wrote a poem about it with a line that went,

Who hung the gun on One-Lung McClung?

Paul Rogers wrote a lot of poems. Both he and Walter Gordon wrote a lot of them. They had some good ones. I got a big kick out of them.

It's been rumored that I could smell Germans and that this came in handy in Normandy because I could smell them before I could see them. Well, that's true in a way. I seemed to have an uncanny sense of smell when it came to finding German soldiers. In later years I've had German people ask me if I could actually smell Germans. Well, that just sounds wrong—there's no implication that the German people have a particular odor. The German soldiers wore a lot of leather—all their webbing, their boots—much more than we did. Where we had plastic webbing, they had leather. When they were damp and the wind was right, I could smell the wet leather. If you've ever walked into a tack room with wet saddles hanging in there, you know that smell. I don't remember if there was a specific time that it came in handy, it's been so long ago. But I would imagine that when I was out on patrol

I'd stop and sniff. If I could smell Germans, it got us in a better way than not.

After Ste. Mère Église we found out where E Company was, so we took off cross-country and joined our outfit. I don't know what happened after we left, but apparently the Germans moved out and the 505th was able to take the town.

Ed Tipper

Out of the plane, the opening shock was so great it ripped my musette bag off. I went down almost immediately. I went right through a tree and landed unhurt. I had my rifle in three pieces in my pack and was holding my bazooka—I don't know how I was able to hold on to it, but I did. I had my weapons but very little ammo.

Here's the result of being well trained: a small battery in the stock of my bazooka provided a charge to ignite the rocket when the trigger was pulled. Immediately upon landing I checked the bazooka by pulling the trigger. The light was supposed to light up but didn't. The opening shock had snapped open the battery latch, pulled the batteries out, then snapped it back together. Fortunately, I had checked before I had tried to fire at any of the enemy. I tossed the bazooka away.

When I landed, I heard another guy shout over to me. We had these passwords, "welcome," "flash," and "thunder," but instead of using the password, he yelled "Tipper!" How he knew it was me, I wasn't sure, it was dark. It was Frank Mellett (he was later killed in Bastogne). Mellett and I started walking. We met some troopers, probably five or six more. I didn't know any of the guys we were with. We eventually wound up with about eighteen men. I didn't know any of them except Mellett, but we had a sergeant in charge. We met one German patrol and had a short firefight. They had too much firepower for us, so we backed off. We didn't have any automatic weapons, just rifles. They did. They didn't pursue us.

Ed Joint

When I landed, who do I find on the ground next to me but Joe Lesniewski, my friend from Erie, Pennsylvania? There was no one else around.

It was quiet—you wouldn't think a war was going on. We took our chutes off and needed to decide where we should go.

We followed a ditch. Then we met some guys from 82nd Airborne, six or seven of them. They had ammo and everything, so I said, "I'm going with them." I figured we weren't going no place the way we were headed.

In Normandy I got a little concussion. They were lobbing those shells over five, six, seven miles into France. Me and three others were walking across a field, and boy, something hit me. It knocked me out. The guys thought I was dead. One guy says, "He's dead, let's get the hell out of here." Another guys says, "No, I'm not leaving without him." So they waited a little bit and I came to. It was a concussion. It scared them, and it scared me, too, but I was okay. That was during the first day, first hours, after jumping.

Clancy Lyall

When I jumped in Normandy it was with the 2nd Battalion, 506th, Headquarters, heavy weapons. I landed about eighteen miles from our drop zone, close to the town of Ste. Mère Église. I had my M-1, trench knife, and about four clips of ammo with me when I landed—that was it. My musette bag and bandoliers were blown off from the speed of the jump. I got some ammo off a dead trooper pretty soon after that, so I was okay.

The Germans had flooded the lower lands. I landed in a swampy area, water up to my waist. I got out of my chute and picked up my buddy John Campbell right away. Neither of us knew where the hell we were. We heard Germans coming, so we hid under a little footbridge until they passed, then kept going.

We moved toward the sound of firing because we figured paratroopers would be there. Soon we hooked up with some guys from B Company, 508th. We stayed with them for two days and fought as they were taking Ste. Mère Église. Some guys from Easy Company, Battalion headquarters, came past us, so from there we went back over to Headquarters and joined the rest of Easy Company just before the Battle of Carentan.

Ste. Mère Église—that was pretty bad. The Germans opened up on us with artillery and small-arms fire while we were still in the sky. The flak was so thick you could walk down on it. Most of the 508th landed right on top of the town. Quite a few Germans were there when they landed. I remember seeing a couple of our guys hanging in trees, all shot up.

While I was fighting in Ste. Mère Église, a German popped out from behind his cover across the street. He looked pretty young. I aimed at his knees and hit the lower part of his leg. A couple of his guys came over and helped him away. That was fine as far as I was concerned, just as long as they weren't shooting at me. Truthfully, I never wanted to kill anybody. I know I did—don't get me wrong. But I was never bloodthirsty or anything. Anytime I could, I would shoot to wound, not kill.

Buck Taylor

Being second-in-command, I was the pusher, the last one out of the plane. It was dark when I landed and very quiet. I was in this little hedgerow field. I rounded up Rod Strohl, Shifty Powers, and Bill Kiehn. We tried to figure out where we were exactly. There were no streets or roads around that we could see to get our bearings. We decided to head east. One of our objectives was to get to a landing area in the east and lend a hand to stop German reinforcements believed to be there.

We soon came across a little dirt road and began following it. I still hadn't fired a shot or seen any Germans. Dawn was just breaking when we came across an officer from the 502nd who had been dropped in the wrong place. He had half a dozen fellows from his platoon with him. We talked for a few minutes. It was daylight then. Suddenly we heard a truck coming down the road. We could hear it before we could see it, and knew by the sound that it wasn't one of ours. The truck came into view. It was filled with Germans. This officer from the 502nd barked some orders. He was really on the ball. One of his guys had a bazooka, and as soon as the truck was in range he blasted it. We headed toward the truck. Dead and wounded Germans were scattered all over the place. That's when I decided we should move on. The officer outranked me and I knew he would have us standing guard over the prisoners and wounded for the rest of the Normandy campaign. So I said, "Excuse us, we're going to try to find our unit," and we kept moving.

Frank Perconte

On D-day I landed near Ste. Mère du Mont. There was a river there, I remember. You've got to think, the plane's going 150 miles per hour. There are twenty guys in the plane. So from the first guy out the plane to the last guy who jumped, you were at least five miles apart when you landed. But we got together and kept going. I was with Lipton, Boyle, Luz, and Christenson. Later on we met up with Winters.

Forrest Guth

I landed in a meadow with cows all around. Luckily I didn't land on one. Walter Gordon was with me. We found John Eubanks. Floyd Talbert came along a little later. The four of us went on together. We were way off target, about 2½ miles away from where we were supposed to be—near Ravenoville. All we knew was that we were supposed to head to the shore, so we headed west to get to the Channel.

We didn't encounter much hostility that first night. We were supposed to avoid fighting that first night if we could. So if you saw any enemy, you tried to circumvent them. You could get pretty good hiding places in the hedgerows.

It gets light quite early that time of year. The next morning we kept going. Lieutenant Tom Meehan had become our company commander after he replaced Captain Sobel. His plane, with twenty-one men aboard, was loaded with torpedoes and blew up when hit by enemy fire in the first hours of D-day. The remains crashed to the ground near Ste. Mère Église. Everyone on board, including the entire company headquarters, was killed.

That's what we found the next morning, the four of us, although we didn't realize at first whose plane it was. The plane was out in a field beyond where we had landed. It was all torn up, burned, pieces of aluminum, dead bodies, so we didn't spend much time there. This kind of thing happened and you didn't dwell on it, you just got back to business. I had a camera and took a number of pictures. When we got back to England I got the film developed. They decided it must have been Meehan's plane by the description of the area it had landed in. I guess if we had known it was Meehan's plane we would have had a tougher time with it.

When you were fighting you never had time to dwell on things. But when we got back to England, that's where it affected you more. You saw guys who were missing. You wondered what happened to them. You got that feeling like, what am I doing here? You had more time to reflect. But I never had any second guesses about enlisting. I don't know what it was, but when you were with this group of men, you became brothers. You never wanted to be away from them, you wanted to help them. In fact, I never got the feeling like we might not make it. The only time I was close to that was in Bastogne, when things really got rough. Other than that, we thought we were invincible.

We kept walking after we saw the plane. After a while we came across a group of the 82nd in a barn and fought alongside the 82nd for a few days. There were probably fifty guys from the 82nd. It was good in the sense that the Germans were just as confused as we were.

Ed Pepping

We were dropped much lower and faster than anticipated. On the way down I remember seeing burn holes in my parachute from the bullets going through. I came in backward and landed in the middle of a field. I didn't have enough time to pull up on my risers and alleviate the shock of landing. The back of my helmet hit the back of my head. I didn't know it at the time but I had cracked three vertebrae and received a concussion. All I knew was that I kept blacking out and coming to. That blacking in and out happened all the time I was there. I have a lot of blank spots in my memory of Normandy. I can remember only about half the time I was there. It comes in bits and pieces.

When I landed, I had nothing except a knife. As a medic I never carried a rifle anyway, but the speed of the jump and the opening shock had ripped all my medical equipment off me. That was very frustrating. It had taken weeks to pack the equipment, but the frustrating part was that I had nothing to work with. You can imagine, a lot of the wounds seen were catastrophic.

As medics, our job was to do whatever we could do. On the first day I was on my way to join the guys and was called into a building being used as an aid station. We had no evac at the time. A guy had a big sucking chest wound, a wound they had only told us about but never seen first-hand. The only thing I could do was close the wound up as best I could. I couldn't stay there to see that he was evacuated. I don't know if the man lived or not. That was the way it was. Time after time we saw guys lose legs and arms, chest wounds, guys all shot up and bloody. A man can bleed to death in a couple of minutes. If it hadn't been for the wonderful doctors we had—the guys who had some serious medical experience—we would have lost so many more men.

You have to realize that a medic is no doctor. Our job was to reach a wounded man as quickly as possible out on the field, get him stabilized by bandaging and giving him morphine, then get him back to a doctor—if you could. But if you don't have any bandages or morphine, what can you do? You scrounge around and find whatever you can. When you come across catastrophic wounds—what can a medic ever do about those? It's not like I had a first-aid book with me or could call up a doctor on the phone.

That same day, the first day, I went to a church in Angoville au Plein that was being used as an aid station. One of our guys had found an abandoned German jeep somewhere and was bringing in as many casualties as he could. I helped him out for quite a while. The people in that church have never taken the blood stains off those pews. They contacted me a few years back to ask me if I wanted my name put on a memorial there. I said, "Heck, no. All I did was bring people in."

Outside of Beaumont, there was a lot of fire going on. Lieutenant Colonel Billy Turner, 1st Battalion's commanding officer, stood on top of a tank turret and directed fire at a .75. He was hit in the head by a sniper's bullet and collapsed. Since he was at the front of a six-tank column, the whole advance halted, exposing the column to enemy fire. I ran over and leaned headfirst into the tank's turret where he had fallen. With the help of the tank's crew I pulled the battalion commander out just before he died. It was an agonizing moment. Lieutenant Colonel Turner was a good man and much revered. At least the tank column could keep moving again.

I never did get back to my unit. The last thing I remember was being in Carentan with three others, walking headlong through town in an attempt to reach E Company. All I knew was that they were meeting fierce resistance and needed medics. The next thing I knew, I was in the hospital with a cast on my leg from ankle to hip. I have no idea why. I have no recollection of how I got wounded. There was no record of anybody picking me up. One moment I was trying to get back to my unit. The next minute I was in the hospital in a cast.

In the hospital I got the Purple Heart, the Bronze Star for my actions trying to save Lieutenant Colonel Turner (I never knew who recommended me for it), and the Croix de Guerre. Somebody stole my uniform, all my equipment, my medals, and everything I had.

They wouldn't send me back to my unit because of my condition. They figured that because I was still in and out I either had a concussion or was a victim of combat fatigue. They ran me through all these tests. A doctor determined I had a severe concussion and had cracked three vertebrae in my neck. Those were causing the blackouts.

That was all I needed to know. Five of us decided to go AWOL, left the hospital, and went back to the 506th. I was with the unit for fifty-one days trying to get set up to go to Holland. It's funny—for those fifty-one days I am still counted AWOL, even though I was back with my unit. After that time they sent me to the general hospital in England to serve in the seriously wounded ward. I was still blacking out occasionally.

Working in the ward turned out to be one of my favorite experiences. Sometimes we worked two to three days straight on the guys, if a convoy came in, but it felt like we could actually do some good for the men. The doctors and nurses took me under their wing. I got so I could give penicillin shots without waking a guy up. That felt important. It was an honor to serve in that ward.

It's true, we saw some horrific things in the ward. Some guys were in really bad shape. The Germans had a land mine called the castrator. It was a long bullet about eight inches long. They stuck it in the soil, and all that could be seen was the tip of the bullet. Guys stepped on it, and the blast went up the leg. One night we had thirty-four men wounded in this manner. Some lost legs, some had their lower legs shattered. You can imagine it.

I stayed with the general hospital in England until I was transferred to another general hospital, in France. There, I helped the chaplain. When I was a kid, I had found out that I was immune to almost all the common diseases. So the chaplain had me go into the communicable-disease ward to talk to the guys.

After that I operated a switchboard for trunk lines throughout France. I don't know how I got hooked up with that, but I took to it naturally.

Ed Tipper

We started moving toward Ravenoville. At the southern edge of a village stood a compound called Marmion Farm, which was being used by the Germans as a headquarters and supply depot. The compound consisted of three two-story buildings in a horseshoe shape. My guess is that there were sixty or seventy Germans holding this place. I think many of them were still asleep when we crept up. They had trenches dug all around the place, but I'm not sure if the trenches were manned. They didn't seem well prepared.

Three different groups of Americans attacked the farm, virtually all at once: our eighteen men; a second group, with about seven Easy Company men; and a third group, led by Major John Stopka of the 3d Battalion of the 502nd. The men called Stopka the Mad Major. He was a total wild man, yet he was much respected and knew what he was doing. Besides Mellett and me, the other men from E Company involved were Floyd Talbert, C. T. Smith, David Morris, Daniel West, Walter Gordon, John Eubanks, and Forrest Guth. After the attack we held the place, functioning as one group.

The initial battle was very quick, maybe five or ten minutes. I don't think there were casualties on our side. We took the buildings, and the Germans mostly disappeared or surrendered. Soon after that, the Germans started to get organized and began counterattacking the farm about once every hour. We didn't have any automatic weapons with us. Nobody had even a tommy gun.

The location must have been on the American maps as enemy targets, because we started getting fired on by the U.S. Navy just off the beach. I don't know what size shells they were, but the whole ground shook. I don't know how anybody can survive continual bombardment. The three shells that hit just about finished me off—I couldn't believe what was happening. We produced orange flags and orange smoke, which identified us as American. Thankfully the shelling of the farm quickly ended.

We stationed men on the roof of the farmhouse, which the Germans had not done when they had possession of it. Our men, yelling stuff like "About a dozen of them coming at six o'clock," were able to spot the positions of the Germans as they counterattacked. We held the place all that day and the morning of the next.

One German machine gun stationed down the road was really giving us problems. Stopka asked for volunteers; men from his company quickly agreed. The men gathered about twenty German prisoners and marched them down the road toward the machine gun. The fire stopped. One of the Americans hollered out in German to the machine gunner, "You can surrender or leave the machine gun there and walk away. If you don't, we're going to kill these prisoners. Which is it going to be?" Almost immediately the machine gunner opened up into his comrades. I think all were killed, as were a few of the American volunteers. The rest made it back to safety all right.

Early the next morning one guy entered the compound, hands raised. We were all up and awake, expecting an attack. The guy yelled in perfect English, "Don't shoot, men. I was lost, but now I'm all right." Immediately one of our guys killed him with a single shot.

We were all astonished. "What in the hell did you do that for?" someone said.

"Look at the boots," said the man who killed the German. It was true—this guy wore an American paratrooper jumpsuit but had German hobnail boots. He was a German who knew how to speak English. I don't know what he was hoping to do. Probably his commander had told him to get as close as he could to us, maybe mix in with our group for a while to find out what was going on. He was as good as dead anyway. He stood on grass when our man shot him, but if he had gone in any building the sound of his boots on a stone floor would have given him away. There was no way he could have succeeded.

Close to noon we saw about 150 men on the horizon, walking toward us. It was like something out of a movie. At first we weren't sure if they were Germans, but they turned out to be the seaborne infantry who had landed at Utah Beach. Some accounts say they arrived at Marmion Farm at dawn, but that is not true; they arrived about eleven-thirty or twelve o'clock. Regardless, it was a good thing because our ammunition had run dangerously low. I doubt if we could have held the place much longer.

Shifty Powers

Normandy was a lot of fighting, a lot of killing. But I'll always look upon myself as fortunate that I got to jump out of a plane on D-day compared to the guys who came in on the beaches. They had it really tough.

After the jump, I landed and met up with Buck Taylor and Bill Kiehn. We didn't know which way to go, but we had a general idea. We spent most of that night with the 82nd. The next morning we split off. As we walked down this road we saw a glider in a field. We figured somebody might be hurt or need help, so we went over to the glider to check things out. The glider had a jeep in it, reared up on its rear wheels, just about perpendicular. There wasn't a soul around. "Let's get that jeep," Taylor said. "We'll ride to the beach."

That sounded like a good idea to us. The jeep had some braces on it; that's the reason it was stuck. So Kiehn said, "Let's take some C-4, put a little charge on it, and blast it out." We were all trained in explosives. Kiehn took a little chunk of C-4 and put a cap in it. We walked off and hit the charge. We didn't realize that the jeep had been leaking gasoline. It blew up—everything caught on fire, the jeep, the glider. Kiehn looked at me and grinned. "It's a good thing Sobel didn't see that," he said.

Captain Sobel wasn't our company commander by then. I saw him after D-day. He was standing next to a river, so I went down, saluted, and spoke to him for a while. Sobel asked, "How did it go, Shifty?"

"It went all right," I said. "We did our part of it." I shrugged. "Popeye got a hand grenade popped on his butt."

"Serves him right," Sobel said. It sounds harsh now, but I understood what he meant, even then. It wasn't the idea that he didn't appreciate Popeye as a soldier. It was the idea that everybody had been so well trained it was a shame anybody got hurt.

CHAPTER TWELVE

The Battle of Carentan

Buck Taylor

It was D-day plus three or four before we finally found our way to Easy Company, just as they were getting ready for the attack on Carentan. Winters said, "Where have you been?" It was a friendly comment, not critical, though he clearly expected to see us earlier. I always got along well with Winters.

A lot of fellows were still missing. We organized into our proper platoons and squads as best we could. Carwood Lipton was there, and Winters had him take over as company first sergeant. Then Winters turned to me and said, "You take over the 3rd Platoon." So that was my first job as platoon sergeant, and I stayed in that role throughout the war. There was a great bunch of guys in the 3rd Platoon, a very close-knit group of fellows. I couldn't say enough good about them all.

I was wounded three times in the war: the first time happened just after Carentan. A grenade came over a hedgerow and caught me lightly in a leg. It wasn't that bad of a wound. I probably should not have been evacuated, but at the time they were trying to keep the aid stations clear, expecting a lot of casualties. So most of fellows who were as lightly wounded as I were evacuated. Carwood was, too. We were almost ready to go back to England, anyway. We just got there earlier than the rest of the guys. I spent about two weeks in a hospital in England. That's where I lost my camera. I had a 35mm camera with me and had taken a lot of pictures in Normandy. I had it with me when I got to the hospital, but when I checked out I forgot it hanging on my bed and never got it back. I don't remember what any of the pictures were that I had taken.

Joe Lesniewski

Carentan was a real hornet's nest. This was where I really found what war was like. There were eight or nine of us going from door to door and house to house. It was horrible to hear all the shooting. There was a lot of killing going on. One guy got a blast directly in his face.

Not long after that, Winters came up and said, "I need five guys for a patrol—you, you, you, you, and you." He pointed at me to go. Albert Blithe was one of the other guys. We were supposed to check out a house. We heard there were snipers in there. We got about twenty-five yards away from the house and all of a sudden—wham—Blithe gets hit. The bullet hit the back of his neck, and a piece of his collarbone came out. I had two T-shirts, one in my right pocket, one in my left. If I needed a clean shirt, I always had one. I took a shirt out, turned Blithe over on his front because the hole was so big in his back, and stuffed the shirt in the wound to stop the blood flow. We took turns carrying him back to the hedgerow, where the medics were ready to take him out. While we were carrying him, the Krauts were still shooting at us. We could feel the bullets go by our ears, but nobody got hit. They must have been blind. That was one hell of a bad one.

After that we didn't do too much until we got ready to be sent back to England. Boy, when we got to that beach, there were lines and lines of supplies, food, you name it—they had it. There must have been three rows on the beach thirty feet high, about half a mile long, maybe one to two miles. They were coming in constantly with all the stuff. It was really a sight to see.

Forrest Guth

We found E Company near Ste. Mère Dumont. It was just before we went into Carentan. Carentan was really the first battle where I saw a lot of action. We had to have that town because it was on an important route to the beach. That was a pretty tough one. We went in with hand grenades and got the Germans. It wasn't too hard, but the next night, they returned. They took back Carentan and beat up the town with all the shelling and bombing, so we took it back from them. After the Germans were driven out, we found some wine and helped ourselves to it.

There was a crossroads beyond Carentan that was identified as Dead Man's Corner. An American tank had been disabled there. Some of the crew were climbing out, and a man was shot. He hung over the edge of the tank for days. We couldn't get in to retrieve the body. So if someone was sent out on a scouting mission, you'd say, "Well, you go up to Dead Man's Corner and take a left," or whatever. I saw it. What did I think? My thoughts always go back to the parents—here's their kid who wouldn't be coming back. I got this feeling all the way through. It didn't matter if I saw a dead American or German, I always figured he belonged to somebody. You knew somebody was going to miss him.

Around the end of June we headed back to the beach to get on troop carriers to head back to England. We had no idea what would come next. Just before we boarded the ship, a number of us jumped in the Channel. It was our first decent bath in weeks.

Clancy Lyall

We attacked Carentan. Man, we were really fighting there. Me and a couple other guys could see around the corner of a building to a downstairs area with some Krauts in it. We decided to throw grenades at the target. As we rushed around with the grenades, I ran around the corner and was stopped flat by a German. I plowed straight into his bayonet. His weapon stuck fast in my gut. We were both frozen, still standing up—I think he was as scared as I was. I shot first. As he fell backward he pulled his bayonet out of my stomach. I put two rounds into him. I wasn't shooting to wound then.

I crumpled next to the German, blood spurting out of my stomach, and jammed myself with a morphine syrette. About twenty minutes later, a medic ran over. He gave me another hit of morphine. They put me on a stretcher and took me back to Omaha Beach. I got two shots of morphine there. Then I got another three shots as we were heading back across the Channel. Man—I was flying like hell. Turns out, the wound in my belly was very fortunate. The bayonet had not gone that far in. If you look at your belly button, the bayonet punctured to the right of that, down about an inch. It missed all the vital organs. Just a lot of blood.

After I got across the Channel to the hospital they gave me another hit of morphine every two hours 'round the clock for four days. I had never smoked or drank before, so when I took morphine, I was very high. Coming down, it felt like my guts were ripping apart. They lowered the dosage down to one hit a day. About a week later I was off of it, but my mind still demanded more. I didn't want to carry this with me, so I asked them to put me in a rubber room to dry me out. They did. That was the worst four days of my life. I was cramped, bent over, throwing up for the first two days solid. It started easing the third day. Late on the fourth day my body didn't want any morphine anymore. After that whenever I got wounded I would not use morphine syrettes. Whenever I was issued syrettes I handed them over to a medic right away.

When I was hit, I went to the 92nd General Hospital in England. Two wards down from me was a big ward for the merchant marine. You'll never guess who I saw.

I thought the world of him. I knew his voice. He was a big man, about 6 foot 2, maybe 240 pounds; nobody else sounded like him. I walked out of the ward I was in and heard this loud Scotch brogue. It knew instantly it was my father.

Dad was in the hospital for hypothermia. A first mate by then, he had been making a run to Russia on his ship, taking high octane gas over, when his ship had been torpedoed. They had to abandon ship. He had drifted on the North Sea for two days.

Dad couldn't believe it. He saw me and gave me a big hug. We got hold of one of the orderlies and liberated a bottle of Scotch. We shared it around with the ward. (I think we were all in worse shape leaving the place than when we came in.) Dad and I talked of Mom and everything at home. It was mostly small talk. We hugged a bunch of times. I gave him a Luger I had with me in the hospital. One of the wounded troopers, I think it was George Luz, had given it to me. Dad wouldn't put the Luger down. He thought it was a really great gift.

Over the years my father was torpedoed a total of three times. They lost a lot of people on those shipping runs, but Dad made it through the war. He became a captain later on and lived until 1956. Meeting up with him in the hospital in England was one of my best experiences ever.

From the hospital, I went back to Aldbourne, to the 2nd Battalion. Easy Company had lost two machine gunners, so they sent me and another gunner to take their place. I was assigned to the 1st Platoon, where I became a machine gunner in the 3rd Squad. Mike Massaconi was the other one.

Earl McClung

Carentan was a tough battle. We ran into Germans as we got into town. A tough tank outfit was in there. They had tanks. We didn't. We didn't have any antitank weapons. We had bazookas, but one bazooka wouldn't stop the Mark IV; it wouldn't even slow it down.

It was a battle right from the start to the finish. We took it house by house. You come up to a house, throw a grenade in, and when it explodes, you follow it in. If there's anybody in there they either run or you have a shoot-out. It's a slow process. It took us a couple days to get through the town. Were there civilians in the houses? Not too many. We found a few in basements, but most of them had got out of there when the fighting started.

Then the Germans counterattacked through the north. That's when our tanks came in. We took a couple of bridges north of Carentan. We ended up being in Normandy over a month. Then we went back to Aldbourne for replacements and supplies. Going back to England from Normandy—it was a fairly triumphant feeling, but we had that also before we went.

Ed Tipper

Carentan was my last battle. Everything felt by the book. We didn't have everybody there, but maybe a hundred men from E Company. We had weapons and ammunition by that time. It felt like we were in good shape. I had a functioning bazooka by that time to make up for the one I discarded upon landing.

We attacked the city. I was involved in clearing out houses. I didn't get far with that. At the first house we cleared I was standing in the doorway when a mortar shell landed at my feet and exploded. Everything was finished.

When you clear houses, you do it with two guys. You throw a grenade in a door or window, then go in and take control of the situation. I didn't have a grenade in this first house we came to, so I just kicked the door in and went in. Nobody was in the house, so I went out onto the back porch. There was a small structure in back, probably an outhouse. I called out in German to come out with hands up. Nobody answered, so I put three shots into the outhouse. The backyard had a stone wall all around it, fairly high, probably five feet or so. There were no Germans anywhere, nobody at all. So I came back out through the front door. Joe Liebgott was covering me on the other side of the street. I told Joe that the house was clear.

All this time the Germans had been retreating and had planned this. They apparently knew the exact distance to this location and to where our guys were. They waited until we occupied the location and then sent mortar shells in. Eight or ten of our men were wounded all at once at this place.

I was standing in the doorway when this blast hit me. It knocked me back. I didn't feel any pain, though my right eye had been destroyed by the concussion and both my legs had been broken. Strangely enough, I was still standing and I didn't drop my weapon. I turned around and looked at the house. I didn't realize what had happened. I thought there was a German somewhere back in the house I had missed who had thrown a grenade in. I thought, I'll be ready for him. After ten or fifteen seconds the German didn't come my way. But Liebgott did. He ran across the street. "You've just been hit by a mortar shell," he said. "Sit down." I reached up. My helmet had been blown off. My head felt like a watermelon, swollen and mushy, and blood was everywhere. I was in shock, and my muscles had all tensed—that's the reason I was still able to stand and control everything. I sat. Several of the guys had seen the hit and thought I was dead. Eight or ten months later I visited Floyd Talbert's parents back in the States. They wrote to Floyd and said that Ed Tipper had come by to visit them. He wrote back, saying, "That's impossible. He was killed. I saw it. Whoever's claiming to be Tipper is someone else." He couldn't believe I was still alive.

Large pieces of shrapnel had flown into my left knee, right hip, and left elbow. The shrapnel in my knee and elbow had both gone through the joints. My tibia was broken in my right leg. My fibula was broken in my left leg. Small pieces of shrapnel had hit my legs below my knees. I thought I had lost my eye, but it actually wasn't gone. Shrapnel had split my upper eyelid in half and created a ridge in my eyebrow. I could see nothing out of the eye.

Lieutenant Harry Welsh was the second man who ran up to me. Liebgott and Welsh both risked their lives to help me. Mortar fire was still pounding the street. As shells went off they both ducked down to flatten out. Welsh had some morphine and gave me an injection. I couldn't walk by myself, so they helped me get up. I hobbled on the leg that was not so badly injured. Still under fire, they got me down the street a block and a half to where an aid station had been set up. I was fortunate I was so close to the aid station.

Somehow they got a jeep to the aid station. It had stretchers on each side and on the back. They evacuated me and two other wounded men back to the beach. The Germans shot at the jeep as it was going down the road, even though the jeep had Red Cross markings on it. The jeep driver went like mad. He sped up and braked hard, avoiding getting hit. I was on the stretcher on the rear of the jeep.

I was pretty sure I was going to survive. One of the first clear memories I have was worrying about my eye. My God, I thought, I won't be able to get a driver's license. I won't be able to apply for a lot of jobs. They sent me to a hospital in England, where a doctor said they might be able to save my eye. I doubted that from the first time I saw my eye in a mirror. The eye was almost all bloodshot, and necrosis [death of cells and living tissue] was setting in. I was not surprised several weeks later when they told me the eye needed to be taken out.

Dewitt Lowrey

I have no memory of how or when exactly or where I was when I was wounded. Major Winters has sent me a copy of a ten-dollar bill that all the men signed at Carentan that has my name on it, so I know I was there.

Shrapnel hit my head and took me out of commission. I remember lying on the ground, paralyzed on my left side. I couldn't get up or move or keep up with the fighters. I lay on the ground a long time.

Medics picked me up. We were still under fire. An ambulance carried me to some field hospital, I don't know where. I remember a nurse on either side of me with a pair of scissors. She cut off all my clothes and I lay there on a cot like that until a doctor came by. I think it was the next day I was carried by amphibious jeep out to a boat. I was on one side, another boy was on the other. I remember seeing planes in the air. I'd come to, then black out, then come to, then black out. They took me to a hospital in England where I had one surgery, then back to the States where I had more surgery.

I had bad seizures for years, but I was blessed, I'll tell you. I haven't had one in a pretty good while. It's been several years now since I've had one.

CHAPTER THIRTEEN

R&R in England

Joe Lesniewski

At the end of June 1944, we left Normandy and got on a boat heading back to England. There were hundreds of boats going both ways with supplies and troops. It just boggled my mind, all the boats—just hundreds and hundreds of them. The boat we were on was fairly small, maybe a hundred people. It didn't take long to get back to England, maybe an hour or so. I just stood on the deck somewhere watching all the boats.

When we got to England, we went to base camp and got seven days' leave. They told us go wherever you want, just make sure you're back at the camp on the seventh day, otherwise you'll end up in the clink.

I went to Birmingham, where I knew some people. Then I went to London. Back at home I used to work for a couple who lived across the street from our house. The lady had two sisters who lived in London and I got a chance to meet them. We had a good day together talking about life back home.

Back in Aldbourne, a lot of replacements were brought into the company. I didn't pay much attention to replacements. Mostly I just kept together with the guys that were with me from before we went into combat.

In Aldbourne, we spent our time in more training, then getting new clothes and fixing things up. There was a lot of work to do at the time.

Bill Wingett

All the way through the army I always had a tool—a hammer, a punch, a hacksaw blade, a pair of pliers, a couple of screwdrivers, and needles and thread to repair harnesses. I was continually making modifications to things like musette bags—mostly for myself, but if anybody came along with something to be fixed, I was always happy to do it. One musette bag I remodeled so it could triple the amount of machine gun ammo you carried. That can be pretty handy on landing.

We had one guy, Johnny Martin, a sergeant in the 1st Platoon. His mother sent him a battery radio when we were in England. We didn't have small radios then. It had flashlight batteries in it. The radio had tubes in it. Johnny took the radio out on a night problem [training exercise], and it worked great. A couple days later it wouldn't play anymore. So I fixed it. Really, all I did was open it up, found a broken connection, and soldered it. When I ran into him at a convention in the early 1980s, me fixing his radio was the first thing he brought up to talk about.

CHAPTER FOURTEEN

The Fight of Our Lives in Holland

Frank Perconte

Holland. It was a summer day. A nice, warm day. Holland was flat as a pancake. That was an easy jump there. In fact, we were there just last May on a tour bus. I have some good friends who live there today.

Buck Taylor

The jump for Market Garden took place in daylight, September 17, 1944. It was an easy jump, with good weather. We landed in a field. We organized, got together, and headed out on our planned route.

The first obstacle was to take the Wilhelmina Canal. We were supposed to capture the bridge. Unfortunately, the Germans had already set the bridge with explosives and blew it up just as we arrived. We were delayed on the side of the river most of the night but got over the river the next morning and moved into Eindhoven.

As we were crossing a field on the way into Eindhoven, a replacement named Lieutenant Bob Brewer got shot by a sniper as we approached the town's first buildings. He was a big, tall officer and really stood out of a crowd. One shot rang out; Brewer went down. I ran over to him. Rod Strohl had already been there. Brewer lay face down in the grass, bleeding profusely from the neck. I thought, Well, he's gone, and made the mistake of saying, "Let's get moving. Brewer's finished." Wouldn't you know it, he heard me say that. Brewer lived. After the war he and I became good friends.

In 2007 I visited Holland to dedicate some memorials. Dutch war reenactors drove us around in World War II jeeps while we were there. As we approached the city of Eindhoven I told the driver of my jeep about the loss of our officer, Lieutenant Brewer. He was very elderly and said, "You mean Bob Brewer?" The driver knew him. He was able to tell what happened to Brewer after we left him in the field with our medic. Brewer was taken to a city hospital. The local doctor who treated him became a friend, and the two continued contact after the war.

As a platoon, we've also talked about this after the war: this sniper who shot Brewer, if he had had a machine gun with him, he could have mowed the whole 3rd Platoon down before we could have gotten out of there. The sniper was probably set up in an outpost on the edge of the town, placed there to watch for the Americans. He only fired one shot, then probably took off to CP [command post] to tell them that we were coming. But he could have really raked us if he had wanted to.

We continued on into Eindhoven. It was a great welcome. All the people were on the streets, waving, cheering, hollering. A lot of the fellows were invited to Dutch houses by the families and got a good meal that night. No C rations for once.

We moved out of the city, toward the north. The British 1st Airborne Division had been cut off in Arnhem, and nobody knew their status. So we started up what they called Hell's Highway—the single road that goes up from Eindhoven through Nijmegen and Arnhem and up into Germany. The plan was to capture this road and protect it. Then the British would come up the road with tanks and go through Nijmegen, which the 82nd was holding, then proceed into Germany. Well, it didn't work out that way. The British 1st Airborne Division really got clobbered. They lost most of their men, captured, wounded, or killed.

Al Mampre

When I jumped into Holland somebody came through my chute and I free-fell for about seventy-five feet. Boy, that ground came up at me fast. When I hit the ground the other man landed on top of my chest. I'm still messed up today because of that.

My lower back was in a lot of pain, but I got up and kept going. Just before Eindhoven, Lieutenant Bob Brewer was shot through the neck. I ran out to where he lay in the field. He looked like death warmed over. I got some plasma out of my kit and got it into his vein, which had all but collapsed. I heard bullets crack. We were still under fire. In my good bedside manner I leaned over to Brewer and said, "Lieutenant—are you still alive? Because if you're not, I'm leaving."

Brewer was still alive. That's when I took one just above my bootline. The bullet peeled the flesh off my leg all the way down to the bone. My lower leg looked like raw steak. A couple other guys came out to help, and they were hit, too. The bullet had cut the nerve, so I couldn't straighten out my leg. I dumped some sulfa on it. Some Dutchmen ran out—boy, they were something else. They put Brewer on a ladder and ran toward a house. I got back to the house and started looking after Brewer. I had given myself some morphine by then and felt like I was going to throw up. I motioned for the woman in the house to bring me a pot.

Meanwhile, our guys got the sniper. We got ready to leave the house so we could evacuate Brewer. As we stood outside at a crossroads, not clear about which way we should go, shots came in again. I dove into a German foxhole, a round one. The Dutchmen started running down the road with Brewer on a wheelbarrow. One Dutchman came back, pulled me out of the hole, and threw me on another wheelbarrow. By that time I was really in and out. I started throwing up over the side of the wheelbarrow. But eventually we got to an aid station. One of the first things I did when I got there was donate a pint of blood. I hadn't lost much, relatively speaking, and they needed it desperately.

Earl McClung

After we jumped, I was first scout and out front about a quarter of a mile. I just got across the Wilhelmina Canal and was down behind a big shade tree, and the damn bridge blew up. The way it happened was I ran across the bridge, got behind a tree, and was looking back toward them coming up the road, maybe two hundred to three hundred yards from it—that's when the bridge blew up. The tree protected me from flying debris. So I was across already, but the rest of the guys didn't get across until the next day. I was lucky I got behind that tree before it blew up. The timing of that explosion—if it had been just a few moments later they would have got the whole damn company; a few moments earlier, they would have got me. The way it worked out, it didn't get anybody. It stopped us, but nobody got hurt. We could talk across the river, but there wasn't anything anybody could do. So I just lay down behind the tree and went to sleep. There were no Germans around. By that time they were long gone.

The next morning the company got a bunch of doors from barns and wood and made a makeshift bridge to get across. The canal was about a hundred feet wide maybe. Barges could go up the river. The bridge had been made out of wood and cement.

I got hit in Holland under the knee with a piece of shrapnel. The medics bandaged it up and I limped around for three or four days, but that was it. I was never evacuated. Luck has a lot to do with it. I think only two of us went all the way through without being evacuated—Shifty Powers and myself.

A guy named Donald Moone was my second scout. I was out in front of him about a hundred yards, he was in front of the company about a hundred yards. I went into Eindhoven ahead of the company. People were cheering and hugging you; I didn't know what to do. So I turned around and went back to where Moone was. That's when Moone and I came up, and a truckful of German 88s showed up. Suddenly there were no civilians around; they all scattered. Moone and I knocked out the truck. That was about all the fighting we had in the town of Eindhoven. Moone had a rifle grenade, and he hit the truck in the radiator. That stopped it. We chased Germans around the buildings. Two of them were shot. I know a civilian who said, "I waited five years to see Germans die on the streets like that. Now that I've seen it, I don't want to see any more." After that, the celebrating started again. The people just mobbed you. You see pictures of that. Little kids coming around—we gave them our rations.

We started out toward Nuenen. That's where we started hitting it. Men started getting killed. We ran into a bigger force than we were. Paul Rogers, a mortar sergeant, had two guys with him carrying ammunition. Paul got wounded. The guys on either side of him got killed. So that wiped out our mortar squad right there.

What's it like to be under heavy fire? Well, you don't know whether you're mad or scared. You can't fight artillery. Small-arms fire—it doesn't bother you at all; you can fight back. But when you get in an artillery barrage, you can't. Me, I get more angry than scared. I can't do anything about it. There's nothing to fight. You never know when the next one's coming. Guys you know are getting killed.

Clancy Lyall

Market Garden was the first daylight jump into combat that we had made. I felt very visible. If you jump at dawn or nighttime, no one can see you. But in the daytime you're jumping from five hundred feet or so and bang, you're on the ground in just a few seconds. In the daytime they can shoot you in the goddam door of the plane. As it turned out, there were no Germans around, and the most dangerous place to be when we landed was the drop zone because of all the helmets and equipment raining down on us.

We got into the little town of Zon. There was one German 88 there. It fired one round down the middle of the road. That was the only problem there. The next day we started getting a bit of flak. We advanced into Eindhoven. Mike Massaconi and I took my machine gun up on top of this two-story warehouse. We had no idea what kind of building it was. From up there I had a field of fire of three intersections, and if anybody came we could get them good. Suddenly the Germans fired a mortar through the skylight of the building. We heard glass breaking. I shuffled over and looked down the hole. Inside I could just make out cases and cases and cases of something and a big brown vat. I bent down to get a closer look. Goddam, it was a Heineken beer factory! We had a jump rope with us, so I shimmied down, hand over hand. I tied off two bottles at a time and Mike pulled them up and lowered them over the side of the building to the rest of the guys. Nobody drank the beer just then, as we were still in a combat zone. So we put the bottles in our jump pants pockets. But the first break we got, we all popped a bottle. Every time I go to an Easy Company reunion I have a bottle of Heineken.

After we secured Eindhoven, we took off up Hell's Highway. We ran into a lot of Germans then. There was a flock of them—two or three panzer divisions and a lot of paratroopers. Those were the Germans that had got past the Brits and made it out of Normandy. They had gone to Holland to refit, and the Brits jumped right on top of them. There were a lot of skirmishes going up that highway. You look at the old cowboy and Indian movies with Indians shooting at covered wagons as they're going down a road—that was exactly what was happening, except it was tanks going down the road. The Germans had their 88s set up and knocked the tanks off like ducks as they went along. It was a hell of a thing to see.

There was another sight I'll never forget. Every day at ten, two, and four, the Brits got out of their tanks and make their bloody ass tea. It happened every day, no matter what kind of fighting was going on. If you ask me, the Brits were brave as hell but silly as shit.

At Veghel, that was a hard day for me. We were on both flanks of the British when the Germans attacked us. They came at us with all kinds of stuff—half-tracks, artillery, I don't know where they got it all from. We ran into an apple orchard to take shelter behind trees. That proved a mistake. The Germans sent over these TOTs (time over targets) that blew up in the air right over us, hitting the trees, knocking off branches; the shrapnel rained down. Foxholes were no use. You just prayed you didn't get hit. That went on for about six hours. I got quite shaky. After we broke through I never got under or around another tree again. Even at Bastogne. I'd go lay in a puddle before I'd lay under a damn tree.

Bill Wingett

I jumped, broke my leg, and was shipped to the hospital. That was it. Are you familiar with farming? When they're plowing and make a turn, it creates those open furrows. That's where I landed, in a plowed field where they had been making a turn. I landed with one leg on top of the sod and one leg in the hole. It wasn't a bad break—I could barely walk on it—but I did anyway. It was three miles to the bridge, and I walked that far. The bridge was gone when I got there. Colonel Strayer set me up in a machine gun position and said, "You stay right here and wait." A couple of days later a British ambulance came by. I wasn't all alone that whole time. There were troops coming and going. I wasn't in pain. I probably could have even gone on. They sent me to a Catholic hospital in Brussels.

Frank Soboleski

My unit had come in later, so we stayed in Aldbourne, England, and waited to jump into Holland to join Operation Market Garden. I was in the 506th replacements when I did that jump.

It was a beautiful, sunny day in September when we jumped. I landed right in a big cow pie. What a grand entrance.

Shifty Powers

I've thought about this story hundreds of times since the war: We came up to this little town in Holland with Germans in it. We were going to take the town, but we got there real late and didn't have time to do it before dark. We dug foxholes and stayed put overnight. Somewhere early the next morning a guy hollered, "There are two Germans with two American prisoners, and they're walking right down the road!"

I grabbed my rifle, lay down, and spotted them. Sure enough—two Germans walked on the outside with two American prisoners in the middle. I thought, This will be easy shooting. I'll shoot the German on the right first, then get the one on the left. Then I got to thinking—That town is full of Germans. If I can see those guys walking down the road, I'm sure the Germans can see them, too. If I shoot those Germans, the Germans in the town will open up on those two American prisoners.

I debated and debated what to do. Finally I watched them go out of sight down the road. I've thought about this often—maybe I should have shot those two Germans. But if I did, there would have been four dead people in the middle of that road, all for nothing. I'm glad I made the decision I did.

The next day we took the town. We took some German prisoners and got some American prisoners back, too. I never did find out for sure, but I hoped that some of the guys we got back were those two Americans they had walking down the road that day.

Forrest Guth

Coming down, I had a malfunction of my parachute. It was twisted. The chute had not been properly packed. Or maybe it had been packed in damp conditions; we hadn't jumped high enough to be able to use the reserve. We had jumped under five hundred feet, so my main chute opened, but didn't open completely. You try to shake out the twist if you can, but there's so little time. I couldn't do a lot and came down fast. I just hoped for the best. I hit with a thud. I hit on my left hip and back and was knocked out. I don't remember much, just hitting hard and seeing stars. I was paralyzed in leg and back. I couldn't move.

Medics came along, gave me a shot of morphine, and put me in a cattle barn. That was the extent of my fighting in Holland. I stayed for a day or two in the barn until the field hospital was moved up. When I woke up there was my old hometown doctor. Boy, was I surprised to see him. He was thirty-five or so. I thought he was too old for service, but sure enough, he was there.

They packed me up and took me back by ship to England, where I went to the hospital. I had hit the spinal cord and broke a disc in my back. They stretched me out in the hospital but didn't operate. (I didn't have my back operated on until about ten years later. It got to the point where I couldn't walk or sleep or function—that disc was rubbing on my spine for quite a while.) I stayed in the hospital in England for about eight weeks, then came back to Mourmelon, France, and waited until the troops came back from Holland.

When I rejoined Easy Company, my back still hadn't healed, but I wanted to be back with my company. They gave me medication for the pain. I insisted that I wanted to go back. Sometimes guys would go AWOL from the hospital just so they could go back to their own unit. If you didn't, they'd send you to a replacement depot and you might get sent anywhere. So it was always good to get out on your own and get sent back to your own company. Was the injury enough to be discharged? Yes, I could have been sent home to the States to heal; I'm sure of it. But I just wanted to go back to my company. Nobody had any idea we were going to Bastogne next.

CHAPTER FIFTEEN

Defending the Island

Buck Taylor

Our last two months in Holland, October and November 1944, were spent defending "the Island," the strip of land between the Rhine River on the north and the Waal River on the south. We spent most of our time there in a defensive position on the southern bank of the Rhine. The Germans had the high ground on the northern side and had the advantage. It was a bad place for us to be. We couldn't move around much in the daytime.

The only action I have a clear memory of there, was going across the river in boats to bring back some British wounded who were hiding out. One officer had come over, a swimmer, and said they had two hundred plus British airborne troops over there, some wounded, and he wanted to get them back over. So we got these pontoon boats and brought them to the dike at night. We took the boats down to the edge of the river. It was quite a haul, as they were quite heavy. It was mostly just the 3rd Platoon involved. The action worked. No shots were fired. The only problem was that the British were so happy to be rescued that we couldn't keep them quiet when we brought them back over the river. The Germans were right on the other side and could have started firing, but they didn't.

I was wounded for the second time in Holland in a convoy going down Hell's Highway back toward Eindhoven. Art Youman (one of my platoon sergeants) and I were on a motorcycle together. He was driving, I was on the back. The road was wet. Suddenly the truck ahead of us jammed on the brakes. The whole convoy was stopping. Art hit the brakes and we slid sideways under the back of the truck ahead of us. Bang! For about five minutes I was paralyzed and couldn't move my legs. Gradually the feeling came back. They put me in the hospital in Nijmegen, where I spent a week. The company had been relieved by then and was heading back to France, so they came by and picked me up. I never knew the exact diagnosis—they never tell you these things in the military—but it turned out to be some sort of back injury, a compression fracture of the lower spine. I could walk, but it was painful for quite a while after that. It still gives me a fit today.

Joe Lesniewski

We went across on pontoon boats and got to the Island. There were people ahead of us who knew exactly where to put us. They put me with Ed Joint and put us in a barn along with one other fellow, I don't remember who. Ed Joint and I got to be good friends. About a week later we were in another barn with Shifty Powers, Jim Alley, and I think Earl McClung.

We were sent out on patrols. You had to go to a certain area. One was to a house maybe a half mile away from where we stayed. We would spend the night in the house, observing out the windows. You needed to situate yourself in the house so you couldn't be seen from the outside. It was jet black in the house. You couldn't see anything in front of you except when the enemy shot a flare—they were about three hundred yards away from where we were. We went on patrols to that house for about two weeks.

Another time a runner came over and told me and four other guys to go to see Captain Winters, who sent us on another patrol. I think the guys were Art Youman, who was patrol leader, Jim Ally, Rod Strohl, Willie Wagner, and me. Art sent me up the dike to observe any enemy over the top. I said okay, got about nine tenths of the way up, took my helmet off and put it on the barrel of my gun, then lifted my helmet over the barrel of the road. Nothing happened, so I climbed up higher and looked across the road. One of the enemy shot a flare in the air. It lit up the whole area. As I looked across the road, there was a German soldier directly in front of me with a potato masher grenade. He threw it at me. I ducked as fast as I could. The grenade hit my helmet and bounced off. I hollered to the guys, "Live grenade! Get the hell away from here!" The thing exploded. Every one of us got wounded. Jim Alley got hit thirty-two times. In 1994 he went to the hospital again, even this late in life, and they still found a piece of shrapnel in his body.

After the grenade exploded I hollered to the guys, "Get moving! Get going as fast as you can go!" I had eight grenades on me, so I started throwing grenades in the direction of the enemy—throwing them in one direction, then another, so they'd confuse the enemy. It didn't take long, and I heard screaming, hollering, crying from the enemy. As soon as I threw all my grenades I started moving. Back at the command post, Winters took one look at us and said, "O my God, get to the hospital, all of you."

They put us in a rubber raft and took us back across the river, where a six-by-six truck was waiting for us. They took us to Eindhoven, to a hospital. Every one of us was bleeding pretty hard. I got hit in the neck. My wound was not very big, but the wound was right next to my jugular vein, so they told me that it was too dangerous to take out. So that piece is still in my neck. About ten years ago they took an X-ray of the area and said the metal has all been grown over, so it's still better to leave it in. But I set off metal detectors in airports all the time. I get a charge out of that wherever I go.

I was in the hospital in Holland about five days only. They took all five of us there, but we weren't on the same floor. I didn't know where the other guys were. I was in my hospital bed on the fifth floor when I heard a loud roar of motors. We were informed that some enemy dive bombers were coming in our direction. I heard they bombed the northern end of the hospital, but I can't confirm it because right after that they took me downstairs, so I didn't see it. After that, I was sent back to the Island, and pretty soon after that we were sent to Mourmelon, France, by train.

Earl McClung

The Island meant patrols. It was strictly a holding position. The Germans were across the river on the high ground, so you didn't move in the daylight. If you sneezed, they were on you with an 88. You moved at night. The 101st Airborne Division was attached to the British XII Corps, and the British were making the calls. Our position didn't make too much sense, at least to me, but that's what we did.

I think everybody was getting plenty of sleep. We were sleeping in barns and buildings. But we were wet all the time, so a bath or a change of socks would have been great, but we didn't have that, either. It was a long time to be under fire, but the guys stood up pretty good, I thought.

Clancy Lyall

This is where we had some problems—they called it the Island, but it was really two dikes. We set up a defensive line. In front of us was a dike much higher than ours, where the Germans were. If you got up on your dike in daytime, they killed you, so we couldn't do hardly anything in the day. Just bayonet charges. But that was kind of silly. There was this one charge we made where the OP [outpost] had seen a whole bunch of Germans in the high grass, so we were going to rout them. We ran maybe three hundred yards toward the Germans, hollering, screaming, shooting, doing some good. We were smack dab in the middle of the two dikes when we saw another huge bunch of Germans coming toward us like ants over a hill. It was maybe ten against one. That was the first time I ever heard Lieutenant Dick Winters cuss. He said, "Oh, shit." The Krauts began firing at us; their mortars were zeroed in perfectly. We got the hell out of there. One of our guys was killed that day; twenty-one were wounded.

That was when I got blown off the dike, wounded by a mortar round. It happened just as I reached the top of our dike. We had a foxhole on the reverse slope. Just before I reached our foxhole a piece of shrapnel hit my leg—nothing big, nothing bad, but it burned like hell. The hot metal went right through my boot. Luckily it didn't hit any bones, just went into the calf of my leg. Gene Roe dug into me to get it out. My leg went numb for a while, so I didn't feel a lot of pain. I could still hop. I think

Burton Christenson grabbed my arm and helped me get to a house where an aid station had been set up. They evacuated me to Brussels to an English hospital.

I stayed in the hospital a while, then rejoined the company in Mourmelon. Two weeks later, we were in Bastogne.

CHAPTER SIXTEEN

Respite in Mourmelon

Buck Taylor

After seventy days on the front line in Holland, the 101st was sent to
Mourmelon, France, to rest and refit. We arrived in France on November
25, 1944, and stayed in an old French military base. It wasn't fancy, but
for a while it meant we had some hot food and were able to just sit down,
relax, and take life easy. We had gone for more than two months in Holland without a bath or shower.

Shifty Powers

We got our back pay but we didn't have any place to spend it in
Mourmelon. So there was a lot of gambling going on. I was never much
of a poker player, though I liked it.

There'd be about six or seven of us sitting around in one of those old
barns, playing poker. Now, when you're playing poker, you've got to concentrate. One of the guys took a hand grenade, screwed the top off, and
poured the powder out. He put the grenade back together and loosened
the pin. While we were playing poker, the guy came in and worked the
pin so the grenade popped off his vest and fell on the floor. "Live grenade!"

he hollered. Everybody in there dove anywhere he could. Money and cards flew everywhere. The guy who dropped the grenade ran off. It was all a big joke.

Here's the funny thing: while we were at Mourmelon, several guys tried the same joke. (Nobody stole the money when the poker players scattered—everybody knew if he did, the guys would catch him and he'd get whupped. It was just to aggravate somebody.) It didn't matter how many times different guys tried the joke, the results were always the same. If someone hollered "Live grenade!" you automatically took cover.

Henry Zimmerman

As a replacement, I was sent overseas in November 1944. Some of us went to one unit, some of us went to another unit. I happened to end up with Easy Company while they were in Mourmelon.

Some of the guys didn't like replacements very much. One day, I had just gotten out of a shower when this guy, he had just been working on something greasy, came up and rubbed his greasy hands all through my hair. I said, "You sonuvabitch, get back or I'll knock you on your ass." So he and I got into it and had a fight. The guy was supposed to be an amateur boxer. The next day he came to me and asked me what rings I was wearing. He had a couple of cuts on his face. I was pretty tough back then. After that, the guy and I got to be the best of friends.

Joe Lesniewski

Winter was coming, so they took most of our summer clothes away in preparation to get new gear. I turned in my boots to get new ones. I have small feet—size 6—so they didn't have any boots for me right away because they were too hard to replace, they said. So I just went without. I found an old pair of shoes lying around, size 8½, much too big for me, but I wore those in Mourmelon.

On December 17, a lot of the guys had gone into town that day to buy souvenirs. I went to the movies, but for some reason they had a real show there that day with live people—Marlene Dietrich, Mickey Rooney, one of the Williams girls. While sitting there, the lights suddenly went up, the captain comes in and says, "Go back to your barracks. Be ready to move out in an hour."

I still didn't have any boots. What could I do? The old shoes I had wouldn't work—I couldn't run in those. I had some heavy wool socks, so I put them on, then wrapped some burlap sacks around my feet with some leather shoelaces I had. They didn't come off, and worked pretty well. I think there were three guys from E Company who wrapped their feet like this, without any boots at all. In the end, those burlap sacks saved my feet. Some of the guys with boots, once they got wet, the boots froze. They couldn't even take off their boots, and they ended up with frostbite. After I saw some of that, I was glad I didn't have boots.

Earl McClung

As soon as we got to Mourmelon, I left and went to Paris. I didn't wait for a pass, but I was known for that—I was a good combat soldier, but the worst garrison soldier in the whole damn world. What did I do in Paris? Man [laughs], what do soldiers usually do when they go to town?! My wife's sitting here—that's all I'm going to say!

I got picked up off the street, some guy with a bullhorn was hollering, "If you're from the 101st get back on the truck." So I jumped on the truck. They just picked us up in the clothes we were in and that's how we went to Bastogne. I was wearing my ODs and looked like hell. I got back in time to put on fatigues. No warm clothes. No coat. Just that. We had no idea where we were going.

Herb Suerth Jr.

The year before Bastogne, I had been sent to the Blue Ridge Mountains for additional infantry training. It was late January, maybe early February, very cold, and we went there on winter maneuvers. Someone had told us that the sleeping bags the army issued were no good below thirty degrees. The guy said, "If you really want to stay warm up there, you better wrap another blanket around the inside of your sleeping bag. And get ahold of all the socks you can." So most of us did that and we were fairly comfortable then.

So a year later in Mourmelon it was a Sunday night, and guys were just coming back from passes. Sergeant Buck Taylor came into the barracks and said, "Guys, we're going up!" I grabbed my sleeping bag and started wrapping blankets around it and sewing them in. A couple of guys asked what I was doing and did the same. My bag was original issue and hadn't even been used yet. By sewing the blankets in, I was able to stay warmer in Bastogne—as long as I was in the bag, anyway.

Frank Soboleski

In Mourmelon I was assigned to Easy Company, 2nd Battalion. The platoon assignments were alphabetical, so by the time they got down to the *S*'s I was put into the 3rd Platoon and assigned to Sergeant Shifty Powers. We talked about hunting. He had been an avid hunter, too, so when he found out that I had done a lot of deer and bird hunting he said he wanted me to be his first scout. From then on, he and Lieutenant Ed Shames would just point at me and thumb me to go on patrol whenever they needed reconnaissance.

One day, without warning, we were told to load up. We were moving into Bastogne to replace the Allied troops who were being overrun by the Germans. The Germans were really putting up a last-ditch effort to take Bastogne. Seven roads came into the town, so it was a strategic transportation, communication, and supply hub. The Germans were totally overwhelming the troops we had there, who were stretched out too thin to be effective. We needed to hold the line to close down the German advance.

CHAPTER SEVENTEEN

Frozen Hell

Shifty Powers

Bastogne—I hate to talk about that place. It was a lot of fighting, just a lot of fighting.

Forrest Guth

Bastogne was about fifty or sixty miles from Mourmelon. There was no time to get airplanes for us. So they gathered a gang of stake-body trucks, similar to cattle trucks, and got the MPs from Paris to round up everybody from the division to get everybody back from leaves and truck us up to Bastogne.

We went north through Bastogne and established our defense, December 17, 1944. We dug our foxholes in a heavily wooded area; we dug right through the ice and frost. As the shelling went on, you deepened your hole. We went on scouting trips. We could see Germans down in valley below us, set up with their guns and tanks. They were shelling this area. Most of the shelling happened at night. Someone would get wounded and you wouldn't find who until morning. Everything was torn up. Trees. Terrible explosions.

We wore our green fatigues and jackets. You didn't have many extra pairs of socks, so you had to be careful to not get wet feet and get frostbite. There were three of us in a foxhole. We threw everything in there to keep warm—cardboard, canvas, pine boughs—whatever you could find to cover up. Everybody was dirty. You smelled. You put water in your helmet to rinse off but you could only heat water in daytime because you didn't want fires to show. I didn't get an overcoat until the middle of Bastogne and we were resupplied by air.

Joe Lesniewski

When we got up there, a fine drizzle was falling. We got out of the trucks and saw something that we'd never again see in our lives. It was our soldiers retreating. I couldn't believe it. As they retreated they were mumbling, "Don't stay here, go someplace else, the enemy's going to kill us"—stuff like that. We found out later on that the 28th Division lost something like 7,000 killed, and the 106th Division got a worse beating than the 28th, maybe 8,000 to 9,000 killed. The Malmédy massacre had just occurred, where about 120 American prisoners of war were executed by the Germans. What a sight that was—every one of us felt so bad seeing our guys walk the other way like that, but it made sense when you knew what they had been through. Some of our guys had tears in their eyes. We didn't have much ammo. So as guys were retreating, we took any kind of ammo they had.

Our officers had a place picked out to set up. So they told us to "dig fast and dig deep." We had time to dig our holes. There were three of us in the foxhole I was in, about 2½ feet deep, maybe 3 feet wide, maybe 5½ feet long. We cut down some of the trees and put logs over the foxholes, then cut a slit between two parts of a tree so you could see through if any enemy came in our direction. Then everything started. First it started to snow. It didn't seem so bad. It snowed all day December 17, 18, 19; we ended up with 2 to 4 feet of snow. Kept coming down, coming down, coming down. It was like seeing a movie; you can't believe that something like that was happening, but it was happening to us.

The cold was there from the beginning to the end. It started out not too bad, but as the days and nights kept coming, it got colder and colder. It started out about five degrees above zero [Fahrenheit]. As time went by, the temperature dropped to ten degrees below zero, Belgium's coldest winter in thirty years. Can you picture yourself there? We were a bunch of comedians, the airborne, the things that we laughed about to each other—how cold it was, how dirty we were.

Alex Penkala and Skip Muck were great guys. They had taken me under their wing when I first got to the company. We played guitar together. They were good friends. They were hit directly by mortar fire while in their foxhole. They just disintegrated. You couldn't even find flesh or blood, that's how badly hit they got. Out in Bastogne, there was no use sitting down and crying, because there were other guys that you needed to worry about. You knew death was going to happen along the way. That's how I felt: I couldn't help those guys anymore. But I still pray for them. I'm a Catholic and go to church every Sunday. I keep in touch with Alex's family to this day. I still pray for Alex and Skip; that's about the closest thing I can do.

Believe it or not, I didn't think much about praying when I was in a foxhole. After Normandy, when I went back to England, I went to church every Sunday until we went into combat. I had a friend who went with me and we'd pray. Outside of that, you really didn't have any time to sit down with a rosary and pray out of a prayer book; everything you did was in your mind. You can pray without moving your lips. I don't recall if any of the guys had Bibles with them. I kept a small rosary and I'd pray off of that once in a while. But things were so hectic. You had your mind, so that's what you used to pray.

I felt prepared to die. I never worried about it to this day. If I'm going to die, I'm going to die. Whether I get blasted out of a plane or a car runs me over or I die of old age, it's never bothered me. I felt that God takes care of you one way or another. If something's going to happen, then Somebody is going to take care of you.

Henry Zimmerman

Bastogne. You wouldn't believe it. If we didn't hold them there, the Germans could have won the war. Hitler was close to having the atomic bomb then, and if he'd-a got it, he'd-a used it. We were stubborn—we weren't going to give in to him.

Bastogne was very, very cold, the coldest winter I've ever spent. Snow up around our rumps. Two or three guys in a foxhole. It's a wonder we didn't freeze to death. You'd hug one another just to try and stay warm. Some of the guys lost their feet because they got completely frozen. I have problems with my feet even today because of that. Thankfully, I had grabbed an overcoat when I was back in Mourmelon. I didn't know where we were going, so I just grabbed it.

One of my closest friends in the company was Frank Mellett—he was from Brooklyn. I saw Mellett get killed. We were fighting near Foy. When I saw that, I was crying. I had a lot of tears in my eyes. He and I were very good buddies. It's hard when you're fighting and you lose a good friend. We prayed a lot. Believe me, we did. We prayed for a safe return home.

Popeye Wynn was another good friend. And Walter Hendricks—he and I used to sing together. The Germans were always shelling us. During the shelling we harmonized as loud as we could. Both of us sang at the top of our voices to let them know they weren't getting to us:

> *I'm gonna buy a paper doll*
> *That I can call my own.**

That's the way it went. You made a joke wherever you could, just to let the Germans not get to you. Once, on the way into Berchtesgaden, we came up on a house where there was women's clothing. Hendricks put this dress on and acted like a woman to make a joke. He was an Indian and had a really smooth complexion. I don't think he had any whiskers. But I don't think he fooled any of the guys. We all had a good laugh.

You always tried to keep your morale up. There are many events from the war that took place that I cannot and probably never will get out of my mind.

Once in Bastogne, Buck Taylor and I came across the body of a dead German soldier. He appeared to be about twelve or thirteen years old. Buck and I buried the boy.

---

*"Paper Doll," written by Johnny S. Black, 1915, lyrics as recorded by the Mills Brothers in 1942.

Buck Taylor

I was one of the lucky ones because I had a hooded sweatshirt that my parents had sent to me back in Holland. I put the hood over my head with the drawstring pulled tight around my face with my helmet on top and, boy, that made a big difference against the cold.

Walter Gordon, a good friend of mine, was the 3rd Platoon machine gunner. He had a bigger foxhole than most because he had his machine gun with him. At one point we were on the forward edge of a lightly wooded area facing across an open field. A country road ran across our front. The road was elevated just enough so the Germans on the far side could come right up to the road and look over without being seen. We didn't realize this at first, but that was how Gordon got shot. Gordon was just getting back into his foxhole when somebody saw a head across the other side of the road. Only one shot rang out and caught him in the shoulder and spine. He was paralyzed. It happened on the twenty-fourth of December, Christmas Eve. That shot marked the beginning of an attack the Germans made on us. It proved to be their mistake. The next day somebody counted twenty-three German bodies on the other side of the road. I took a Luger from one. I still have it today. I just gave it to my oldest son about a month ago.

Clancy Lyall

We made our defensive perimeter in the Bois Jacques woods. The next day we woke up and snow was coming down like you never saw. I was wearing my same old green jumpsuit—it wasn't designed to keep out the cold. I had an M-1 and a bandolier, a few K rations, a field jacket, and a towel around my neck. After a while I was able to find an overcoat. I took one from a dead GI, one of ours, an infantry guy.

To stay warm you got close to each other. You can't make fires. If you're lucky enough to have a blanket, it gets wet so it doesn't do much good. You never take your boots off and leave them off. If you do, your feet freeze up. In the nighttime we went on patrols, so those help you stay warm. You never really sleep, you get two, three cat winks then hear a round and that wakes you up. You got used to going without sleep. After a while you can walk sleeping.

For shelter, we found tree limbs to put over our foxholes. I knew guys who put frozen German corpses over the top of their holes to insulate against the cold. I never did. Your hands got so cold, guys urinated on their hands to warm them up. You did the same thing with your M-1. If your bolt was stuck, it wouldn't fire. What the hell are you going to have it for then? So guys pissed on their rifles, jacked the bolt back a couple times, and it was all right.

You couldn't shower. You were so dirty you smelled a guy from twenty yards away. But everybody smelled the same, so what the hell. There was only one time in my life I smelled worse. Years later, in Korea, I jumped and landed in a rice paddy. They had put human feces in there and I landed in that sonuvabitch. I bathed and I bathed but it took me months to get rid of the smell. It was like a skunk had sprayed me.

One day in Bastogne I got hit. I had no place to go. It was just a graze across my forehead. Maybe a little bit better than a graze—it put a line across my skull. They bandaged me up at an aid station. I got a cup of hot coffee and spent the night. The next day I was back in my foxhole.

Things got a bit shaky around that time. I have to say something at this point: airborne outfits that go into combat are supposed to be relieved within three to five days. But it never happened; not with us, anyway. Normandy was thirty-four days combat. Holland was seventy-four days combat. When we got to Mourmelon, it was right into battle again. By the time we got into Bastogne, we were all flaky to start with. Then we were forty days combat in Bastogne. If it wasn't for each other, I'm sure a lot of us would have gone crazy. That's where the cohesion comes in. We were brothers.

Me and Mike Massaconi were in a hole in the Bois Jacques woods. Snow was all around, and I saw a goddam bird stick his head out the side of my hole. I told Mike to look at it, but there was no bird there really. Mike gave me a hug and brought me down. That's what I'm talking about. You're flaky after all that combat. Crazy. One little thing sets you off. I swear to Christ I saw that bird. He opened his beak and all. The Germans were shelling the living crap out of us at the time. I'm scared like everybody else. If it wasn't for Mike I would have charged the light brigade or something. But he calmed me down. After that I was fine—actually, I wasn't fine, I carried that with me for many years. I got to a point after the war where I started drinking a lot. When you drink you forget your nightmares. But then you wake up and you have to go worship Mother Hopper and you've got a damn headache and you still remember it. So it took me a long time to get out of that. I'm telling you— in Bastogne I got so calloused I could sit on a frozen corpse and eat a K ration. But after the war I used to have these dreams—I was afraid I'd roll over in bed and strangle my wife. The dream I remember most is of the bayonet attacks. Running headway at the enemy, rifles out, and they're running at you. I can see their faces. I remember the blade going into a man. I had nightmares about the concentration camps we saw in Germany, too. There was the stench of it, the skeletons walking around— they come up to you and hug you, I'll never forget the reality of those experiences as long as I live.

Frank Perconte

I was this side of Bastogne, just outside of Foy. That's where I got shot. The bullet hit me in the thigh and just missed my pecker by a couple inches and went out my butt. It was my left leg. Everybody says Perconte got shot in the ass, but that's not true. When I got to the hospital the doctor [confirmed the point of entry for the bullet]. I was fortunate.

I came back and rejoined the company about two weeks before the end of the war.

Ed Joint

We were sent out to take a machine gun position. It was just before the Battle of Foy ended. I was running up a hill and got hit by shrapnel in my right arm. I went flying up in the air; I didn't know at first what hit me. Somebody hollered for a medic. They put me on a stretcher and took me to a field hospital. They couldn't do nothing with it there, so they took me back and put me in a hospital in Paris. A medic said, "You can go home now, soldier, you ain't going to fight no more." But twenty days later I hitchhiked back to Company E to find them. They were just getting ready to go to Germany, to Berchtesgaden.

What made me want to go back and fight? I don't know. They thought

I was nuts. But as a young kid, you're not scared. They were my outfit, my friends. They asked me at the hospital why I wanted to go back. I said, "It's my outfit up there." I know it sounds crazy, it's just like jumping out of a plane. I don't know how many times people have said to me, "Boy you must have been scared to death to jump out of an airplane." But jumping out of a plane is like recreation, it's nothing—it's the stuff they put on you and the people shooting at you that's the problem.

When I came back to my unit, half of the guys were gone. I don't think there was a guy in my squad or platoon who was the same. It had changed a lot. It was different guys, but it was just another day. Some guys had been saying that if they could last through Normandy, they could live through the whole war. But I don't think none of them were saying that then.

Bill Wingett

Just back from the hospital in Brussels, I pulled into Mourmelon 1½ days before we piled on trucks for Bastogne. We drove for quite a while, we only got off that truck for piss call—I think we only did that twice. I didn't have hardly any of my equipment. When our guys were coming south when we were coming north, I never hesitated saying, "Hey, I need that." So I got to Bastogne with a couple good coats and a rifle, borrowed from the guys who were retreating.

After some time I had to go to the infirmary for my feet because they were frozen. They were shelling the infirmary while I was there. But I was never shot. I was one of the few. Did I ever think I was going to die? I can only remember a couple of times thinking "this might be it." But I do not remember any time that I felt like hunkering down in a foxhole and covering up my head in fear. Understand this: I'm not a religious person. I believe in God. I'll say more than that—I *know* there's a God. And I know that there's got to be several occasions that I displeased God, whatever form He's in. But I never felt the need to get down on my knees and pray that I wouldn't die. I don't think it ever crossed my mind that I wasn't going to go home—not while I was in a foxhole, not while sitting on the line somewhere. I always figured tomorrow was coming and I was going to be there. I never had a doubt that I wouldn't go home.

Early on in our training, it could have been Sink, or Sobel, or Winters, somebody said, "Determination is the answer." I took that to heart. At Bastogne we were cold. We were hungry. But we had to get the job done. A job ought to be done right if you're going to do it at all.

Herb Suerth Jr.

Bastogne was the coldest place I've ever been in my life. My wife and I have a cabin up in Wisconsin today where we often spend some time in winters, and even now, sitting in the warmth of that cabin, I'll look out at the snow-covered pine trees and shiver. It's just a reaction.

A lot of the struggle in Bastogne was trying to keep your feet dry and warm. It was a twenty-four-hour-a-day exercise. If you weren't vigilant you had trench foot within hours. I was a bit lucky because I had been previously issued galoshes, rubber overshoes, with clips. They weren't perfect. Your feet would sweat in them because they were enclosed, and get wet from the inside out. But they did keep the snow off and keep your feet from being soaked from the outside in. I never wore the burlap bags a lot of guys put on their feet.

If you changed your socks three to four times a day, you could keep your feet pretty dry. You dried your socks with body heat by putting them in your helmet or wrapping them around your waist. I had six to eight pairs of socks. I kept them with me all the time and never put them back in my personal bag. You wouldn't wash them—hell, no; you just dried them. It was hard to get water because you had to melt snow to get it, and fires were too dangerous. You couldn't even keep water in your canteen at night because it froze. One of the things I learned back at the Blue Ridge [in training] was to always have a needle and thread with me to repair gloves. That proved handy at Bastogne because your gloves stuck to the rifle barrels and ripped because of the cold.

I was wounded when an artillery round landed next to me. Both my legs were broken. I spent three months in skeletal traction. They drill a hole right through your knee, put a wire through all the bones, then put a U-shaped brace over that. At the end of that brace they hook up a wire. That goes up over the end of the bed and put weights on it to keep your legs set straight. Talk about painful. You've got to realize that by now all

of us have tremendous leg muscles. We've been running, hiking, climbing, exercising—it takes a lot of weight to overcome your thigh muscles
so the bones can set properly. If you ever want to interrogate an enemy
soldier, just put him in skeletal traction. About the third day he'll tell you
anything you want.

They used maggots on my legs to eat away the dead flesh. I guessed it
worked, because I kept my legs. At one point they had talked about am-
putating them. Altogether, I was in the hospital for eighteen months—
three months in traction, then another six months in bed, then months of
rehabilitation after that. It took a long time before I could set a foot on
the floor. The first day I did, I stood up. The next day after that I walked
across the damn hospital floor on a pair of rolling parallel bars. Ten days
later I was out on a weekend pass. They fitted me for a set of braces that I
wore for about three months after that. I worked at rehab eight hours a
day until I finally healed.

Al Mampre

I rejoined the company in Mourmelon, right before Bastogne. Driving up to Bastogne, I thought, "Well, this is the way to go—on trucks—
no jumping this time." I had no idea what was ahead. I was put with
regimental headquarters and stationed on the edge of Bastogne across the
paved area from McAuliffe's headquarters.

To explain our position as medics a bit more—we really didn't receive
much medical training. It was almost the same training I had received
back when I was a Boy Scout. When we were out in the field or in combat
and a guy got hurt, we just used our heads and tried to figure out how to
best help him. One time a guy was in a tree using Composition 4 [explo-
sives]. It went off. I rode to the hospital with him with my hand on his
chest to keep him from sucking air. What else could I do? You really
didn't know a lot of the time. You had your equipment—your morphine,
your penicillin, your bandages—but that was it.

For some time in Bastogne a guy tried to install a communications
line on a wall. A shell came in; he got knocked off the wall but went right
back on the wall. Another shell came in and knocked him off the wall

again. He went right back. That happened several times—I don't know if he ever got the line installed.

Another time I was in a room and bent down to tie my shoe. A German artillery shell blasted right into the room, flew over my head, and landed close by. It was a dud. I never could explain that one. In fact, there were plenty of things in combat I could never explain. Once I saw a guy get hit in the head with a mortar shell. It bounced off him and exploded. Bang, he went down, stunned but not a scratch on him. Another guy was shot through the forehead. The bullet traveled up and around his scalp, over his hairline, and out the back side of his head. He had a concussion but was otherwise fine.

No matter how crazy it got I always tried to keep a sense of humor. In Bastogne we had captured a German kid. He was about seventeen and spoke some English. One day I was joking around with him and said, "Hey, why don't we change uniforms. Think about it: if I wear your German uniform they'll send me to the States as a captive—then I'll be home. If you wear my American uniform, we're going to go to Germany, you know that, then you'll be home."

He thought about it for a moment and smiled. "Ah, the hell with you," he said. "I want to go to America. You go to Germany."

Frank Soboleski

They backed up the trucks and said, "Get in." They drove us to Bastogne and dropped us off at the crossroads.

We could hear the rumble of heavy artillery, big explosions, and small-weapons fire as we advanced into the woods. We dug foxholes as fast as we could. Herb Suerth and I ended up digging and sharing one foxhole together. We were together until Herb got hit by shelling. I was out on patrol at the time and didn't know it until I got back. Some of my other good buddies were Don King and Babe Hendricks. I didn't spend much time in a foxhole, just during the shelling.

I remembered what my father had said once about how to keep your feet warm in cold weather: "Keep your feet dry and your footwear loose." So I found a rubber boot on a German foot sticking out of the snow one day. It was that old-fashioned kind of boot that had metal snaps all the way up. I dug around until I found the other. I cut the bottom of my wool coat off, took my leather boots off, and wrapped my feet in strips of wool from my coat. I put on those rubber boots and had no trouble with my feet being wet or cold from then on.

Bastogne was hell. In places the shelling was so intense that there were no more trees, only tall stumps with jagged tops. Whenever the shelling stopped we had to be ready to shoot because German soldiers would attack on the ground under the shelling. We watched German tanks roll in behind heavy shelling—the tanks hovered over foxholes and pivoted back and forth, crushing the bodies of screaming men—you thought you would lose your mind. Other times the enemy captured, tied to a tree, and tortured a man out on patrol, trying to get someone to come out and help him so they could spot and kill the unit. We knew there was no surrendering. It was kill until you are killed.

One day we were fighting an advancement of German soldiers that had come in behind their tanks. They were dressed in white outfits that camouflaged them in the snow. All we could see was moving snowbanks coming toward us, except for what appeared as black sticks moving toward us, too. They were the Germans crawling on their bellies with white sheets on and their rifles in front of them across their elbows. I shot into them steadily with my Thompson submachine gun. We were all doing the same when I noticed that the foxhole to the right of me had stopped firing. I hollered over to them, "What's wrong?" I wondered if they were out of ammo. No one answered. I kept firing until I was out of ammo, then jumped into the foxhole and found a soldier slumped over his machine gun. I pulled him away from it and saw that he had been shot in the neck clear through to the back. I was sure he was dead. I hollered "Medic!," grabbed his machine gun and ammo, and jumped back into my own foxhole. I figured that a German had a fix on him and would keep shooting in that direction. The soldier who was shot got help from a medic and was taken back to England for medical care. He was later sent back to the States and lived a long life. I didn't know that he had survived until I was reading Ambrose's book. I was happy to know that I had taken part in saving a man's life.

I was injured in Bastogne but not enough to ever be pulled out of combat for medical help. One day, during a confrontation in the woods, I was crawling on my belly like a frog, my rifle cradled over my elbows in front of me. Suddenly I felt a very warm spot on my butt. Someone hollered, "You're on fire." I looked to see my back pocket on fire and felt my flesh burning. A medic crawled over and pulled a large chunk of burning metal out of me, cut the cloth away, and poured sulfa on my butt. The fire from the shrapnel that had landed and embedded in me was out, so I just kept crawling. Later, I was awarded a Purple Heart for that injury— and I do have a chunk of my butt missing to this day. Other than the shrapnel in my legs from a lot of other shelling that I was in, I was never injured bad enough to be out of combat. I never lost a day on the job.

General McAuliffe got a letter from the German commander telling him to surrender his troops because they had us surrounded. McAuliffe answered with one word: "Nuts." When the German officers who had delivered the message asked what it meant, Colonel Harper, who had delivered the message to the German officers, said, "It means 'go to hell.'"

We soldiers felt the same way. The Germans had surrounded the wrong outfit.

CHAPTER EIGHTEEN

Blood

Buck Taylor

On January 13, 1945, word came down to leave Bastogne and go into a defensive position around Foy, a small village six miles northeast of Bastogne. It was all still part of the larger Battle of the Bulge.

We moved toward Foy, walking through the woods. We started at daybreak and moved out of our old positions, getting ready to attack the town. Everything was covered with snow. Just at daybreak the platoon ahead of us came across a big log-covered bunker with somebody undoubtedly sleeping in there. They threw a couple grenades in. As this was happening I looked to my left and saw something move about twenty-five to thirty feet away. I realized it was a German in a foxhole covered with a blanket. I did a dumb thing. I had my tommy gun, and still moving forward, I pumped about three rounds into him and finished him off. What I should have done was take him prisoner and ship him back to Headquarters for interrogation. It would have been nice to find out what we were up against.

We moved on through the area. It was very quiet as morning grew to afternoon. I walked over to the side to our right flank to see what was going on there and met up with some troopers from another company. As I stood there talking to them, a couple shots rang out, just random. One caught me in the leg and I went down; that was the third time I was wounded. They took me back to the aid station and loaded me in an ambulance that evening. In many ways that was the end of my career with Easy Company. A few hours later that night—they call it the night of hell—the Germans really bombarded the company with artillery. That's when several of the fellows were killed; Herb Suerth was wounded in both legs. I was back in the aid station that night when it all broke loose.

The bullet that hit me had torn into the nerve that went down to my foot. It didn't sever it completely, but the wound took forever to heal. I spent eleven months in the hospital and rehab. From the aid station they took me back to England, then shipped me back to a hospital in the States. I had one operation in the general hospital in England, then another operation in the States. For a long time I had no feeling in my foot; it was all numb. After a while I could hobble along. In the end, the nerve pretty much healed.

Shifty Powers

This incident is strange: a guy in the 2nd Platoon, Frank Mellett—he and I didn't get along real well. We never fought or anything, it was just a conflict of personalities. He was a good soldier and all, but he was a Yankee and I was a Southerner. So it was just a conflict we had.

Easy Company was getting ready to take this little town of Foy. Each night we covered our foxholes with pine boughs. The night before the attack on Foy, it snowed. Early the next morning I crawled out of my foxhole, looked around, and couldn't see a soul. I was the only person standing. The only thing I could see were mounds, just like I was standing in a cemetery. In a few minutes somebody popped out of one of those mounds just like he was coming up out of a grave. At least I knew then I wasn't all alone. Then another guy came along and said, "Who was doing that shooting last night, Shifty?"

"I didn't hear any shooting," I said, but when he said that it reminded me of a dream I had had during the night. In my dream Frank Mellett was behind a tree and he and I were shooting at each other. I could just about picture where he was.

I had to think about that. I had a little old .62 pistol, and when the guy left, I pulled it out of its holster and looked at it. Rounds were hard to get for those, so I knew exactly how many I had. Sure enough, the pistol had been fired twice during the night. I had no idea what I had shot at. I got to worrying that maybe I had shot Frank Mellett in my sleep. Finally, Frank popped up out of one of those holes. I was tickled to death to see him. But later that day, when we took the town of Foy, Frank Mellett was killed in the attack.

Clancy Lyall

We were told to attack and clear Foy.

Taking Foy, I had some bad thoughts. We were going across a wide-open field. About halfway across the field I started to sweat. The Germans were dug in with their foxholes and tanks. They started firing at us. It was like cutting grass. You could hear the zing and the tang. That's one of the goddam scariest times I've ever had, taking Foy.

Foy is where Lieutenant Norman Dike was relieved of his command. Now, you have to understand Dike. Out of West Point, he was assigned to the regiment. He had never had a combat command, never even been in combat, but for him to get a rank he had to lead a combat company. So battalion sent him to Easy Company. Thank God he wasn't around very much. Anytime he was around, it was awful. He was shot in the shoulder while taking Foy, near a haystack. That's when Ron Speirs came running across the field, like you see in the movie. Winters had sent him in to relieve Dike.

I always figured that Captain Speirs had the right outlook on life: *Don't worry about it, you're dead already. You just keep on moving. If it's your time, it's your time.* One time I was really shaky and one of the chaplains talked to me. He said, "What's the matter?"

"I'm afraid of getting killed," I said.

He said, "Do you believe in Jesus?"

I said, "Yes, I do."

He said, "Clancy, that's what's important. You don't need to worry about dying. You may go home and sit in a chair and die that way. We all die. But everybody has something to do before being taken. You do that."

That stuck with me. Ron Speirs was the same way. I liked him better than Winters, to tell you the truth.

When the war was all over, I stayed in the service, this time with B Company, 508th, because E Company, 506th, had been disbanded by then. I took my wife with me back to Frankfurt, Germany. The army sent us there for three years, 1947 to 1949. We were the only airborne combat unit left there. Our specific job was to counteract the Russians. If you gave them an inch of territory they'd always claim a foot.

When I got to Germany, my wife and I had a nice two-bedroom apartment. We were also allotted a driver and a maid. So I went and found an old German paratrooper from the 6th German Airborne to work for us. He and his wife were living in a bombed-out building with just a sheet stretched across the opening of the building. Their children had been killed. I got them out of there, got them ID cards and new clothes, and they came to live with us. All their belongings fit into one paper sack. We had two bedrooms and only needed one.

They were a very nice family. The man's name was George Stinz. He and I swapped a lot of stories back and forth. After the war, everybody was friends. Hell, why not? We were both paratroopers. The only thing different between us was the language. He had God and country, he was drafted, he had his job to do. (Not the SS, mind you; that's different. I'd shoot an SS man in the head if I had a chance.) George had worked as a stamper in a boot factory before the war; then he got drafted, and away he went.

George had been a sergeant in the German Army. He was at Bastogne, fighting against us. I had long talks with him and asked him once why they didn't just roll over us at Bastogne—they had eight divisions around us. He said, "We never knew what you had. Every time we attacked, a whole bunch of artillery came on us."

Joe Lesniewski

Just after the attack on Foy, Lieutenant Winters told me to go on patrol. I was about three hundred to four hundred feet away from the company, walking by myself on patrol, still in full sight of the guys at all times. If there was any of the enemy spotted, my job was to immediately give them the slug. Shelling started. It wasn't a massive amount of shells or anything right then, just one at a time. I never even expected to get hit. It was usual to get shelled randomly—every now and again a shell would come in. It just happened that two landed close to me.

I was hit with shrapnel and got two wounds: one on the right shin-bone, the other on my left knee. A medic had a little bit of sulfa powder and dumped that on. He only had one piece of cloth, so he wrapped that around my right leg. A couple months later I talked with the medic after I got out of the hospital. He said, "Joe, I'm sorry I couldn't give you any more than I did—that was the last that I had." It wasn't Gene Roe, it was another medic. Can't remember the name.

Even though I was hit, I was still walking. The injury didn't seem that bad. No pain, really. So I just kept going and stayed with the company. They didn't take me to the hospital then. Several weeks later, on March 3, I noticed something bad was going on. We had moved to Hagenau by then. The wounds on my legs were festering, scabs were forming from my ankle to my knee, on both legs. An infection soon set in, and it spread from the bottom of my legs up to my knees. You've got to realize that for three months none of us had any change of clothes that whole time. We would relieve ourselves—it sounds funny to talk about it—but there was nothing to help you clean yourself up. The odor from your body was terrible. Everything was so filthy. Dirt was just caked to your body.

So when my legs got so bad I talked to the medic and he sent me to a holding area. I was there for about two weeks with nobody coming around to look at me or anything. Finally I nailed down another medic and said, "Hey, I gotta get this taken care of." This is when they sent me to Germany; still nothing was happening. This is when I blew my top. I showed the guys my wounds and they couldn't believe how bad everything looked. The doctors wanted to amputate my legs. I got hold of one of the captains and showed him my legs. He said, "O my God, that's horrible." He made arrangements for me to go to Liège, Belgium, to a field hospital, which was a bunch of long tents filled with wounded, but quite good medical care. When they brought me in, the nurses took a look at me and couldn't believe what they were seeing. They wanted to know how long this had been going on like this. One of the doctors there got the idea that my legs were so bad they should amputate. There was a Major Myers from the 101st in the area. He took a look at me, then said to the doctors, "The next time I come over here I better see those legs still on him—nobody's going to touch him."

My legs were so bad—can you picture a lot of loose hamburger? Put it on your legs in the place where the skin is—that's what my legs looked like. It was pus and scabs from my ankles to my knees. Nurses and doctors at the field hospital were really good, like angels from heaven. They gave me three shots of penicillin per day, five hundred thousand units. So they were really pumping me full of penicillin. Altogether, I was in the hospital eighty-eight days. Gradually I healed up.

When I was in the hospital in Belgium, Captain Speirs sent mail home to my parents marked, "killed in action." Speirs was company commander at the time. I was a bit of a loner, often put on patrols by myself. It's feasible that he heard I was wounded and didn't see me, so he assumed I had been killed. The mail came home to my mother, but my sister intercepted it and held on to it without telling them anything. I continued to write letters to my folks, so that's how my sister eventually knew I was still alive. She never told them.

Frank Soboleski

Around the middle of January, the sun finally came out and we were able to get supplies flown in to us. General Patton's tanks could move toward us, so we were up and on the move, no longer in defense around Bastogne. We pushed out in all directions, making the circle around us bigger. We took Foy and Noville and kept chasing the Germans. They were on the run.

During the short time we were occupying Foy I attended a service by a warrant officer at a small church right in the town of Foy. The church had a blown-out wall, so we just stood outside that wall for the service. The warrant officer asked us to join hands and bow our heads for prayer. He thanked the Lord for bringing us this far and asked Him to help us continue to defeat the evil still ahead of us on our way into Germany. He prayed for the men we had lost in battle and for those who were injured and had to be sent back home.

In December 2007 my wife, Renee, and I came back and visited the small town of Foy. We found the same little church. It had been rebuilt after the war. There, I spoke to a Belgian man, Joel Robert. His father was nine years old when Easy Company was in Foy in 1944. One of the GIs had asked his father if he wanted some chocolate. It was the first time his father had ever tasted chocolate. It's very possible that I could have been that man, because I have always loved children and have always not liked chocolate.

In the middle of January 1944, we went through the city of Bastogne, now secured. We were traveling in trucks and on foot. There wasn't much left of Bastogne, just piles of bricks and rubble where buildings used to be. There was extensive damage to the town, fallen buildings, wrecked tanks, tipped-over trucks, but it was very quiet, no sounds of artillery or explosions. There wasn't much snow now, just mud and water.

As our group walked, Lieutenant Ron Speirs hollered at me, "How many men are in your group?"

"About thirteen," I answered. "Why?"

"I've got a political duty to take care of," Speirs said. "Round them up and follow me."

The thirteen of us went to what used to be Bastogne's town square. The citizens of Bastogne had made a platform with steps up to it. A Belgian officer, a Dutch officer, and a French officer, all in uniform, and a couple of city officials waited on the platform. They marched us up the steps one at a time. The Belgian officer kissed each one of us on both cheeks and placed the Belgian Fouragere on one of our shoulders. The Dutch officer presented each of us with the Dutch Order of William. The French officer awarded us the Croix de Guerre with Palm. They had a box of brass plaques and presented each of us with a commemorative plaque.

We thirteen paratroopers were given these honors and awards as representatives of the 101st Airborne. I couldn't understand a word said during the presentations, but we had no trouble knowing what they meant. It was a highly emotional time. The people were just so appreciative for what we had done. They wanted to celebrate our victory and their freedom with us before we left the area. I still have the braids on the jacket of my old uniform and have the brass plaque hanging on the wall of my home. I have always been proud to have them as a gift from the people of Bastogne.

When I returned to Bastogne in 2007, we found the people of Bastogne have a huge memorial celebration every year. They are still so grateful to American veterans, and pass on their gratefulness to each successive generation by teaching their young people to never forget the price of freedom. In 1956 the city of Bastogne built a huge memorial on a hilltop in the form of a star. It has five points, and along the top of each point are the names of all of our states. In the center of the star, on large walls, the story of the Battle of the Bulge is engraved in large letters. Across from the memorial they built a museum dedicated to the battle.

The whole city of Bastogne is a living memorial to their liberation by the United States. Every year during the three-day celebration, hundreds of reenactors dress in vintage American uniforms. They live in tents all over town and drive American jeeps, tanks, and trucks just as they were in 1945. In the town square, which is now named McAuliffe Square, they have a large American tank and a statue of General McAuliffe. A couple of blocks away they have a large statue of General Patton. When you are there they make you aware, wherever you go, that they haven't forgotten, and they can't do enough for you. If you are a World War II veteran who fought in Bastogne and return in later years to visit, the people in Bastogne will plant a new tree with your name next to it on a brass plate in the Peace Woods.

On that same trip in 2007 we visited the Bois Jacques Woods with Herb Suerth and Ed Shames. Herb and I had our picture taken together standing in our old foxhole. As I stood in the woods, an eerie feeling came over me and I started to become misty-eyed. As I looked through the replanted trees I thought I heard the sounds of tanks approaching and the outline of them in the mist. I couldn't wait to leave.

But what strikes me most strongly about that visit was how the people there are so filled with gratitude. We often hear about how America should stay out of wars in other countries. But people who live under oppression are thankful to be freed.

Earl McClung

The whole time I was in Belgium, I never did see the actual town of Bastogne. Right when we got there, they turned us loose on the outskirts.

We walked from there to the road south of Foy and dug in along the woods that ran along the road. We got our ammunition from the guys coming down the road as we were going in. I never did get an overcoat. We set up in this bunch of woods along this road south of Foy.

The real bad shelling—night of hell—that's what I called it, was when Guarnere and Toye lost their legs. Muck and Penkala just disappeared— the shell came in and you couldn't even find any piece of them. We were a sad-looking outfit, but we kept on going. I was on outpost that night, so I lucked out like a bandit.

Around the end of January 1944, we were sent to Alsace to take up position along the Moder River. We were put in boxcars for the trip. There was straw in the cars, but it was still very cold. Paul Rogers was platoon sergeant then, and we pulled into a little French town or some-place. He says, "We got to have some heat. We've been freezing to death for two months." There was a guy sitting around a potbellied stove in the middle of this station. I don't know what he was doing; he was part of the train outfit. So I turned to another guy and says, "You got leather gloves, put them on." The train was going pretty slow, so we jumped out, walked up, and got the stove still going full blast with the coal in it, and put it in the boxcar. The guy just sat there looking, like "What the hell you guys doing?" But we got Rogers his heat, anyway. That warmed us up. Paul always says, "We were the only boxcar in that whole damn train with a potbellied stove."

A little later we stopped in a railroad yard. I shot the lock off a railway car. There were 10-1 rations in it—new stuff. So we ate good from there to Hagenau. They had bacon in there, lots of good stuff, ground coffee, a lot of food. After two months we finally had a good meal.

CHAPTER NINETEEN

Enemy Across the River

Forrest Guth

After Bastogne we went to Hagenau, about seventy-five to eighty miles down the river. We went there by truck and set up in this little town. The enemy was right across the river from us. Sometimes we shelled them. Sometimes they shelled us.

After Hagenau there were about twenty-one original E Company guys left. They put the names in a helmet to draw a thirty-day furlough back to the States. They had done this a few times already. This time I was the lucky one. All the guys were happy for me. I came back on a hospital ship, a nice, clean ride back. So I returned to the States. I promised a few guys I would see their families. I saw families of Carwood Lipton and Bob Mann. It was a particular treat to see the families of these guys. Lipton was married and had a boy. I informed his family of what was going on.

When I got ready to go back to the company, the war had ended. I wrote a letter to Captain Speirs to get me back, but he said, "Don't you worry, they're over here getting drunk and killing each other." So I waited at Fort Benning, where I helped train new recruits, all the time thinking we'd go to Japan. But the war ended there, too. Of course, we all felt relief. But it was a big disappointment when I couldn't go back to the guys.

Norman Neitzke

I joined Easy Company in Hagenau. It was just before my nineteenth birthday. We celebrated in the cellar of a house with one candle going. We were stationed in a three-story house near the river with the Germans right across the river from us. Mostly we did guard duty and went on patrols. Being in a house, we were fairly comfortable at that time. The Germans sent over artillery once in a while—that was about it. Did the guys get me any presents for my birthday? No [laughs]. The Germans missed us with their artillery—that was present enough.

I didn't know much about Easy Company at the time. Most of the fellows were very good soldiers, concerned about what was going on and what we needed to do. We replacements listened to the old-timers. That gave us a lot of assurance—they knew a lot more about war than we did, that's for sure. They spoke in generalities about what had happened in Bastogne, Holland, and Normandy. As replacements, we were very much in awe of the old-timers: Pat Christenson; Jim Welling; Lieutenant Jack Foley; our squad leader, Tex Coombs; Bob Rader; Clancy Lyall; Don Malarkey. I was assigned to the 2nd Platoon.

The old-timers had mixed emotions toward replacements coming in this late in the war. Some were very helpful. Others appeared concerned at our presence. After a while I figured out why: They had gone through three campaigns. A bunch of new replacements coming in was an indication that the unit's strength was being built up again, which meant they needed to be ready for another campaign. So there was concern.

In some ways, Easy Company was a company of replacements by then. There were certainly a lot of us. Many of the old-timers had been wounded, killed, or were in the hospital. Some were able to rejoin the unit. The old-timers made a very good core. We were proud to know them.

One night we were told to make a patrol across the river to get some prisoners for interrogation. I provided backup on guard duty. I lost a pair of good, heavy underwear because one of the boats tipped. The guys all came back with wet clothes. I had an extra set of underwear, so I loaned it to a guy. I never got it back. That's how it went. I didn't mind.

In our courtyard we kept a 75mm howitzer. Our guys would lob a few shells over the river to keep the Germans on their toes. We got some coming back at us, too. The first time I saw that, I couldn't figure out why our guys shot so fast, then ran down to the basement. Then the German shells came over, so I figured out why pretty quick.

The Germans had a big railroad gun from World War I that went off on us quite a lot. It was camouflaged pretty well and we couldn't find out where it was. But we always had a good feeling whenever our P-47 fighter planes flew over to look at the Germans. Nobody would be shooting the railroad gun from the German side then, because the Germans didn't want to be spotted. It was always a relief to see our planes overhead.

For guard duty you challenged anybody who came down the line. I gave them the password, and they were supposed to give me the password back. One time I was guarding on a road in front of a building and heard some fellows coming toward me. I gave the password, but they didn't give the password back. I did it again. Again, no answer. I thought, "Uh-oh." So I took the safety off my rifle. Right about that time a shell came in, and we all went down. Then I heard the guys come up cussing in English, so I knew they were on our side.

I pulled guard duty two hours on, two hours off, 'round the clock. I never had a chance to sleep very well, but it could have been worse—we could have been sleeping in foxholes. We slept inside the basement of a house. It rained a lot in Hagenau, so being inside was pretty comfortable.

We manned another guard post in a three-story building. We were on the second floor, set up with machine guns on top of a table with sandbags around. From there we watched with binoculars and could see if anybody was coming across the river. You imagine a lot of things when you're up there.

Bill Wingett

Once in Hagenau, I had been out for two days scrounging around for food. I had gathered several rabbits, three or four pigeons, and a turkey.

Behind the place where we were set up was a tennis court that was all enclosed. I put our food in there and went out again, looking for something to eat. This time I found a bunch of canned food—peas, carrots, even a little bit of canned meat. So I came home to cook it up, and my goddam cage was empty.

I searched around, asking questions, and found that the 2nd Battalion officers' mess had all my stuff. I found where they had hid it and took the stuff back. The only thing I didn't find was the big bird. I went back down and put it all into a nice pot of stew—the whole damn thing. Me and my buddies ate. Was 2nd Battalion ever mad! They had probably been bragging around about what a meal they were going to cook.

In Hagenau I got to know Private First Class Antonio Garcia, a replacement, another real great guy. We were billeted in the same house. I got to know him better after the war. He brought his daughter to a couple conventions, and he'd take her out on the dance floor. Man, that sonuvagun could jitterbug.

Henry Zimmerman

In Hagenau we looked for things to eat. We found goats and rabbits, anything that was good eating, skinned it, and cooked it over an open fire.

Don Bond

We were the first group of replacements to join a paratrooper outfit on line. The 101st had taken so many losses in Bastogne they were short-handed.

Hagenau had been a pretty good-sized town, about twenty thousand civilians before most of them left. The city lay on the banks of the Moder River, a tributary of the Rhine. The river was fast-flowing, maybe fifty yards wide, maybe more—too big to throw grenades across, anyway. Things were run pretty smoothly in Hagenau by the time we replacements got there. You just did what they told you to do and you were all right.

Three cobblestone streets ran together there at a big intersection. One of my jobs was to make sure phone lines were laid in okay and working right. Mortars came along every so often and messed them up. I went out with the message center chief a lot when the lines got messed up; he knew what to do. He went out and came to where the line was blown in two and spliced it together. You've got to be careful. One day a line was blown in two right in the middle of that three-way intersection, mortars had been landing there most of the day. So we went out there, knelt down, spliced the line, and checked it to make sure it was fixed. We ran back under the doorway. We had just got back when the Germans hit that exact spot with about eight mortars, just *boom, boom, boom.* A second or two earlier and we would have got it.

I didn't go on the patrol across the river. I just took the men who went over to a house near the river where Captain Speirs and I had gone earlier to black out windows. The men stayed in the house until it got completely dark, then they went over in rubber boats. I came back to company head-quarters alone.

I've never told this story to anybody until years after the war: Earlier, when Speirs and I went to check out houses, we looked at several to pick out the best one. It was dark and we had tape, paper, and candles with us. Finally we decided on the best house across the street from the canal-bank. Now, it was critical to the patrol that no noise be made in that area, but when Speirs and I were blacking out the house a mongrel dog nearby eyed us and started to bark. That's a dangerous situation. It can really draw mortar fire or machine gun fire from the enemy—both on us and on the men who later did the patrol. We hushed the mongrel as best we could. He shut up but every once in a while he barked. I could see Speirs shake his head. We finished our job of blacking out the house. The dog let loose into another long bark. Old Speirs pulled out his .45 and let him have it.

Frank Soboleski

While we were in Hagenau, there were rumors that the Germans had broken through at Alsace. Easy Company was told to go fill the gap. We went by truck through many villages to Alsace-Lorraine. I was promoted by Speirs to a buck sergeant and assigned seven men. I had to find quarters for my men and myself. On the way there, we came to a house and a woodshed. I walked up to the door and knocked on it with the butt of my rifle. Out came an old man, older than my dad, with a big, sweeping mustache. His hands were in the air and he motioned by pointing to the woodshed and shaking his head. I assumed he didn't want to have to leave his house. I felt sorry for the old guy and pointed my finger at my chest and then away from his house.

He motioned toward his mouth with his thumb, meaning he had nothing to eat. We gave him some of our rations; then I got a better idea. I make the sign of deer antlers and jumping. He shook his head no, so I motioned rabbit ears and hopping. He pointed to my gun and nodded his head but indicated he had no shells. He led me around a hedgerow and pointed to large rabbits. They were red Belgium hares. I shot one, and he took it in to his wife. They cooked it with potatoes and shared it with us. We moved out the next morning, still traveling toward Alsace.

I was on guard duty one evening, and another guard from another checkpoint came over to get me. He had an old lady with him who carried a gunny sack but wouldn't let him look in it. I asked her in Polish, *"Sho ta miash?"* (What is that?), pointing to the bag. She answered, *"keat."* Sure enough, she pulled two smoked cats out and held them up. She motioned with her hand that she had small children to feed by showing how tall each one was. I gave her as much of our food as she could carry.

After about two weeks we traveled back to Hagenau.

One day in Hagenau, things got quiet for a while and I happened upon a dappled-gray horse. I got my buddy to drive me alongside the horse in a jeep while I lassoed him. I noticed he had numbers on his hooves. He must have been a Polish cavalry horse, because he was so well trained I could do anything on him. I rode into town and someone threw me a purple top hat so I put it on my head. At a reunion in Atlanta in 2006, my wife and I ran into Easy Company member Jim Alley in the hall of the hotel. The first thing Jim said was, "Hey, Frank, where's your dappled-gray horse and purple top hat?" That sure brought back memories from sixty-two years ago.

On February 20, 1945, Easy Company went into reserve and was sent back to Mourmelon. On March 15, while in Mourmelon, the 101st Airborne received a reward after a division parade before the most brass we

Hank Zimmerman in uniform.
Courtesy of Henry Zimmerman

A young Joe Lesniewski.
Courtesy Joe Lesniewski

We found German officers' uniforms in Berchtesgaden and put then on, then took our picture. We had had a bit to drink at the time. FROM LEFT TO RIGHT: Ken Mercier, Pat Christensen, Clancy Lyall, and Earl Hale. *Courtesy of Clancy Lyall*

Don Bond in uniform.
Courtesy of Don Bond

Buck Taylor, 1945.
Courtesy of Buck Taylor

Camp Toccoa, 1942. FROM LEFT TO RIGHT: Buck Taylor, Salty Harris, Ledlie Pace, and Walter Gordon. *Courtesy of Buck Taylor*

Guard duty, Kaprun Austria, 1945. Two German MPs (either end), Norman Neitzke (the tall one), unidentified Easy Company man. *Courtesy of Norman Neitzke*

Shifty Powers.

Courtesy of Shifty Powers

Norman Neitzke, Germany, 1945.

Courtesy of Norman Neitzke

Ed Joint, 1943.
Courtesy of Ed Joint

Earl McClung, after first enlistment.
Courtesy of Earl McClung

Normandy residents out to greet us on D-day morning, June 6, 1944.
Courtesy of Forrest Guth

Roy Gates, paratrooper.
Courtesy of Roy Gates

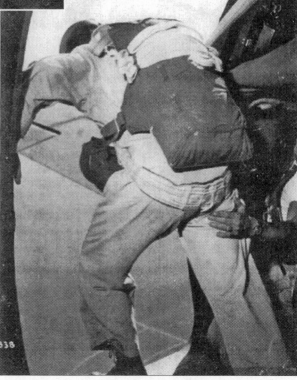

Training jump—stand in
the door . . . go!
Courtesy of Bill Wingett

Devastation in Carentan.
Courtesy of Bill Wingett

A picture of the scarf that Bill Wingett found on a dead German pilot who was shot down on the beach at Normandy. *Courtesy of Bill Wingett*

The picture found by Bill Wingett in a dead German pilot's pocket who was shot down on the beach at Normandy.
Courtesy of Bill Wingett

Rod Bain in Austria at end of war (notice champagne bottle by his ankle!).
Courtesy of Bill Wingett

Coming home aboard the USS *Wooster Victory Ship*, Boston Harbor, Thanksgiving Day, 1945. *Courtesy of Bill Wingett*

Al Mampre, then and now.
Courtesy of Al Mampre

Dewitt Lowrey at Toccoa.
Courtesy of C. Susan Finn

Robert Burr Smith and Skip Muck.
Courtesy of C. Susan Finn

FROM LEFT TO RIGHT: Ed Pepping, war years. *Courtesy of Ed Pepping;* Forrest Guth in Normandy. *Courtesy of Forrest Guth;* Frank Perconte, in uniform. *Courtesy of Frank Perconte*

Skip Muck.
Courtesy of C. Susan Finn

George Luz Sr. (on right with cigarette) and a friend playfully roughing up a buddy at Toccoa.
Courtesy of C. Susan Finn

1946 reunion, New York (LEFT TO RIGHT): Buck Taylor, C. Carwood Lipton, Shifty Powers, Ed Shames, unidentified, Herb Suerth Jr, Bill Guarnere. *Courtesy of Elaine Taylor*

This photo was taken after we took Berchtesgaden after we scrounged some gas and got the plane off the ground for a short time. *Courtesy of Frank and Renee Soboleski*

Frank Soboleski and Tom Gray going hunting on horseback
in the mountains after the war was over.
Courtesy of Frank and Renee Soboleski

ON LEFT: Soboleski; ON RIGHT: Soboleski and Blue Hale, "Tex."
Courtesy of Frank and Renee Soboleski

Formal portrait of Robert Burr Smith.
Courtesy of C. Susan Finn

Frank Perconte.
Courtesy of C. Susan Finn

Easy Company on a march at Camp Mackall.
Courtesy of C. Susan Finn

Easy Company at war's end, Zell am See, Austria, 1945.
Courtesy of Frank and Renee Soboleski

ON LEFT: The Easy Company monument in Foy.
BELOW: Foxhole on the edge of the field at the Bois
Jaques woods. They are all still there.
Photos courtesy of Frank and Renee Soboleski

Easy Company takes Hollywood. FROM LEFT TO RIGHT: Lester Hashey, Frank Soboleski, the back of Buck Taylor's head, Herb Suerth, Earl McClung, the back of Babe Heffron's head and Shifty Powers. *Courtesy of Frank and Renee Soboleski*

Frank Soboleski.
Courtesy of Frank and Renee Soboleski

Frank Soboleski's medals.
Courtesy of Frank and Renee Soboleski

Ed Tipper.
Courtesy of Ed Tipper

Herbert Sobel and son.
Courtesy of Rich Riley and Michael Sobel

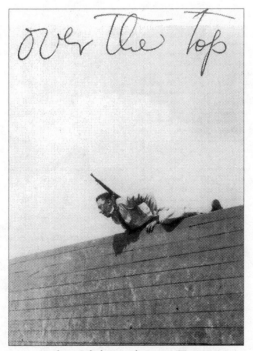

Herbert Sobel, over the top at Toccoa.
Courtesy of Rich Riley and Michael Sobel

Mr. and Mrs. Herbert Sobel.
Courtesy of Rich Riley and Michael Sobel

Herbert Sobel with his son.
Courtesy of Rich Riley and Michael Sobel

Dewitt Lowrey, Camp Mackall, 1943.
Courtesy of Rich Riley

Dewitt Lowrey, Camp Toccoa, 1942.
Courtesy of Rich Riley

had ever seen. General Eisenhower was there, along with General [Maxwell] Taylor; Lieutenant General Sir Frederick Morgan; Lieutenant General Lewis Brereton; President Roosevelt's secretary, Stephen Early; and Major General Matthew Ridgway. They drove past the whole division, then climbed up on a reviewing stand to give speeches. General Eisenhower announced that the division had received a Presidential Distinguished Unit Citation for its performance in Bastogne, the first time in the history of the army that an entire division had been so cited. Each man was given the commemorative medal representing the Presidential Citation with cloverleaf.

CHAPTER TWENTY

Meeting a Defeated Aggressor

Norman Neitzke

From Hagenau we went to Mourmelon for a few weeks. It was nice to get away from the front. On a sunny day you could look at the sunshine and not be concerned that anybody was shooting at you.

Nothing much happened in Mourmelon. While there, the 17th Airborne was supposed to jump over the Rhine into Germany. We were supposed to be their backup. Their jump was a success and we were not needed.

From Mourmelon we headed into Germany. We rolled through France and Belgium. All this time we saw a lot of American flags on the road. Then we rolled into an area where there were no American flags. That meant we were in Germany.

We had some hard-core Nazi troops that kept firing at us, but the majority of German soldiers we met were giving up in droves. They knew the war was just about over.

When our men found the concentration camps I was in the group that went to get food. We found a cheese factory nearby and loaded all these cheese rounds on a truck; they looked like spare tires. But then our company surgeon stopped us and said that if we distributed food too quickly the people would die, they had been starving for so long.

Frank Soboleski

We moved into Germany on foot, on tanks, in DUKWs [amphibious vehicles], and over pontoon bridges, moving swiftly. All along the way the Germans created pockets of resistance to hold us back and hold some ground so they could regroup and retreat. There were too many smaller battles to count.

Constantly, we took prisoners and sent them to the rear for interrogation. They came out of the hills, seven abreast in endless columns, no weapons, tearing off any insignias they had so as not to be recognized as any specific unit when they surrendered in large numbers. There were so many of them at a time that it actually scared us. We were really outnumbered at times.

One night a small group of us were warming up K rations in a burned-out building next to a river. On the other side of the river were more burned-out buildings. Behind that was a house still intact. The officer in charge decided we should get a rope across the river at dusk and pull a small rubber raft over to see if there were any Germans in that house. They asked for someone who could swim. I volunteered and stripped to my underwear. The men greased me down with axle grease to keep out the cold, and I slipped into the water, almost as cold as Rainy Lake on the Canadian border back home. I swam across and tied the rope to a piling that had been part of a warehouse. As several of the men pulled the raft over to the other side, one German soldier about fifty years old and two about sixteen years old came out of the house with their hands up. Not a shot was fired. There were no more Germans around. When the older German saw me he said, "I could have shot you anytime when you were swimming over. I didn't because I've never fired this gun. I didn't want to be a soldier. I had no choice, but I knew from the beginning we wouldn't win this war. Everything was too fast and we were too spread out without enough supplies." He spoke pretty good English. They were all glad it was over and they could go home. We sent them to the rear as prisoners and were on our way again.

We couldn't help but notice that in Germany there seemed less damage to the buildings and homes than in other countries we had been through. Many of the German people seemed to be living in relative luxury—beautiful homes in immaculate condition, plenty of food and material goods.

Late in April 1945, Easy Company came to Buchloe in the foothills of the Alps, near Landsberg. We went on patrol. It was a clear, still day with no wind at all. We were spread out going through the woods when we smelled a putrid odor. I looked at the other men a little ways apart from me and saw that they had the same questioning look. We kept walking in the same direction, and the smell got stronger as we approached very high fencing. It was about twelve feet high with posts about eight feet apart and four feet of tipped-in barbed wire around the top. Between the posts was extra-heavy fencing like chicken wire, but so much stronger, like quarter-inch welded grating. The posts were made out of unpeeled trees, just cut and put in the ground. The wire fencing had been buried deep in the ground so no one could dig under it. It was a big compound, planned out with low buildings about twelve feet apart and a space for elevated guard posts that covered each twelve-foot space between the buildings. There were rows and rows of buildings. Some buildings were just three-sided sheds.

As we got closer we saw the open side of some of the sheds. Stacks of bodies were piled there, probably waiting to be burned to render out the fat. We approached cautiously. We smelled another odor now: horrible, sickening, sweet, putrid—it was burning flesh. What we saw then was the most unbelievable sight I have ever witnessed: human beings, some standing like mummies, most lying on shelves in buildings, live bodies mixed with dead bodies, all together on shallow shelves so hundreds of them would fit in the buildings. There were also piles of bodies burning. The constant sounds of low moaning and crying could be heard. The sound made you want to plug your ears to get away from it. I became sick to my stomach, as did many of us.

The people we saw were mostly adults, but some could have been as young as ten or twelve years old. The only food anywhere was a few buckets of discolored water with dippers. It might have been some kind of broth or boiled grain water. Some people had yellow armbands that signified they were Jews. Others could have been Polish or Austrian. Most prisoners were naked or had striped rags hanging on their bodies. We saw no evidence that they had any clothes for the cold winter that had just passed. How man can do such a thing to man is beyond comprehension.

Later we learned that the Germans had locked up the camp and fled immediately before we got there. Some of our men said later that they had found a boxcar full of rotting dead people. They could hardly talk about it. Many of them were still vomiting when they got back to camp.

Pretty soon our officers ushered us out of the camp. They didn't want us to have prolonged contact with the prisoners because they were full of body lice and all types of infection and disease. The Graves Registration and the medics were rushed in as we were led out. General Taylor declared martial law in the area. The next day he ordered the citizens in nearby Landsberg to go to the concentration camp with shovels and rakes and take care of the dead bodies. The prisoners that were still alive were treated by our health units.

If anyone ever says there were no concentration camps in Germany, tell them it isn't so. I saw, smelled, and heard the agony of those prisoners. It happened, I was there. I am a living witness to it. On that day we all knew instantly why we were there. We saw for ourselves the nature of evil that was being practiced by the Germans. We were told later that this was a work camp, not an extermination camp. It was one of a half dozen or more that were a part of the Dachau complex. God have mercy on them for their unspeakable sins.

Henry Zimmerman

Coming through Germany, I saw the concentration camps. It was sickening what the Germans did. It turned my stomach. These poor people—my heart went out to them. What we had, we gave to them. They were starving. Just like skeletons.

Earl McClung

Something that stands out in my mind—the worst thing I ever saw was one of those concentration camps. These prisoners in there were really starving to death. God, that was really horrible. We walked up the road, they were hanging on the fence, just walking skeletons. Terrible. Terrible. We gave them everything we had to eat, probably killed a few. They told us later we shouldn't have done that because their systems were so starved. The Germans had locked the gates and run. We blew the gates open, then went on through and set up in the next little town.

Clancy Lyall

Moving down into Germany, we were sending patrols out all the time. Near the town of Memmingen, Bull Randleman took two squads of the 1st Platoon on patrol and ran into this huge encamped place. They saw dead bodies all over the yard, so they sent back to tell Lieutenant Winters. We opened up the camp, went inside, and made the mistake of feeding the prisoners we found there. That's when I lost it. I busted into tears. I had shed a couple tears when Don Hoobler died, but seeing those concentration camps was the first time I cried since I was a kid. I didn't boo-hoo, but I just swelled up and tears came down. I felt so sorry for these people.

The prisoners came up and grabbed hold of you, wanting to hug you. Just the smell of the place, that didn't even bother me. What bothered me were the bodies all over the ground. The camp was about four football fields side by side, barbed wire all around. Bodies were stacked everywhere, big ditches dug with bodies thrown in.

We found out later that the Germans knew we were coming. The day before we got there they had left the camp. Before leaving they had shot as many as they could, then got the hell out. There were huge holes dug up with bodies stacked high. We went into the nearest town. None of the civilians knew anything about the concentration camps, they said. That's bullshit because this was a work camp and these prisoners worked in the farms around the area, too. Colonel Sink made the civilians come into the camp to bury the bodies. That was about the grandest idea I ever saw.

A couple days later we found another camp, near Muhlhausen. A train track ran up through the woods, so we followed that. We weren't the first there. Some armored outfit had already taken it. We walked into the big shower system where they put the cyanide in the shower heads. One of the inmates showed us how they put the bodies in this huge oven and raked the ashes out. It was a twenty-four-hour-per-day job, every day, killing all these people. This was the work of Hitler's SS. Who could do that? People had to be insane to do those things.

CHAPTER TWENTY-ONE

Toasting Victory

Frank Soboleski

We kept moving forward until we got to Berchtesgaden. Easy Company's 2nd Battalion was the first to reach it, on May 5, 1945. We took the town and secured the Berchtesgaden *hof* for the regimental headquarters.

Hitler had already killed himself, and his officers knew the inevitable was upon them. We came on it from all sides of the building. We kicked in doors with our rifle butts and were ready to fire. The officers came out to us with their hands up. Nobody fired a gun.

One officer came right up to me. He said he wanted to surrender and handed me his Luger with both hands outstretched. It was still in its holster. He spoke good English. He said that he had gone to school for eight years in the United States. When he went back to Germany to visit his parents the Germans said he had to fight with the German Army or be killed. I took his weapon and saw to it that he was delivered with the other German officers to headquarters. Lieutenant Speirs gave me a permit to keep the Luger and send it home. It was immaculate. It had never been fired, still in its beautiful leather holster, still with the Cosmoline in it.

It was an exhilarating time at the end of the war, and all of us in Berchtesgaden felt it. The fun and games began. Everyone was shooting in the air, looting, drinking the best wine and champagne in Germany. Things were running amok. To the victor belong the spoils, and spoils they were. The place was bursting with money, currency from a dozen countries, and art treasures from all over Europe. It was stuffed with booze, jewelry, and famous cars. Hitler's silverware was split between Winters and Welsh, who were both still eating with it in their homes forty-five years later.

I soon tired of the revelry. Not being drinkers, I and Tom Gray, who was a family man and also didn't drink, looked for a different kind of fun. We found an abandoned German airplane. We scrounged around for some gas, put it in the plane, and got it about six feet off the ground. As soon as it ran out of gas, it dropped back to the ground. Then we grabbed a motorcycle and rode around until we found some horses. We got our hands on a jeep and rounded up the horses, about six of them. They were steeplechase horses, beautiful animals. We took them to a nearby stable and got them corraled. Then we decided to go into the mountains to hunt. By that time Jesse Aranda and Dutchy Bauer had joined us in the fun. The four of us found saddles and bridles for the horses, loaded them with supplies, and took off for the mountains to hunt for the red stags that we had seen pictures of at the hof. We camped, hunted, fished, and enjoyed the freedom of being out in the mountains. It was beautiful country. We didn't see any deer, but I shot two loose pigs and found a square tub of honey. We ate that up and spit out the wax.

None of us drank anything except cool, clear water from mountain streams. We had talked about how anything to drink at the Eagle's Nest could have been poisoned. They knew we were coming ahead of time. It would have been a wonderful opportunity to get a lot of us.

Roy Gates

I joined the 101st at Mourmelon, France, in February 1945. From there I went to E Company as a replacement officer. Joining E Company was okay for me. Right away Earl McClung decided I was a good guy, so they decided they wouldn't kill me [laughs]. Far from not being accepted, I found that I was accepted just fine. I got along with the men well. I still do today.

We got in DUKWs, land-sea vehicles, to go through Germany. A guy, Bill McGonical, in the 3rd Platoon, was able to get us the best accommodations in all these towns as we went through the country. Paul Rogers and Earl McClung found a cow and we ate well in that particular town, can't remember which one. McClung, having been a country boy, knew how to butcher it. So we ate well.

Here's a story about Rogers, a hell of a soldier and a little bit older than most of us. He was my platoon sergeant. Just before we reached Berchtesgaden, word came back that a German panzer unit on one of the bridges had its 88s on us—shots fired in anger. We were just outside of Munich. The war was still on at this point, but I hadn't seen any real combat yet. Third Platoon was supposed to take them out, which meant it was my responsibility to lead troops into battle, and goddam—here I was a brand-new second lieutenant in the company saying to myself, God, I hope I can take care of it.

Well, along comes Rogers, who had been through all of this before, his voice cool as anything, saying, "Don't worry about it, Lieutenant. Everything's under control." That really calmed me down. As it turned out, the German panzer was just a mock-up, just a camouflage unit, and there wasn't anybody there after all. But that really said something about Rogers.

Norman Neitzke

Near a small hospital on the outskirts of Berchtesgaden our squad was short on vehicles. We saw a nice black German ambulance and figured we'd liberate the vehicle. This happened quite a bit. For instance, our squad leader, Tex Coombs, drove a German Air Force truck by then. So we hopped in the front of the ambulance but suddenly heard a pounding in the back. A German doctor was delivering a baby back there. He didn't say much, but we figured he could keep the ambulance. We got out and hopped in the back of one of our three-quarter-ton trucks.

Heading into Berchtesgaden, the French armor were beside us. It was a rural area, and as we came up a hill to a plateau, we heard shots. We grabbed our rifles and looked around. The French had caught three German SS troopers. They looked very young, blond. One by one, the French soldiers made the Germans kneel. We watched as the French shot each one in the head. It wasn't that much of a shock for us to see, we had seen people get shot before, but it made you think—you had to wonder at all the French people had been through by then.

At Berchtesgaden we liberated a lot of Hitler's booze. Bob Rader, Jim Welling, Clancy Lyall, and five or six of us from our squad took a van up to Hitler's wine cellar and helped ourselves to the best champagne. We brought down loads of it and kept the bottles in the front room area of a big German villa that we were stationed in. Anytime you wanted a drink, you just walked into the front room and helped yourself. After a while nobody was feeling much pain.

One day Jim Welling and I decided to do some exploring. Across from the SS barracks we found Hitler's tunnels and followed them for quite a while. If an air raid came, the Germans hid down there. We found all kinds of stuff that belonged to Hitler and Hermann Goering. You took steps down to the air raid shelter at the bottom. It was like a regular home office down there with paneled walls, weapons, clothes strewn all around, Goering's size fourteen shoes. Jim took some guns and a type-writer. I took some guns, part of a German SS uniform, and some enve-lopes addressed to Hitler from around the world. I didn't read German very well, but back in the States I took the envelopes to a German barber I knew who deciphered them for me. Unfortunately, none of the letters were left inside the envelopes, but the envelopes had been sent to Hitler from countries all over the world, including the States. If anything, it showed Hitler had a lot of contacts.

We rolled into Berchtesgaden on May 5. May 8 was V-E Day. Some of the guys shot their rifles up in the air. The mood among the men was very elated, but there was also a lot of thought that we'd go to the Pacific before long. A rumor went around that there was already a boat at Mar-seilles, France, all set to take us to the other side. We didn't know when we'd ship out, but we figured it was soon.

Don Bond

I didn't do much in Berchtesgaden except pull guard duty and drink champagne and cognac.

Al Mampre

In Berchtesgaden, I hardly had anything to do as a medic. We set up medical headquarters in a hotel. Some of the hotel staff got diarrhea, and I gave them some medicine to cork them up. Then I had to give them some more medicine to get them uncorked. Once a major was riding a horse and hit his head on a tree. I was called to help, but by the time I got there he was okay. That's about all I did medically.

Henry Zimmerman

When we were in Berchtesgaden, Sergeant Earl Hale sent us out to get transportation. We went out to look for what we could find. We came across Hitler's car, but it had no wheels. We found a bus, but it wouldn't start. We saw a fire truck and took that. On the way back to camp we had a wonderful time ringing the bell. Hale was upset. He didn't want a fire truck.

Earl McClung

I only saw two Germans on the way into Berchtesgaden; one was dead, the other was running. Then we went to a little town close to where the road goes out to the Eagle's Nest. They said they had blown the road out and nobody could get up there. It was just rocks, so I thought, I can climb over them. I went up there anyway. I just walked over the rocks. It was about five miles, but that was no chore in them days. I went by myself. Hitler's house had been bombed—it was just a pile of junk, but he had a good wine cellar in there. That's where we got all that booze. I know I was the first American in Berchtesgaden. Somebody cleared the road eventually and the unit got up there.

From there I went on to Hitler's *teehaus*, on top of the Alps. I climbed to the ridge and got up there. There was no electricity, you couldn't take the elevator. Years later we were over there with a tour and the guide started asking me questions about it. He didn't believe I had been there. I told him about the Persian rugs upstairs and down, which aren't there anymore. The guide said, "You were there all right. The people in the town cut them up in little pieces and took them out."

When I was up at the Eagle's Nest I found some loot hidden in Hitler's garage. I ended up getting into that and got a box full of fifty-dollar bills and sixteen hundred-pound English notes. About four o'clock the next morning search lights came on in the barracks we were staying in. We fell out in our underwear. Our commanding officers went through the barracks and got that money back. Aside from the cognac, that's all I got from the Eagle's Nest. Oh, I got a Luger and got that home through customs; that's the only thing I got.

CHAPTER TWENTY-TWO

Last Duties in Austria

Norman Neitzke

From Germany we moved into Austria at the end of April 1945. All this time the Germans were still surrendering. We headed down the autobahn one way with the Germans coming the other way.

One incident sticks out to me. We had some R & R time in Austria. You could read books, climb mountains, swim, sometimes you didn't know what to do with yourself. One afternoon some buddies and I went about twenty miles away to a lake to go for a row. You always had to carry your weapon with you—many of us didn't want to carry our rifles, so we carried German pistols. I must have rowed longer than everybody else, because suddenly I was all alone in the lake; my buddies had all gone back without me. So there I was twenty miles from the base with German soldiers running all around and all I've got is a pistol.

I walked back to the main road and stuck my thumb out. The first car that came along was a real fancy German Mercedes staff car with the top down. A driver and an assistant driver were in front, with two officers in the rear. They stopped and gave me a ride. It was probably a safer move on their behalf to travel with an American soldier with them. Plus, they probably didn't want any of their soldiers taking a shot at one lone American

GI standing beside the road, which would have prompted an American retaliation.

We rode together for about half an hour. The officers had been schooled in the States and spoke perfect English. They turned out to be part of General Albert Kesselring's surrender team and were in the process of negotiating several surrenders. We spoke mostly of home, no politics. As we drove down the road any German we saw saluted us. I wish I had a camera.

I pulled a lot of guard duty around then. We often stood guard alongside of German MPs, who made sure the German civilians and surrendering soldiers went the right directions. For several days I guarded alongside these two older German fellows. They didn't speak much. They wore these strange collars around their necks. I took a picture of them. Back in the States a friend of mine saw the picture. His mouth flew open. "Do you realize who those guys were?!" he said. They were a specialized German troop, almost like KGB. They had been authorized to shoot anybody on sight, German soldiers or otherwise.

Earl McClung

Kaprun, Austria—I thought I had died and gone to heaven there. My job was to hunt and feed the prisoners that the Germans had taken for slave labor who were incarcerated there. The prisoners were freed by then but they had no place to go. I think they were Polish and Romanian mostly. The job fell to us to feed them. I fed them stag and chamois (goats with little hooked horns) until they were coming out of their ears. So I finally got to do some hunting, like I enjoyed. I just camped out. They saw me maybe once or twice a week.

Shifty Powers

I was there every day Easy Company fought on the line and was one of the very few who were never wounded in combat. That didn't mean I wasn't close a bunch of times, but I never got wounded.

Right at the end of the war, I had my name pulled out of a hat to come home early on a furlough. Four of us won, one from each company:

Headquarters, Dog, Fox, and Easy. As we traveled down the road in the back of this truck, this drunk GI came around the corner at us and crashed into us. I flew out and broke my pelvis and my wrist.

They shot me full of morphine at the wreck site. The next thing I knew I woke up in the field hospital and a nurse was taking my clothes off. I opened my eyes for a few seconds. I saw her take off my boots. When she got to my pants (I had bloused them with condoms, like we always did), she jumped back and gave out a great big squeal. That's all I remember before I went back under.

I woke up again in a hospital tent. I was beat up, black and blue all over. I had a whole lot of stuff I was bringing home, and I lost all of it. I felt so sorry for myself. I raised myself up in bed and looked around. Down the other end of the ward was a cot with a soldier lying on it. He had a complete body cast on, from the top of his head to his toes. All you could see were little holes for his eyes, nose, and mouth. That took care of me feeling sorry for myself. I considered how fortunate I was.

I went to Reims to a hospital for a while and got doctored up some. They put me on a ship and sent me back to the States.

Bill Wingett

In Austria I got detailed with the freight department. I was assigned to a special detail to escort trainloads of displaced persons to Budapest. These were people that the Germans had removed from their homes and taken to Austria and Germany as forced laborers. I don't remember a single English-speaking person. Not all were Jews. We made two trips on this detail. I was the only one, to my knowledge, from Headquarters Company, 2nd Battalion, of the 506th.

The displaced people were put in boxcars. There was only one coach on the whole train, right in the middle, and that was where the troops lived. We had two machine gun crews. I was a rifleman. Our job was to escort those people to their destination, unload them, and return those boxcars, which belonged to the U.S. Army, back to the U.S. Army at Kaprun. But the engines were all operated by Russians, which made this a tricky situation. Every place we stopped, those Russians tried to get away with a boxcar or two. We needed to set up signals to know that the whole train was still there whenever we left. As soon as a train started slowing down we had to have somebody on that first car to be damn sure we didn't have to shoot the engineer.

We had to be pretty mean thinking about it, too. We stopped at one station, and this Russian officer started to get on our personal car. I was on the end of the platform. When he started to get on, I said no. He looked up at me and motioned to a Russian rifleman behind him, who immediately trained his weapon on me. The officer stepped back on the car. I stepped sideways and put my foot on the officer's chest and set him on his ass beside the railroad track. The rifleman looked behind me, and there was another American with an M-1 on him. It was a Mexican standoff. We thought sure we were going to have an awful lot of trouble with that. Every place along that railroad there were flatcars loaded with farm equipment, fire trucks (I remember one row of flatcars was loaded with nothing but fire hoses, coils, and coils of fire hose) that the Russians were taking back to Russia.

When we got to Budapest, we pulled into these railway yards. Alongside were loading docks with warehouses. The Russians were in charge of the station and the displaced people. They unloaded all these people out of the boxcars and all their belongings. The people were taken inside of a building. Then the people were taken out and herded away. I don't know if they ever got their stuff back or not. Now, these people had an awful lot of baggage—trunks and suitcases and bags. They had been taken out of German homes as they came across the country. Whether they had anything that belonged to them or not wasn't part of the question.

Roy Gates

It wasn't all relaxed in Austria. Near Kaprun we heard there were some SS troops hiding up in the hill. When the SS troops got you they took no prisoners. So we didn't either. We got up in the mountains. There was a cabin, and we found out from an elderly lady where the general was. He had been a commandant in a concentration camp and had some SS troops with him up on a hill—I don't remember how many of them. Some of our sharpshooters took care of the troops. In deference to our men I won't say who our shooters were. After a little firefight, we captured the general, still alive. We got him up behind a tree and brought him down to a plane where the cabin was. That's where we shot him by firing squad. About five of us shot together—nobody knows exactly who killed him. That was the first time I saw the back of somebody's head fly off. The war was technically over at this point, but I'm eighty-six years old as I tell this, so if they want to do something about it, they better hurry. It's a true story, and rightly or wrongly, it happened. That's the way war is. I'm sure there are other stories similar to this because we weren't the only ones who found SS troops out in the hills.

Having seen some of the people who came out of concentration camps, I had no compunction about executing a commandant of one of the camps. I can't say I was one who actually liberated the camps, but I was there when we opened the gates. Some of these poor wretches running out were so emaciated they actually died from the excitement of being liberated. I saw it happen several times. These people in the camps—they were like walking skeletons. You could see all their bones. The gates opened and the people ran out yelling, "I'm free! I'm free!" And some of them died right there. I was horrified to see what the SS had done to these people.

Don Bond

When the war was over they started a point system to discharge the high-points men early. Some of the men didn't like the system. You needed eighty-five points to get out. Most of the high-points men in E Company had eighty-five to ninety points, and to reach that you needed to be a three-mission man, wounded probably at least once, and probably have a Purple Heart and a Bronze Star. But there were guys in the air force in England who got a cluster of points every time they flew a mission. So it wasn't a fair deal. I had thirty-six points; I wasn't going home anytime soon.

At Kaprun we heard of some Russian prisoners of war being kept up on the mountain. We got up there and found two Russian men and three hefty Russian girls, each about twenty years old. The Germans had them up there and were working the hell out of them.

This incident happened a few weeks after the war: We were in Saalfelden, Austria, near Zell am See. A civilian approached us and said every time anybody tried to take down the Nazi flag from a little hamlet up there, this mayor beat up whoever tried to take down the flag. The guy who spoke to us had scabs all over his nose and the back of his knuckles. Several of us rode up there in the back of this six-by-six to check things out. Liebgott and Speirs were in the front of the cab with a driver. Liebgott spoke fluent German. We found out everybody up there hated this mayor's guts. He was part of the SS. We located the mayor and started to take him back with us.

Coming back, I was riding in the back of the truck with a couple privates and the mayor. The driver stopped the truck. Speirs got out and told us to get the mayor down out of there. We got him down. Liebgott had a German Luger. He jacked one in the chamber, walked around, and looked at the mayor right in the eye. Boy, that Kraut didn't flinch. He just stood there glaring at Liebgott. Liebgott stuck the Luger between the mayor's eyes and pulled the trigger. The Luger misfired. Right when it clicked, this German went off running down the road. Speirs said, "Shoot him." One of our men shot and missed. I shot about thirty feet over the mayor's head. Another man brought him down. I won't say who.

Frank Soboleski

When I got home from the war and told my mother we were in Zell am See, Austria, I learned for the first time that she had been born there and lived there until she came to America. Later we found that my Aunt Emily had been put in a concentration camp during the war and probably died there. My Uncle Bill had also been in a concentration camp, but was liberated by the Americans. Uncle Bill lived, and after the war our family took up a collection and sent for him. He came to live with us in International Falls, Minnesota, and got a job in the same paper mill that I worked in. He wasn't healthy and lived less than a year. The concentration camp had taken a toll on his body.

While we were in Zell am See, I and Tom Gray ran a riding stable. Lieutenant Speirs gave me a permit to do that to keep the troops busy. Zell am See was a resort town. It was a beautiful place to hunt and fish.

One day when I was running the riding stable, an old lady came up, pointed, and said, "That horse is mine."

"Okay," I said, and handed her the reins. The next day word was out, and more old ladies came to claim their horses. Before you know it I was out of horses and had to close the stable.

We received our mail in Austria. Mail call was still something everybody always waited for. Word from home was so welcome. I had one sister, Lois, who wrote to me and sent boxes of homemade cookies and fruitcake from the time I was in basic training until I was ready to ship home. I never told her until years later that only crumbs were inside her boxes by the time they arrived. I didn't want her not to send them because even the crumbs were good to eat compared to the other food we had.

At the end of July, we were moved by train to France. Our company went into barracks in Joigny. We were starting to break up. Some of us were going home on points. Since the 101st Division was inactivated in November of 1945, I was transferred into the 82nd Airborne before I shipped out for home from Le Havre, France, to New York.

During my time in Joigny, to avoid having to stay busy by being involved in training exercises, I joined the regimental boxing team. I was in the light-heavyweight division. I ended up in the ring with another soldier from another team. He was a Native American and he could really dance in the ring. I sized him up and hit him with everything I had. He just stood there and grinned. That's when I knew I was in big trouble. The next thing I knew I woke up with my head bouncing on the steps as they poured water on me while dragging me out of the ring. That was the end of my boxing career. He came up to me in the dressing room after the boxing match and said, "It wasn't fair for you to box me. I was formerly a Golden Gloves champion in our weight division."

So I tried out for the company choir. I was in the back row singing my heart out when the choir director pointed at me and yelled, "Hey, you with the foghorn voice, out!" That was the end of my singing career.

Next, I joined the honor guard. I got my white helmet, white scarf with the screaming eagle on it, white boot lacings, and white leather belt, and we practiced marching in close order drill. I liked the precision and snappiness of it. Finally I had found a home. I was promoted to a staff sergeant and added a rocker under my stripes and had eleven men assigned to me in an honor guard unit. We served in that capacity until it was time to be shipped home.

CHAPTER TWENTY-THREE

Coming Home

Herb Suerth Jr.

I came back on the *Queen Elizabeth*. I had traveled overseas on the *Queen Mary*, so I joke that I traveled first class both ways. Coming home I was on the promenade deck flat on my back with both legs in a plaster cast from my ribs down. Only my toes were sticking out. I thought, They ain't going to get me in a lifeboat if we get torpedoed. But by then you figure you've made it out alive, so you aren't worried about much of anything.

I landed in America on April 13, 1945, the day after President Roosevelt died. The war was still at its height in Germany and Japan. U-boats were still sinking ships. The *Queen Elizabeth* always traveled alone. It made twenty to twenty-two knots or more, and destroyers couldn't keep up with it.

When I had been stationed in New York, back before I had been sent overseas, we stayed at the Broadway Central, an old rattletrap hotel at the foot of Fifth Avenue near New York University. Nearby was a neat little canteen called the Music Box. I met a beautiful brunette there, Pearl Dufour was her name, a New York model, taller than I was, and we dated all three months I was in New York.

Well, this gal had connections. She had been on the front of *Yank* magazine and a couple others. After I was wounded, I wrote her to say I'd probably be coming home soon but had no idea where or when. Unknown to me, she had someone watch the manifests and found out I was coming home on the *Queen E.*

So we landed at the main dock in New York. All the Red Cross gals came to greet us, and who comes walking in but Pearl Dufour, dressed to the nines. She was the first woman I saw coming home to the States. All around me GIs hooted and hollered. Pearl came right up to me, put her arms around me, and gave me a hug and a kiss. She asked me if I needed anything, something to eat or drink. I said I'd love a chocolate soda. It had been quite a while since I had one. Twenty minutes later here comes a chocolate soda on board the *Queen E.*

Pearl and I corresponded for some time but drifted apart over the years. It was never a marrying thing, we were always just good friends. When we first met, she was a good dancer, and I loved to dance. She knew New York and could get us into any club we wanted to get into.

I was discharged from the hospital May 16, 1946. Altogether I was in the service three years and three months. I saw thirty days of combat before being wounded.

Don Bond

I don't remember where I was on V-E Day, but I remember V-J Day well. We had left Austria by then and gone to Joigny, France. I had come down with tonsillitis and was restricted to quarters. There was a radio there with the BBC on it. The announcer talked about this bomb that had been dropped on Japan that leveled nearly the whole city. I was alone when I heard the report. When the guys came back to the barracks I told them about the size of this bomb. They all thought I was nuts. But they turned on the radio and heard the reports for themselves. I don't remember any big celebration on V-J Day, but we had all figured we'd have to go to Japan next, particularly guys like me who came in late, so news that the war was over was a relief.

The unit was deactivated in November 1945. They sent the guys who hadn't been sent yet over to the 82nd, but they were all being sent home as a unit. I didn't have enough points to be sent home with the 82nd, so after three or four days I was transferred to the 508th and sent to Frankfurt. I was in Frankfurt for Christmas. In January I got a furlough to England. Then I came back to Frankfurt for a few more months. Mostly it was just training and guard duty there. You were on duty four hours on, four hours off. Every other twenty-four hours you got eight hours off in a row. I was a corporal by that time.

One of my jobs was guarding the main doorway to the USAID's [U.S. Agency for International Development] headquarters. Boy, I saw some main brass walk in and out of there. In one shift I counted thirty-two stars come through the door. We didn't stop generals, but we stopped everybody else. A lot of big-name civilians came in and out, too. Once I opened the door for Eleanor Roosevelt.

Norman Neitzke

From Austria we headed back to France, where we were garrisoned in an old stable area. The high-points men were shipped home. The rest of us stayed.

In November 1945, the unit disbanded. They held a ceremony, and the flags came down. I felt a real sense of loss. E Company was our home. Most of our remaining fellows, including me, went with the 508th where we went to Frankfurt, Germany, for occupation duty. I was in Frankfurt about six months, from November 1945 through May 1946.

It felt a bit sad to join 508th, yes, but it turned out that the 508th was good to us, too. In Frankfurt we had a chance to live in a nicer area. I had some relatives over in Germany and was able to meet some of them.

The first meeting happened almost by chance. One cold day I was on a roving jeep patrol with some guys. We came to a town called König- stein. There was a photo shop there and I took some film in to be devel- oped. I gave the proprietor my last name, and his eyes lit up. He called his seventeen-year-old daughter downstairs, who spoke English. It turned out that the man's wife was a cousin to my dad's cousin, who lived in Chi- cago. I became friends with the man and his family. The daughter took me to Frankfurt to meet other relatives. They were all very cordial to me.

It was interesting to meet the other side. Two of my relatives had been in the German Army as infantrymen. They lived in an apartment building in downtown Frankfurt. Fortunately, their building had not been damaged very badly. They were very hospitable and gave me pea soup and crackers. I visited several times and gave them cigarettes, butter, and coffee.

I never felt strange as a German American fighting against Germany. My dad had fought against the Germans in World War I. Ironically, his father, my grandfather, had been in the German Army in the 1870s. But my father felt that you fought for the country you lived in. My family believed that we owed America something. It was our country, and we had been very fortunate during the Depression with my dad in the fire department. We always got a paycheck. Plus, there was a sense of moral obligation. What Hitler and the Nazis were doing was wrong—the aggression, the human rights violations—all that. We wanted to do what was right.

I stayed in Frankfurt until May 1946.

This was something few others have seen: before we left Europe, a buddy of mine, Peter Rosenfeller, and I were heading home and ended up in Bremerhaven, a German port city on the Weser River. We had a layover of a few days, so we walked around the harbor. A German patrol boat was there. We talked to the captain, he was very talkative, and he took us around the harbor in his boat. We ended up next to the U-boat pen area with all the German sailors still down there. I'm sure it was off-limits to us but nobody stopped us, so we were able to get off the boat and walk around the pen area, looking at all the German U-boats. I know the United States had tried to bomb those pens several times, but I couldn't see any damage. The sailors were all very aloof toward us.

We came back across the Atlantic on the *Wilson Victory*, a ten-day, rough ride. We got back on Memorial Day. All kinds of flags waved. We came up the Hudson River and pulled into a dock in New Jersey. A number of us went to New York early that evening. It was so great to be back in America. I took a lot of pictures of the Statue of Liberty. I had looked forward to coming home all the time I had been overseas. I had been away from home for a little over two years. When we had left New York to go to Europe it had been a cold, windy day in January. Now, when we came back the skies were clear, it was a warm day in May, and people were very happy. It was a real contrast.

The following day we took a train to Fort Sheridan, Illinois. A day or two later we were discharged. I got my pay, got my records, grabbed my two barracks bags, then took the train to Milwaukee. I hopped in a cab with some other guys and got to my house. My folks were in the backyard when I pulled up. They were very happy to see me. I was happy to see them, too.

Joe Lesniewski

We stayed in Austria until August, then were sent back to Mourmelon Le Grande, France, where we got new clothes and had a chance to shop. I went to Paris and went gallivanting around. I bought thirty bottles of perfume that I sent home to my sister. She was supposed to distribute the perfume to a bunch of girls that she worked with. But she didn't do it. She gave it to girls she wanted to.

In Mourmelon, they checked how many points you had. I had eighty-five points, so I was qualified to go home right away. I was sent to Antwerp, all by myself. I got on a Liberty Ship. There were nineteen other guys on the ship, all colored guys, all from somewhere else. I was the only white guy. The colored guys were the nicest bunch of guys I ever met. They liked to shoot dice. They asked me if I wanted to join in, so I gave it a try, and we shot dice for five days, just pennies and nickels, stuff like that. On the sixth day a guy says, "Let's shoot dice and see who can win it all, then enjoy the voyage." Believe it or not, I cleaned them out for $298.

On the way across the Atlantic going home we ran into a late fall hurricane in November. We got hit with the tail end of it. That was rough. It tossed our boat around pretty good. The pounding broke one of the ships' plates, and the boat took on water. But we made it back to Boston.

From Boston we were sent to Fort Indiantown Gap, a National Guard training base, where we were discharged. I was there for a week where they check you out for everything. A captain saw my records, saw that I was with the OSS in London, and asked if I wanted to get back in the service and continue on with the OSS. I said, "No, I got other ideas." I wanted to get out and get a fishing camp in Canada. It took ten years before I got the camp, but I got it.

When I was discharged, the captain told the MP to take me to the road outside the base. I thought they were going to take me to a bus terminal or train station, but the MP just took me to the road, stopped, looked at me, and said, "Oh, this is your destination, we don't have any train stations or bus lines around here close."

So I had to hitchhike home—it was about an eight-hour drive. Right around there (Indiantown Gap) was Route 322. I got on the road and started hitchhiking. About half an hour later a guy picked me up and asked where I was going. I got in. We started traveling. For a while we just shot the bull, then I fell asleep. It was about 7:30 P.M.

We got to the intersection of two highways where he was going to let me out. It was about three in the morning then. The guy stopped the car. I took my duffel bags out and got on my way. The guy also got out and went to relieve himself. I put my bags by the side of road and bent down to get something out. Suddenly the guy has got a gun to the back of my neck. He says, "I want that duffel bag and all the money you have."

I had $18 for soldier traveling, $100 in soldier savings, and the $298 I won shooting dice. The guy took it all. He took the duffel bag with all my souvenirs. So that was the end of my military career. Getting robbed at gunpoint.

These days I lecture a lot—I've given about three hundred lectures, schools, organizations, military groups, all over the country. Veterans will tell me similar things happened to them—they were discharged and had to hitchhike home and someone picked them up and robbed them. Some guys must have figured out where the GIs were hitchhiking and knew how to work the system.

Clancy Lyall

I had eighty-one points, just shy of the eighty-five needed to be sent home early. I came home in August 1945. I reenlisted right away, had ninety days off before going back to Fort Bragg, then was sent back to Frankfurt, Germany, where I was stationed for three years. The Nuremberg trials were just starting. When I was in Berchtesgaden at the end of the war I had found a collection of stamps. There were two books, Mike Massaconi took one, I took the other. Within the stamp collection were lists of Nazis, their names, and when they became Nazis. I took the book home after the war, then took it with me when I went back to Germany. I turned it over to the judges at Nuremberg. When it was all over they gave it back. I sent the book home to my mother, who sold it for five hundred dollars. What are you going to do—shoot your mother? Mike kept his a few more years and sold it for something like thirty thousand dollars.

Roy Gates

I was probably one of the last to leave. I was in Paris toward the end, then left for the States from Southampton, England. I had been transferred to the 82nd Airborne by then, and the division came home all together. It was January 1946. We came back on the *Queen Mary*. Conditions were pretty good. We got off the ship, then were sent to Fort Bragg, where I got discharged. Then we were sent to a camp in New Jersey to get new boots and all spit and polished. They had a parade for us in New York on Fifth Avenue, called GI Joe Day. The new boots gave us all blisters. Still, it was nice to march down Fifth Avenue. That's about all I remember about that.

Frank Soboleski

When it was time to leave, I got my orders to ship out for home. We left for the States from Le Havre, France, on the *Queen Mary*. It took her only three days to get to New York Harbor—no submarines to dodge—and then we were taken to Camp Shanks.

As we sailed into New York Harbor I couldn't help but notice the Statue of Liberty. It had a dazzling brilliance in the sunlight, a huge difference from how it looked in the blackout when I left three years earlier.

My unit was commissioned to march in the ticker-tape parade down Fifth Avenue in New York on January 12, 1946, with the 82nd Airborne Division, 505th Regiment.

We were trucked back to Camp Shanks after the parade, and some of us prepared to go home; others were reenlisting. I was sent to Camp

McCoy, Wisconsin, to be discharged. All I wanted to do was to go back home and get a job and start living the good American life. I had enough of war and all its horrors. It was time to just be in the great outdoors without having to look over my shoulder every minute.

Ed Tipper

From England they sent me back to the States to heal. Altogether after the war, I was in different hospitals for about a year while I healed up.

The army fitted my eye with a plastic blank. Then the Veterans Administration sent me to a place in Detroit where they made artificial eyes. But the eye they made me was so bad I couldn't wear it at all. I wore a patch for about a year. Then I heard about a place in Chicago where a guy made glass eyes. I contacted him and he thought I might be allergic to something in my previously fitted plastic eye. I got a glass eye and wore that for ten years. By that time the technology in making plastic eyes had improved to the place I could wear one of those. (Plastic eyes are superior because they won't break if dropped.)

As it has turned out, my wounds I received in Carentan have proved to be very little of a handicap in life. I've been physically active all my life after the war. My right ankle has a limitation of movement. I can't bend it enough to cross-country ski, but I can downhill ski. I got my driver's license, and my driving record has been fine. I couldn't be a policeman, pilot, or miner, but those are about the only jobs I couldn't do. I played four-wall handball for years. The one thing I could never do was play Ping-Pong, because I can't judge depth of field that well. The ball bounces too fast. But overall, it's been much better than I thought.

Right after getting hit, I was in quite bad shape for several weeks. The first week or so in the hospital I had the same dream every night. I dreamed I was still in the hospital and needed to set up a defense perimeter in the ward to repel an enemy attack. In my dream I got eight or ten patients mobile, gave them weapons, and set them up around the hospital. But no attack ever came. We were always ready, waiting, nervous, tense—that was it. I had the same dream night after night—the danger was imminent, the attack was coming, we had to be ready for the attack. That dream stopped after about ten days.

After the war I had a different recurring dream, but one that was not as threatening. I've had it all my life. The dream is that I need to go fight another war. But this time my friends in the paratroopers are all going back to fight another war together. I've had that dream consistently for more than fifty years. It's the same men in my dream that I knew at Toccoa, but in the dream they're at whatever ages they are in real life, no matter when I have the dream. They're all forty-five or sixty or eighty-five—and we're all going back for another battle. In the dream some of the guys who were killed in World War II are alive again. It's not a nightmare, I don't wake up screaming. The location varies—sometimes we're in the States getting ready to go back. Other times we're already in the battle. But we feel in control of this battle. I've never especially thought about what it means. Why are we all together? Why are we going to fight again? I never resist the idea of going to fight again—even when all the guys in the dream are sixty-five years old or whatever. We all appear to be okay with the idea of going back to war and are willing to do it.

The last four or five years I've had a third recurring dream. This dream is about the guys more in the context of reunions. In this dream the war is over. We're just getting together now. We no longer go back and fight a second war. There is a friendship with these guys that will never change. There's a closeness about all we went through. Almost any combat veteran I meet, I feel a connection and rapport with him more than any other person. We're immediately able to talk and get along fine.

CHAPTER TWENTY-FOUR

Lives in Freedom

Forrest Guth

After the war you could feel an economic boom. There seemed to be better incomes for everybody, better living conditions.

I was discharged mid-October 1945. When I had worked at Bethlehem Steel before the war I had bought a newer car, a 1942 Chevy Impala. It was still at home, waiting for me.

I visited my old high school principal. He was very interested in what I was doing and helped me enroll in a teachers' college. I graduated with a bachelor's degree. Then I went to New York University for a master's degree. It was all on the GI Bill. I feel good about the service and about how they treated us after the war.

So I got my education right away and started teaching school in Norfolk, Virginia. They were paying more money in Virginia than they were in Pennsylvania. Over the years I taught junior high and high school industrial arts, drafting, electronics, and woodwork. I always liked to work with my hands. I had a minor in social studies, so I taught a bit of that. I taught from 1949 to 1977, then retired from teaching. I always did some extra work outside and moonlighted as a cabinetmaker. When I retired from teaching I went full-time as a cabinetmaker. I finally gave it up in the early 1990s. I still do a little bit now and then. I have a hobby of carving songbirds. I also repair and refurbish antique cars. Right now I have a '67 Mustang convertible, a '29 model A Ford, a '74 Triumph Spitfire, and an '84 Corvette. I've done a number of other cars over the years that I've sold. They grow on you. But I'm slowing down now. I'm getting too old for that stuff now.

When I started teaching in Norfolk, my future wife, Harriet, was teaching across the hall. We got married in 1949 and have two children, a son and daughter, and two grandchildren. One is a navy pilot in Afghanistan.

The guys from Easy Company that I get together with, whenever we get together, we always talk about fun things, never the hard times.

Clancy Lyall

Why did I reenlist? I liked that kind of life. Not the combat, mind you. But I liked the military. It was hard, but it was good. When I was sent back to Frankfurt in late 1945 I was a squad leader, then a platoon leader. We left there and came back to Fort Mackall. That's where I was in the Recon units, the precursor to Special Forces. We did six weeks desert training, six weeks of mountain training, six weeks jungle and swamp training, then six weeks of commando training.

Korea came along and I went with the 187th Airborne and made two drops in Korea. After that, Indochina. Then I got hurt pretty bad, so that ended my career. I was a master sergeant when I resigned from the military in 1959. I jumped in a practice jump and came down aimed straight at a wire fence. I oscillated to miss it, came down wrong, and tore the hell out of my left knee. I was about ready to get out of the army anyway. I was tired of the bureaucracy. I've never felt the army owed me anything.

After I got out I moved to Florida and worked as a marketing director for Carvel Ice Cream. I worked there for quite a while. Then about eight years ago I had a heart attack, so after that I drove a van delivering food to various seniors' sites. I just retired this year. Why not keep working? I enjoyed it.

I got married for the first time in 1946. We had three children. My oldest son retired from Special Forces here not too long ago. The next son died. My daughter lives in Florida. In 1971 I married the wife I have now. She has three kids, so we've got six kids total, nine grandkids. So here we are.

Ed Tipper

I was discharged in August 1945. I had a total of two years in E Company and one year in army hospitals.

When I came out of the army I walked with a cane and wore an eye patch. The thing I remember most was the tremendous response of everybody I met to do everything they could do to show support for the military. Maybe the support felt exaggerated to me because I had clearly been shot up and wounded. Whenever I ate at a restaurant I went to the cashier and there was almost never a bill. Or the waitress nodded her head and said, "A gentleman over at that table has paid." Of course, I was home a year ahead of everybody else. But that sort of thing happened to me a lot.

The war opened doors for me. It was always my goal to get into the University of Michigan, but my high school record was spotty and I didn't qualify. I had an admissions interview and they stretched the rules for me—just did everything they could—to get me in. I didn't have any problems academically once I was in.

I might not have received all these courtesies if I had come home later. But it's been the same way with Easy Company and the Band of Brothers. We were just one airborne company among many who served in World War II. For some reason we got the benefits and credits when so many others haven't.

I wanted to get out of Detroit and go somewhere with mountains and fresh air. Detroit was a place to move away from. I graduated from the University of Michigan, then went to Colorado to get a master's in English at the University of Northern Colorado. My career goal was to become a high school teacher. When I graduated from my master's program I had difficulty finding a job, so I worked in construction for a short while. I had been told by my university counselors that I could never teach because I was blind in one eye. They thought that the minute I got in front of a classroom the kids would run around to my blind side, misbehave, and I wouldn't be able to teach them. I soon got a job teaching. I taught thirty years, and that never happened.

Before the war I had been dating a girl from the University of North Carolina. Her family was fairly wealthy. Her father was sympathetic with me, but her mother felt that with my background and my ambition to become a teacher, I was not the man for her daughter. I can understand that. The girl and I had planned to get married after my first year of college, but the objections of her mother became obvious and we broke up. It all worked out for the best.

I stayed single for a long time. I dated and was even engaged at one point, but I think I was always expecting too much. My career continued to go well, though. In 1961 I was one of about thirty high school teachers who won a national award for excellence in teaching. It was called the John Hay Fellowship, and it included a full-tuition scholarship plus my yearly salary paid to me to attend UC Berkeley for that year. I went on that and temporarily became a member of the faculty at Berkeley.

Teaching was always my first focus—it was the only thing I really ever wanted to do. Still, almost all teachers need to find ways to make additional money. In my midforties I bought a small apartment building and ran it on the side. I did well with it, and it never distracted from my teaching. Pretty soon I had two apartment complexes and was doing quite well.

By age sixty-one I was still single. One of my former students, Ronald Ross, and his wife, Mary, headed to Costa Rica when Ronald got a job there as a professor of linguistics at the University of Costa Rica. I liked to travel, and after I retired went down to visit them. I loved Costa Rica and spent a couple weeks there, then came back a few years later to stay for a few months. When I came back, my friend's wife introduced me to a friend of hers, Rosie, whom she had taught school with. Rosie had just returned to Costa Rica from a four-year British government scholarship in genetics.

Rosie was thirty-four. I was sixty-one. That alone raised eyebrows, but if you didn't look at the obvious differences such as our age, we were extremely compatible. We dated about a year. She was the woman of my dreams, and I didn't back off. We were married soon after. More than twenty-five years later we're still together. The marriage has been very successful. My wife is phenomenal. She's the best thing that ever happened to me in my entire life.

We married February 12, 1983. Our daughter, Kerry, was born December 11 that same year. I was afraid she was going to be born on December 7, the anniversary of Pearl Harbor. Kerry is simply amazing. At age ten she got her black belt in karate and at age twelve was Colorado State champion in her division, winning more than thirty consecutive matches. She's the young woman shown talking about me on the Band of Brothers video series, the segment entitled "We Stand Alone Together: The Men of Easy Company." She had just finished high school at the time. She went to Denver University and is now a law student at Northeastern School of Law in Boston. Kerry seems to be successful in anything she tries. I am so thankful for my family today.

Earl McClung

I got home December 1945, just a day or two before Christmas. On the boat ride home, there were two little Victory Ships and a little flattop in convoy. We hit a big storm; it was terrible. The one little Victory broke in half. They had to load all the people on the other Victory. That's when I got sick. Everybody was sick. You might stand the motion, but the smell will get you sooner or later. Even on deck they were sick; that's where I stayed. I was sick for eight of the twelve days it took to get back.

We landed in Newport News, Virginia. I was put in charge of ten to twelve men to get them to Fort Lewis, Washington. Whenever that happened guys would scatter from here to the West Coast—as soon as they saw a liquor store they'd get off the train. So I loaded them on the train and told them, "I got your service records and I'm going to Fort Lewis— I don't give a damn what you do. Your records will get there—that's all I can tell you." I never lost a man.

The first Christmas home, it was kinda scary back home. It's hard to say. The kid who left wasn't the kid who came home. I had a pretty rough time of it. I had dreams. I'd be sound asleep and somebody would touch me and they'd end up in the closet, with me choking them. I was pretty dangerous even to touch. I got in fights. I was angry all the time. I didn't know what it was. I knew I needed help, and the only way to get it was to go back in. A little hair of the dog that bit me to get me straightened out. So in February 1946 I reenlisted for another eighteen months. I was okay from then on.

I was sent back to Fort Benning. I was an NCO in the school troops battalion. We jumped for OCS [officer candidate school] and stuff like that all over the country. Then they put me as a weapons instructor in Greenville, South Carolina, for power pilots they were making into glider pilots. That's where I spent my last eight months. I got married during my second enlistment. My wife was in the service. We met in South Carolina and got married before we were discharged.

I got out of the service then, and I was better. At least I wasn't wild and crazy, like I was before. My mind was working better. I didn't have the dreams anymore. Most of the stuff I've shut out. It's funny, but you can shut out things from your memory. Some of the guys talk about things that I was supposedly there for and I have no recollection of it.

I came back and done just a little bit of everything. I worked in a trucking garage for a while, then as a mail carrier seventeen years, then I ruptured my back and had to have a spinal fusion done. They said I wasn't going to be able to work no more so they retired me from the post office. So I went up to the Colville reservation and went to work for the police department, then transferred into the game department and retired as a game warden in 1988.

My wife and I had three children. One boy was lost in Vietnam. A daughter was killed in a car wreck. So we still have one. We have a grandchild and two great-grandchildren.

Every year we have our Easy Company reunion, and I go to that. I keep in touch with Shifty Powers. Paul Rogers, Jim Alley, and I stay in pretty close contact.

Joe Lesniewski

I remember my first Christmas home, December 1945. I didn't have any civilian clothes to wear yet. Where I lived, every store was sold out, there were so many vets coming home buying civilian clothes. So I wore my uniform for about six months before I was able to get a suit, a couple pair of pants, and some civilian shoes.

I had a brother in the military. He spent most of his time in North Africa and came home alive. It was good to see him and my family again.

After the war, I worked for GE for a while, then quit and took my test at the post office. I worked as a letter carrier for thirty-four years. I've been retired for the past twenty-five years.

I was an avid fisherman my whole life. I did almost all my fishing in Canada. We got a fishing cabin, me and thirteen other guys. We always went in groups of threes or fours. None of the guys went there alone. The people who owned the fishing camp had a set of rules: you had to be a fisherman, and you couldn't get drunk. So we all got along together really good.

All those years we went to the cabin we did a lot of fishing and got some big fish. We enjoyed life. I could have been with the OSS or the FBI, but I didn't want either one. I wanted to fish. We went to the cabin every week. It was called Camp Adanac—Canada spelled backward. We'd go there every week on Friday and stay there until Sunday and spend our vacations there. We had a group of guys that were out of this world. We all got along like gentlemen.

I have six children and nine grandchildren. No great-grandchildren yet. Everybody's doing good. They've got good jobs. I married my second wife, Phyllis, in 1974, and we're together to this day.

Frank Perconte

After the war I came back and worked in the steel mill in Gary. But I didn't stay there too long because some guys told me about the post office. I ended up being at the post office. I was a carrier for about thirty years.

I got married, yes. I had married Evelyn on a furlough from Camp Benning. I had met her here in Joliet. She was pregnant when I left for the service. When I came home my son, Richard, was eleven months old. What was that like to see my son for the first time? Well, you didn't stop crying—it was really something else.

We just had the one son. We have two grandchildren, two boys. Evelyn died about six years ago.

What kinds of things do I do now? [laughs]. I don't do nothin'. I'm retired. All I do is sit on my ass and watch TV.

There's nobody from Easy Company who lives in this town, but we have conventions every year, and I go to them. Herb Suerth calls. In fact, he just called the other day. They've got a trip planned for Europe and wanted to see if I could go. I said yes.

Norman Neitzke

The overall mood toward veterans was quite good. I think we all felt some uncertainty, but mostly people were hopeful. Everybody was trying to go back to college, get jobs, start over. They were building these victory homes very quickly.

I went to college on the GI Bill and went to work in sales for the Omar Bakery Company. I bought a house, got married, and raised four kids. My wife and I have nine grandchildren today. The bakery went out of business after nine years, so I went to work for New York Life for five years selling life insurance. Then I opened my own insurance agency until present day. I'm not quite retired yet. I've been in insurance for about fifty years total. I've had some health problems recently, so I'm slowing down. I'll be eighty-two next month.

Our family has been very fortunate. My wife, Lucille, and I have done a lot of traveling. We've been back to Europe for four trips, Hawaii four trips, and Alaska once. A lot of this was done on military flights. I spent thirty years in the 84th Reserve Division in Milwaukee and was discharged as an E8 master sergeant.

Ed Joint

When I got home, I didn't feel like I belonged. None of the people were there that I knew. They had moved or died or joined the service. It was strange. I didn't feel at home. None of the guys in the neighborhood—all the guys I used to play basketball with at St. Patrick's—none of them were there anymore.

Once in a while I had nightmares about the war. I'd jump up out of bed—I didn't know what I was doing. I still get them strange things, even to this day. I don't remember specific nightmares. Sometimes I see people and no one's there. I don't talk about it because I figure people will think I'm crazy. So I don't say nothing. Maybe it's cause of the concussion I got back in Normandy. I wake up frightened and I'm ready to fight. I want to hit something, a door or something. I go after the people I see, but then the people aren't there. But I don't get that too much anymore.

For a while after the war I didn't do much. I had a sister in Oakland, California, and we took a trip to see Florence, my sister. It was really nice.

When I come back, it was in the summertime, and there wasn't much work around, but I knew a guy who knew another guy who was the post-master of Erie, Pennsylvania. My friend set up an appointment for me to interview with the postmaster and talked to the guy for me. I had the interview. The postmaster says, "When do you want to start?" I says, "To-morrow." He says, "How about today?" I took a civil service test, passed it, and went into the post office. I worked there thirty-two years.

Joe [Lesniewski], he was from Erie, same as me, but I didn't know Joe until France. We got to be good friends. After the war, I didn't see him for a while. Then one day I was out delivering mail on the street, and a guy was blowing his horn at me. I said, "What the hell?" It was Joe. He says, "How can I get a job like that?" I told him the postmaster's name. If you were a vet they'd put you at the top of the list. Lo and behold, a couple weeks or a month and Joe's working there.

Our families got together once or twice throughout the years. We still see each other as families, but mostly we talk on the phone.

While I worked at the post office, I took a part-time job as a stagehand in the theater here. We did road shows, Broadway shows, rock shows. I worked there thirty years along with my other job, just quit a couple years ago, which is pretty good considering I'm eighty-four years old now. I don't do nothing now. I'm lucky I'm breathing [laughs].

My wife, Sally, she's one in a million. I married her fifty-eight years ago. We've got four girls, ten grandchildren, ten great-grandchildren. A slew of them. I've been pretty lucky. The place is loaded on Thanksgiving.

My wife and I are still involved in the Catholic Church. My wife sings in choir and I usher. I haven't been there in a couple weeks because I fell down a flight of steps and fractured my wrist. Boy, it's taken a long time to heal. I missed a step and went down the rest of the flight.

I don't know if you can define success; everybody defines it differently. But I got a house, a nice wife, four good kids, and my health. I couldn't ask for anything more than that.

Bill Wingett

I came home with the 75th Division in November 1945. We came home on the USS *Wooster Victory*. I arrived on Thanksgiving Day in Newport News, Virginia. Nobody knew I was on the way home or when I was coming. Ten days after I got home that girl I had been dating broke up with me. It took her that long for her to tell me that I wasn't the guy for her.

After the war there wasn't anything to do in agriculture, so I went into wood. Then I reenlisted and went back into the 82nd Division. Altogether, counting the Reserves, I was in the military for twenty-two years. I did 167 jumps.

After I got out, I traveled around the country for a little over three years. I had a 1939 Plymouth coupe, a dog, and a two-wheel trailer with everything I owned on it. I put 512,000 miles on that car. I had a job in every state in the Union except Maine. Hawaii and Alaska were not states then. I was at loose ends—I didn't have any particular place to go. I didn't have a girlfriend, and I just wanted to see the country. I did a lot of things then that you couldn't do now. In the middle of the night, I'd just drive up alongside of somebody's barn, park my car, and go to sleep. You wouldn't dare do that today. They'd call 911.

I learned a whole bunch, too. I got a better education than almost anybody gets in college. I did every kind of a job that you could name. I worked as a carpenter, for an undertaker, in auto body shops and service stations, once I even worked as a carhop at a drive-in. I took whatever job I could find to put gas in the car. Gasoline was only twenty-five or twenty-six cents a gallon. I didn't stay in any one town for very long. I stayed in Pennsylvania for about two months while I worked for the undertaker. I was going out with his daughter, but then I got to thinking, Who the hell wants to be an undertaker? When her dad started talking that way, well, it was time to pull stakes.

I got out to Los Angeles, and my dad was living there then. I got a job with an outfit that built fancy stairways. I built an apartment in my dad's backyard. Then my brother Allen showed up, and we both went to work for a Hungarian fellow who had a cabinet shop. I learned a whole lot from that old boy. I learned a whole lot that I thought I already knew.

I met a girl in Long Beach—a waitress. Her name was Grayce, but I called her Peg. Then she quit and went home to Minnesota. I took a vacation, followed her, and talked her into getting married. We've been married for fifty-five years. Peg and I have four children and two grandchildren.

We came back out to California. I built modular homes for a while. Then one night the plant burned to the ground, so I was out of work. That's when I went to San Jose. I worked for Hall Machinery setting up woodworking equipment. Then I got a job in a cabinet shop. Should have been a one-man cabinet shop, that's all he had work for, but he had three people working there. I worked for him a couple months. Every Friday I had to wait until Tuesday or Wednesday the next week to cash my paycheck. Finally one Friday I said, "Jack, this is the last paycheck I want to get this way." He said, "Okay, okay." Well, come Friday night, he gave me another paycheck with nothing there to cover it. I went out the next day and got another job in a retail lumberyard. I went back to the cabinet shop and said, "You got the money to cover this paycheck yet?" He said "No." So I said "Okay," and went and picked up a skill sander, an electric drill, and a router, and said, "Well, I'll hold these until you got the money." He started to argue but I said, "You can protest all you want, but that's the way it's going to happen." I never saw the man again.

I worked for the lumberyard until 1961. Then we moved up to Oregon and I worked for a prison, manufacturing furniture. A couple hundred men under you—it takes some doing to keep a couple hundred men heading in the right direction, and if they're inmates, it takes something more. Right away I ran into snags. They had a six-week training period. They kept getting off the subject—they wanted you to learn about the forest camps in the summer and when women prisoners take showers. I knew I wasn't going to get to watch them take showers, and I made it known that I didn't give a damn about that. 'Course, they disagreed with me and asked me questions about that in the final exam. I didn't bother answering them. But I got the job anyway. I found that mostly you needed to be a bully and be threatening the inmates all the time. That builds resentment more than character. So I only stayed there for about four months, then told them they could take their bureaucracy and shove it.

Then I had a year of tough going. People in Oregon thought at the time that if you came from California you didn't know anything. I got a job at a big cabinet shop, part of the paper mill in Salem. I ran into a lot of situations where I did things differently. Where I had to, I changed to their way. At the same time I built myself a shop and got all the equipment. It took about five years to really get going. Then I worked for myself and operated a cabinet shop. In addition to the shop, for twenty years I did property maintenance for a real estate company. Now I'm retired and I still work in my shop. I'm eighty-six and I still do things like make special moldings for antique houses and for people who are restoring stuff. I'm not as nimble in the fingers as I used to be, but I can hold a hammer, and I do what I want, when I want to. I enjoy it. I just can't see myself not doing anything.

Herb Suerth Jr.

When the war was over I went back to Marquette University. I met Monna, the girl of my dreams, two nights before we started classes in September 1946. We dated off and on all the way through college. She was in nursing. I went back to engineering. For some years it was all homework and lab courses. We graduated from Marquette University in June 1950 and were married that October. We had nine kids and fifteen grandkids. Seven of our kids went to college, and one started his own business at eighteen. We lost our oldest son from complications due to cancer in August 2007.

I worked in the industrial and technical marketing field. I had a bent toward sales and marketing more than technical engineering. For about ten years I worked for GE and learned a lot there, then was in a number of different fields. I ended up as general manager of a large, privately held industrial laundry.

Roy Gates

Reentry to civilian life was good for the most part. I was still enjoying the libations we got from the Eagle's Nest. Drinking grew into more of a habit for me as time went on. But for a job I did pretty well. I became a factory representative for a division of the Norton Company, a supplier of sandpaper, sanding belts, polishing products—stuff like that. I had a territory and was with them for a few years. Then I went to California and got into the collections business. I had a friend in the industry, and for a while had my own agency in Dallas, Texas. I did okay.

I was married three times, once for thirty years, but none worked out. Maybe it's because I went to Texas A&M. At the time I went it was all-male, all-military—maybe that's why I've never been too good with women [laughs].

I drank pretty heavily until I was about forty years old. Then enough was enough already. I've got forty-five years of sobriety coming up this year. I don't blame war as contributing to my alcoholism. My father was an alcoholic, and I think heredity has something to do with it. But I think the availability during the last part of the war sure helped. I'm not blaming it on Hitler or his hideout, but we had pretty good access to booze for a while there. Then when I came home in '46 I hit it pretty good. I went through Alcoholics Anonymous and quit drinking in 1963. AA was a vital part of my recovery. I still go to meetings today. I'm not as gung ho about AA as I was at one time, but it was a great help. I live in the Bible Belt, and AA is a religious organization in many ways. I used to say I was an agnostic and tiptoe around about that, but here again at age eighty-six I'd say I don't really believe. I'm an atheist. I'm not vehement about it, but it's the truth. I think we're here as long as we're here and that's okay.

I didn't have any dreams or nightmares about the war. In all honesty, my war was not as traumatic as some—the guys who really went through the whole bit. Looking back, my days in the service were an experience that I treasure. I'm not sure if that's the right word, but those experiences are something that I'll always remember.

Frank Soboleski

I came back home January 18, 1946, and just went fishing and trapping for about a month. I finally got enough, and went back to my old job in the Insulite mill, but in a different department than I'd been in before. I had a hard time adjusting to civilian life. Everything seemed common and stale. Everybody looked old and everything was too quiet. In the summer I took guiding jobs on my hours off from the mill. I took tourists out fishing on Rainy Lake. I also took extra jobs building houses in town. Then I paired up with a friend and started a construction firm.

The military was bringing back the bodies of boys who had been killed overseas and had been in temporary graves. I helped unload the caskets at the depot at the end of our Main Street. They'd have to be loaded in a hearse and taken to the mortuary or sometimes to their parents' homes. It wasn't a very pleasant task, but I did what I could for all my fallen comrades. Three or four caskets would arrive at a time for quite a while before they were all home. All the small towns around us had their sons shipped to International Falls, and we took care of them as well. I was also involved in the funerals as honor guard and pallbearer. I marched in every parade in International Falls for many years.

I've had numerous exciting experiences while trapping in the north woods. Once I had a pack of timber wolves chase me up a deer hunting tree-stand with my snowshoes on. That was an extremely difficult feat, but I accomplished it in a hurry with the wolves snarling under me.

Another time I was walking the length of a long fallen tree near my hunting shack when I jumped down and landed on the hibernating bear sleeping at the base of the roots. After being rudely awakened, he came up fast, with me on his back. I came off his back and started running in midair. My third and last shot took him down. He was 475 pounds, and his hide made a nice addition to my living room floor for many years.

I also rode a moose that was swimming in the lake when I was out fishing one day. He sunk out of sight with my weight on his back, so I had to swim back to the boat.

During one of my beaver trapping trips I was chopping down a drowning pole and my ax hit a knot, slipped off, and went into my leg on the side of my knee. I cut the leg of my winter underwear off and made a tourniquet. I walked a mile and a half on snowshoes back to my shack, periodically loosening the tourniquet to allow blood flow. The blood spurted over my head each time I loosened it. When I finally got to the shack, I tried putting flour, salt, and baking soda on the wound. Nothing worked, so I grabbed a leather needle and some fishing line, sewed it up with the baseball stitch, and applied duct tape over the stitches. That slowed down the bleeding enough so I could start out for home. I rode out of the swamp four miles on my snowmobile to my pickup, then drove forty-four miles to town to the doctor.

Once I bagged a large deer. It was getting late, so when I got home I stuffed him down the coal chute and stopped in the kitchen to have a quick cup of coffee. I finished my coffee and headed down to the basement to process the stag. As I was walking down the steps I heard a strange ripping sound. There he was, standing at the water heater, ripping off the insulation. He bolted and ran around the furnace in the middle of the basement. I grabbed a two-bitted ax, headed him off, and hit him high across his nose just below his eyes. That knocked him down and finished him off. His horns won third place in the Boone and Crockett contest.

I did some flying over the north woods of Minnesota with a hunting and trapping partner, a bush pilot who owned his own plane. In the winter he put skis on the plane, and we could land anywhere on the ice. Once when we were landing we broke off one ski. The plane spun around in a circle several times before coming to a halt. We fashioned a new ski out of a tree pole and headed home.

Today I have forty acres of leased remote property, a choice hunting ground. Every small game season and later deer season I enjoy hunting on my private grounds.

Shortly after returning home, and during all of the above adventures, I was married for twenty-five years to my first wife, Bertha. We raised four boys and a girl. I built a lake cabin and took the kids hunting, fishing, three-wheeling, snowmobiling, and camping as they were growing up. Two sons, Patrick and Mike, and my daughter, Susie, became teachers. One son, Tim, is a registered nurse, works at a hospital, and owns rental units in the Twin Cities, and the other son, Allen, runs a body shop out West. Susie is married to a colonel, Steve Bolint, general inspector in the 32nd Medical Brigade at Brooks Hospital in San Antonio, Texas. They have one daughter, Jennifer, and one son, Andrew, now attending the Air Force Academy in Colorado. So that makes three generations of military in this family. Tim and his wife, Kathy, have two daughters, Nicole and Alexis. So, I now have four grandchildren from my first wife.

Later, I married a second time. Renee and I have had a wonderful thirty-five years together. We've traveled to just about every state in the Union.

I am a retired shipping inspector from Boise Cascade Paper Company. After retiring I became involved in a new company starting up named Tri-Wood, Inc. I was elected to be on the Board of Directors as adviser for shipping, warehousing, and marketing. I had experience and qualifications from a lifetime of harvesting forest products converted into lumber and paper products.

Henry Zimmerman

I came home, reenlisted into the 82nd Airborne, and spent eighteen months with them at Fort Bragg. Then I returned to civilian life in June 1947. I couldn't wait to get home. I had had enough of war. It wasn't all easy, though, when I got back. I got a job at Phelps Dodge Copper Products and worked a lot of overtime. I was making a hundred a week. I gave it to my dad, and he gave me five dollars per week out of all that money. That's the way it was. It was all about him.

I was dating a girl, Millie; I liked her a lot. I went down to her house all the time. Her folks gave me meals—they were more like a mother and father to me than my father was. One day my dad and I got into an argument. He told me to give her up. I said, "Give her up? Like hell I will." He came at me with his fists. I said, "Go ahead, take a swing—you'll be picking your teeth up off the floor." Then he backed off. I couldn't take my father any longer. I packed my clothing up, moved out, and got a room.

Millie and I married February 10, 1951. We've been married ever since. Today we have three children (a son and two daughters) and eight grandchildren. That's been the best thing in my life—meeting my wife and marrying her and the family we have together.

When we were first married, Millie and I rented an apartment for a while. We didn't have enough money to buy our own place. I was working at Phelps Dodge, but it was government contract work so they kept laying people off. There were a lot of promises of good things to come that never materialized. I picked up odd jobs to keep us going. Finally a friend of Millie's got me a job at Weston Electric. Shortly after that I got another job, with M&M/Mars, the candy company. I worked for them for several months, and Phelps Dodge called me back. This time they promised more money—more than twice as much as I was making at M&M. I didn't know what to do, so I asked my wife. She asked me where I was happiest. I chose M&M.

Turns out it was the right decision. M&M treated us royally. Old man Mars—he ran the place—if it wasn't for him we wouldn't be where we are today. He was my boss, a real gentleman. He owned it. God bless him. He treated his workers really well. It was a nonunion shop, and they always tried to stay one step ahead of the union, so the benefits were far superior to anyplace else. I retired from there in 1987 after thirty-three years of service.

Our son went to North Carolina State University because of their excellent chemistry department. We came down to see him one time when he was working at Southport. I fell in love with North Carolina and said I wanted to retire here. So that's where we live today.

I've been back to Europe five times since the war. The first trip back was in 1976, when I just wanted to see the area. In 1994 I went with an airborne group in commemoration of the fiftieth anniversary of D-day. That time I was overwhelmed with the reception we all received from the people in the towns over there. I did not expect to be welcomed as a hero. In 2001 I went with the HBO group for the premiere showing of *Band of Brothers*. Several years later I went again with my older daughter and her two children. They were interested in where I was during the war. This time, with the help of some locals, I was able to find my foxhole near Bastogne. The last time I visited the area was in June 2005, with a small group. During this visit I was able to piece together many things that in previous visits I was unable to do.

Rod Bain

When I returned to the States, I was quite lucky to meet a young student at Western Washington University in Bellingham, Washington, where I transferred. She and I both graduated as certified teachers. We were married in 1950 and soon found our way to Alaska. We taught at a village school on an island in southeastern Alaska for two years. We had a complement of 4 teachers and some 150 students in grades one to eight. My wife, Donelle, obtained a master's degree in order to teach special education children. I taught in the elementary schools and later became principal of several grade schools in southeastern Alaska. In 1960 we moved to Anchorage with our four children, bought a house, which we still live in today, and began to enjoy the better weather conditions in that city. Each year we enjoyed the three summer months off from teaching and pursued more college courses, traveled, fished, and gardened. In 1975, with our four kids in tow, we flew to Amsterdam and traveled in a rented Volkswagen bus through Holland, Sweden, Germany, Italy, Switzerland, France, England, and northern Scotland, where we visited relatives.

Most years I chased salmon in Bristol Bay, home of the largest run of sockeye salmon in the world. At first I bought a sixteen-foot skiff with a ten-horsepower outboard and worked with one chackle of gear. I drifted with the tides back and forth, gill netting the sockeyes. Bristol Bay is quite shallow, and when the winds blow, it can become very rough. I fished those waters for twenty years and finally bought a thirty-two-foot boat, which was made in the Seattle area and shipped north on a large cargo vessel. I named her the *Donelle B*. She was powered by a 440 Chrysler, a comfortable commercial boat. Some summers when the fish returned in huge schools, the enterprise became quite profitable; other years, not so. I finally turned the boat and permit over to my son Alan, who still fishes the bay.

What beautiful country, this Alaska. I knew then that we would become long-term Alaskans. We are still here—now in Anchorage some fifty-seven years later. We're both retired, lucky to have four children, all born in Alaska, and now we have four grandchildren to boast about. We have been able, very slowly, to own our own home. We have nice cars and a retirement check from Alaska that takes care of all our needs, especially a rare state health insurance plan that is unbelievable.

Buck Taylor

Elaine was there to meet me when I came home. She had stayed very close to my parents while I was overseas. It was the first time I had seen her in a couple of years. During rehabilitation I got a few passes and we went out to Long Island one weekend. We were married when I was still in the rehab hospital, May 19, 1945. She had it all planned. I didn't mind in the least.

After the war I worked for the Veterans Administration in Philadelphia. They had a photo research project under way, and I had had some experience in photography, so they took me on. It was a project they were doing in conjunction with Eastman Kodak, trying to figure out how to reproduce soldiers' X-rays without going through the negative process. We were just about ready to go into production and my boss said, "Let's go down to Washington. I want you to meet some people." I said "Sure." So we went to what looked like a little residential house on E Street in Georgetown. I had no idea what was going on. We went in and talked to the people. They were interested in my wartime experiences. Later on I realized my boss had guided me through the first step of the interview process with the CIA. I had several more phone calls with the CIA. The process went on for a while. It took a year for the security clearances to go through. I resigned from the VA and went with the CIA.

I had no idea what was ahead, but it was a real experience. While training with the CIA I met Bob Brewer again, the soldier who had been shot in the neck in Holland. He was also with the CIA. Of course, we were both under aliases. We became close friends. Altogether I spent twenty-five years with the CIA. I try to avoid talking about any of the specifics of the job—you start talking about it and one question leads to another. I was assigned to the Far East Division. We spent time in almost all the countries over there.

All in all I've had a very good life since the war. Some great experiences. Elaine and I have four children and four grandchildren. We're happy.

Ed Pepping

Adjustment to life back home was more frustrating than I imagined. I had no idea what to do with the rest of my life. I worked for a while, then went back to school at Woodbury University (it was a college then) and took some business and technology courses. For a while I worked in a music store because music was always something I enjoyed. After that I went to industrial design school and got into drafting. I ended up working as a draftsman for the Apollo project, which in the end was a wonderful experience, drafting up plans for ground support equipment. We wouldn't allow anything to get out of that place unless it was letter-perfect.

As a child, church didn't mean anything to me; it was just rituals. I was brought up in the Episcopal Church, but it wasn't until 1966 that I really understood what it was about and decided to follow God. I'm involved with two Christian men's organizations today. I speak to high school students about the war and my faith. I look back on my life, and it's troubling to me how much of my eighty-five years have been so ridiculous. I don't pull any punches. The kids love it.

For many years I figured that since I had been in Normandy for only fifteen days or so before being knocked out that I had let my unit down. So I never kept in touch with any of the guys from my unit. Then in 2002 I was invited to the Emmy Awards, where I met up with all these guys from Easy Company. That got me involved again.

Al Mampre

I came home in September 1945. On November 17, 1945, I married Virginia, a friend since childhood. Our folks had known each other. We're still married today. It's been the best thing that ever happened to me. We have three children and one granddaughter.

I worked for a department store for a short time, then went to Pepperdine University, then to UCLA, then to the University of Chicago, getting a degree in psychology and sociology with a minor in education. I worked as a psychologist and for International Harvester in their training department from 1950 to 1978, while doing private practice on the side. I've been retired since 1978.

Looking back, I think I adjusted to life after the war pretty well. The only hard part has been that I've been messed up ever since that jump in Holland, where the guy landed on me. When I first got back I could hardly carry anything out in front of me. These days I can barely walk. But when I'm sitting down I believe I can do anything.

How did I cope with the war? I always tried to keep a sense of humor. If you didn't have a sense of humor, you were gone. Even today it's like that. My wife has Alzheimer's, and I care for her full-time. Virginia has some good days and some bad days. But you've always got to keep smiling. That gets you through.

Don Bond

I was shipped home in May on a Victory Ship and discharged June 10, 1946. Right after I got discharged I went home to Portland to see my folks. They didn't know I was coming. It was a real surprise for them. We were all real happy to see each other.

I met my wife, Patricia, in 1946. We were married in 1948. We never did have any kids, but we've been married for more than sixty years. We've got lots of nieces and nephews. I went to work in a lumber mill and put in about fourteen years there. I did just about every job there and was mill foreman at the end. By that time it was the biggest sawmill left on the Pacific Coast. Then they sold out to Georgia Pacific and closed the mill down. I had been buying a new Ford every year, so I went down and talked to the guy, who said, "Why don't you sell cars for a while?" So I sold cars for three years. I made good money at it but didn't like it. I went up to Seattle, hired out at Boeing as a machinist, and put in twenty-two years there before retiring.

Dewitt Lowrey

The wound to my head that I received in Carentan meant I had what they call posttraumatic epilepsy. So when I came home from the war they sent me to a hospital in Tuscaloosa. I had one brain operation there that only made things worse. Sometimes I had up to four seizures a day. I don't think anybody could live for too long having those. You twitch and jerk around; nobody can hold you down. They can't tie you down because you'll break your arms.

After that they sent me to Cushing General Hospital in Framingham, Massachusetts. The army had just built the hospital to handle all the wounded coming home. Major Earl Walker, a neurosurgeon, got me straightened out there. They put a plate in my head and I don't know what else—I have a lot of those things where they reconnected the blood vessels and nerves in my head.

They don't put you to sleep when you have brain surgery like that. They put you in a twilight zone where you're hearing but you're not there. I remember smelling something like when you get a tooth drilled. Somewhere during the operation, right below my left knee felt like it was on fire. I started hollering. The doctor told his assistant that he had got my nerves crossed. So they got that straightened out.

I spent a year in rehabilitation. You'd knit, crochet, do things I'd only seen my mama do. I asked the doctor why. He said it was to coordinate your eyes, your mind, and your hands. I did jigsaw puzzles and other exercises. They had a good gym there. A lot of wounded soldiers were in the hospital there.

I was pretty healthy after that. I thank the good Lord for how things turned out. I have a strong faith; I guess I wouldn't be here today if it wasn't for that. With my head injury being what it was, I figured I had two choices: I could quit altogether, or I could keep moving and go down the slow road. It wasn't easy to go down that road. Faith got me through. I'm washed in the blood of Jesus Christ Lord Almighty. He has taken care of me all the way through.

I wasn't better all right away. When I was discharged, I was still having a few seizures every once in a while. The doctor said they'd eventually go away. He put me on medications that I'm still on today. The VA gives me that medicine.

My goal was to become a CPA, then after I graduated to go on to law school and become a tax attorney. I went to business school in Montgomery but couldn't handle it. I had too many headaches. So that wasn't meant to be.

Nobody wanted to hire me. I was still having those seizures, not many, just every once in a while. But I could feel when a seizure was coming on, so I knew I could get out of the way when one came on. This friend, I talked to him, and he said, "Well, let's try it." He ran a shoe business at a fancy store in Montgomery. He gave me a job, and I stayed there for a lot of years. I guess I did pretty well there because I always liked people, and people seemed to like me just fine. If I ever felt a seizure coming on I went back to the stockroom, out of the public eye.

Back when I was still in the hospital I met a girl, Barbara Drew, while out at a café. She was just sixteen then, seven years younger than me. I had never had a steady girl. I had been out with girls before, but one had never made much difference to me than another; we'd just go out and have a good time. But Barbara was different. She was gorgeous. Pretty features. A good personality. A good dancer. Very kind. I said, "Well, this is the one I want to spend my life with." That's the way it's been.

We got married December 28, 1946, and have had a good life together. We have two children, Nancy and Cliff. I think that's the best thing there is. Years later my daughter got a doctorate in counseling. She teaches at a university. My son's a veterinarian. My wife passed away in 1999. Her picture's right here with me on the mantel. I think about her every day.

Doctors checked on me every year. Time and medicine took care of things. My wife was my best doctor. She always kept things really calm and peaceful in the home. As a family, we enjoyed swimming, fishing, going down to the beach. I believe in a close family. If we ever went somewhere, our kids went with us.

Throughout the years, my wife encouraged me to hook up with the guys from Easy Company, but I never went. I've been called one of the "lost ones" from Easy Company. For years Bill Guarnere wrote and sent invitations to the reunions, but I could just never go. I still don't go to the reunions today, but Major Winters, I've talked with him on the phone in recent years. He's a great man, you're 100 percent right there.

Why didn't I go to the reunions? It wasn't that I didn't like the guys from Easy Company, I like all of them just fine. But I wanted to forget as much about that war as I possibly could. That's been my goal: to forget. I think I've done a pretty good job forgetting. That's how I chose to make sense of the war.

Shifty Powers

You would think that after being overseas in the war for a long time that you would crave eating a certain thing that you weren't able to get while you were away—maybe cheeseburgers or milkshakes or steak. Well, you do. But when I came home, the only thing I craved was dill pickles. I'd drive twenty miles to a store that had barrels of pickles in it. I bought them in jars and ate every pickle in them and even drank the juice. That went on for about a year. I told people I thought maybe I was pregnant [laughs], but I wasn't.

I got discharged in a little camp in Virginia and came home. I got a job at the coal mine, picking slate. Back then they ran the coal out of the mines on a belt. As it came by you reached in, got the slate, and threw it out. That's how they cleaned it. I worked there awhile. The company had a machine shop, so I got a job there after a bit. Then I wanted to see what California looked like. I was married by then and had two kids. So me and a couple guys went to California, where I got set up, then sent for my wife and kids to come out and join me. We stayed in California three years. I got a job in a machine shop. It was a government contract but we lost it, so I got laid off and came home to Virginia and started working for the coal company again in their machine shop. That was an outstanding job. I worked there for twentysome years. I was more or less my own boss and could do whatever I wanted, within reason. Even to this day we still have insurance with that company.

After Ambrose wrote the book and they came out with the miniseries, I had retired by then, and down at Wal-Mart one day I ran into a guy I used to work with at the coal company. He said, "How come you never told us anything about those war experiences you had?"

"I never told *anybody*," I said. "Nobody knew anything about those years." Now, I don't know about the rest of the guys, but I never talked about the war. Even my family didn't know anything about it until the book came out.

After I retired I piddled around in the garden, then helped build my house. A few months ago I began having chest problems. Turns out they found another cancer just outside of my lungs. I've been taking all sorts of treatments for that.

These days I've slowed down a lot. My fishing buddy passed away a few years ago, so that slowed things down there. I can't see to fish unless my grandson goes with me to help me with the hooks. I garden a bit. I like to get out on the deck and shoot my rifle. Nobody lives around our house, so it's okay.

My favorite rifle? I like to shoot my M-1. It's nine pounds. I tell my wife, "That doggone rifle has gotten fatter since the war." Ammunition for M-1s is hard to come by sometimes, but my friends will bring me clips. I have a .22 with a scope which helps my eyesight, so I shoot that, too. Then I have a Luger that I shoot, and a .22 pistol, which I like to shoot. As a last resort I have a BB gun out on the deck. I just shoot targets— 'course, I don't hit them all the time, but I hear the gun and smell the smoke, so I enjoy that.

My wife, Dorothy, and I have been married for fifty-four years. We have two kids, a boy and a girl, four grandchildren, and two great-grandkids. Throughout my lifetime, I've never given a thought to having piles of money or being rich or doing anything like that. Now, I worked hard, and if I wanted something, I liked being able to afford it. But to me, success is those happy times with my family, being able to go fishing and hunting, and just getting out in the woods and enjoying yourself, looking at trees, or watching water go across rocks in a trout stream, things like that. That's always what really mattered to me. My life has been good. All the way back, I've always enjoyed it.

CHAPTER TWENTY-FIVE

Thoughts on Heroism

Clancy Lyall

Today I often speak to students in schools. The number-one question I get asked is, "Did you kill anyone?" My answer is, "Yes, it was war, and I know I did. But there's more to the story that you need to know."

Were we heroes? There's no such thing as a live hero. Damn good soldiers, yes, but heroes, no. You do your job and everybody does it with you.

Ed Pepping

I don't consider myself a hero. It was just a job. Sometimes today I get treated as a hero, but I always try to turn it around and talk about the greatness of the guys who served. I'm just me. The people who are heroes are the ones who gave their lives for our freedom.

You know, while we were warming up to take off to Normandy, they replaced me and put Ernie Oats on the plane I was supposed to be on, plane 66. That's always been a sobering fact to me. That's the plane that went down in flames, killing all aboard.* For some reason God chose to spare me. Why? I don't know, but my life's goal now is to help others realize how important it is to know God—that's what my life is all about today.

Earl McClung

Our heroes are over there where the white crosses are. We're survivors over here. None of us are heroes. I don't think you'll talk to a man who says we are. You figure a hero is someone who does above and beyond the call of duty, and when you give your life that's as above and beyond as you can get.

Ed Joint

People come up to you and say you're a hero. I can't claim to that. "I was just an ordinary soldier with a bunch of good guys." That's all I can say about that.

Joe Lesniewski

Being a hero? I don't even care for the word. I'm an individual that had a job to do. I don't feel that I'm any kind of a hero. I'm just an ordinary guy like I'm supposed to be. To me, the work had to be done. I was asked to do it. So I did. When I lecture to kids I tell them the same thing: don't brag that you're anything more than you are.

Herb Suerth Jr.

Do I think I'm a hero? No. The only heroes we have in Easy Company are the guys who got themselves on a KIA list. The word "hero" is

---

*The crew manifest of flight 66 is as follows: Paratroopers: First Lieutenant Thomas Meehan (Easy Company commander), First Sergeant William Evans, Staff Sergeant Murray Roberts, Sergeant Richard Owen, T/5 Herman Collins, T/5 Jerry Wentzel, PFC William McGonigal Jr., PFC Sergio Moya, Sergeant Elmer Murray Jr., Sergeant Carl Riggs, T/5 Ralph Wimer, PFC George Elliott, PFC John Miller, PFC Gerald Snider. Flight crew (assigned to 439th Troop Carrier Group): pilot First Lieutenant Harold Capelluto, copilot Second Lieutenant John Fanelli, navigator Sergeant Bernard Friedman, engineer Sergeant Albert Tillotson Jr., radio operator Sergeant Norman Thompson.

not a word any of the guys would use on anyone they know or on themselves. Everybody did what they had to do at the time it needed to be done.

What would I want today's generations to know about World War II? It's important that we relate World War II to what's going on today. We have to realize there are always going to be people out there who want what we have. The only way this country exists today is because there are 3.5 million men and women (from 1776 to today) who have died in the name of liberty for the United States. It does no good to wish that other countries would simply lay down their arms and be nice to us. It ain't going to happen. Unless you're willing to stand up and be counted for what you believe in, you will lose all of the freedoms that are important to you.

In closing, I think of the family friends, neighborhood buddies, high school classmates, and college dormmates who didn't come home, not to mention the E Company guys who were killed.

Freedom isn't, and never will be, free.

Roy Gates

Heroes? I think they're all dead. These guys who saw a lot of combat, I really respect them, but I think they'd agree with that statement—the real heroes are no longer with us.

Henry Zimmerman

Like Major Winters said, I'm not a hero, but I fought with a company of heroes.

I feel honored that I have been one of the chosen few to tell of my experiences. My hope is that my story and those of others will encourage today's youth to carry on a legacy of freedom for all. I hope we can open the eyes of today's younger people to what is going on in the world and awaken them before it is too late. We are too apathetic today. The dictators we had in the World War II era, they're similar to the dictators of today. Freedom is never free. My message to the new generation is to value the freedoms that you enjoy.

Frank Soboleski

I want to say this: no man comes out of war intact. It leaves lasting scars on the mightiest of men. For the men still returning from wars today, it helps to talk.

After I was discharged from the army I buried any thoughts of the war and resolved to have no contact with the men. My mind was always tormented. Nights for me were long and often sleepless. When I closed my eyes I saw many horrible sights from the battlefield. The only time I escaped was when I was busy with family, work, or hobbies. My body suffered, too. My ears had taken a beating from the loud shelling, screaming meemies, and explosions that I endured for such long periods of time. Today I am totally deaf in one ear and almost so in the other. There are many activities that I just have to avoid altogether because of what they do to my ears. I had suffered from long periods of dizziness and headaches all those years.

In 2001 I got my letter saying that Easy Company and our families were all invited to Paris for the premiere of the *Band of Brothers* movie. My first reaction was to throw it away, just as I had the letters I had gotten way earlier from Stephen Ambrose, but we also got called on the phone and so did some of my kids. Of course, everyone wanted to go to Paris. I said, "No!" as loud as I could. One day my wife asked me why. I told her how I never wanted to remember the war again. She asked a tough question: "How is your strategy working so far?"

I just looked at her and said, "Nothing works."

"Well, why not try something different?" she asked. "What do you have to lose?"

"Okay," I said, "let's go," and it all started.

We gathered up the kids and went to the premiere in Paris and the memorial service in Normandy. There, I experienced the extreme gratitude of the people who attended the service. People came up to us in tears, hugged us, and thanked us for liberating their parents. I discovered that they have been having memorial services and celebrating their liberation every year since the war was over. They never forgot. Since then, my wife and I have attended every Easy Company reunion and have made three trips to Europe. One to France, one to Germany and one to Belgium.

Has talking about the war helped? I still have many sleepless nights, but I don't see the horrors. I still have dizzy spells and headaches, but not anything like they were for all those years. So, I would have to say, yes, it has all slowed down, and the visions are gone. It certainly didn't get worse, as I feared it would. I have really enjoyed seeing some old friends from Easy Company, and I will continue to go to all the reunions as long as I physically can.

Al Mampre

The idea of being a hero is ridiculous. You just did what you had to do.

Ed Tipper

When I was a teenager I took freedom for granted until I got through the army and saw what the Nazis had done in Germany. Then I realized that freedom isn't automatic; it has a price.

World War II was a justified and necessary war. Last year I met five survivors of Auschwitz concentration camp. The things that happened to those people should never have happened to any human being.

Do I think my actions in the war were heroic? No, I don't. I'm even uncomfortable with the word. I was part of a generation of young men who did what had to be done.

Norman Neitzke

I don't consider myself a hero. Most of us were just doing a job: here's a rifle, you guard this—that's not being a hero. I look at the guys who went through Normandy, Holland, and Bastogne as heroes.

What would I want people today to know about World War II? The children today have to know more about what happened in the past or they will be destined to relive it. Kids today don't get enough history. I talk in front of classes of schools today, and the question I get asked most often is, "How many Germans did you shoot?" But often the high school students are more interested in the overall picture. That's a good sign for our country. That's how we figure what life's about.

Buck Taylor

What does it mean to be a hero? I don't know how to answer that. Were my actions heroic in the war? I'll say this: all the heroes are the ones buried over there—the men who never came back.

Don Bond

I think of the guys who started at the beginning and went all the way through as being heroes. I've never thought of myself as being a hero.

Thoughts on war? I think you should stay out of them if you can, but if you get in 'em, you should win. These people right now who're talking about cutting and running out of Iraq, that irritates me. If you're going to do something, do it. Once you go in, you don't change your mind. You've got to win it. During World War II, if somebody wanted us to cut and run, they would have hung him.

Shifty Powers

Nowadays it's nothing unusual to meet people and have them know who you are. They'll say, "You're a regular hero." But we don't look upon ourselves as heroes—at least I don't. We had too many people left over there.

IN MEMORIAM

Norman Neitzke died December 8, 2008, at age eighty-two,
while this book was in the final stages of production.

Shortly after the release of this book's first edition, Darrell "Shifty" Powers
died June 17, 2009, at age eighty-six, and Forrest Guth died August 8, 2009,
at age eighty-eight.

Those Who Have Been Given Much

Marcus Brotherton

In August 1992 I moved to Los Angeles and began a graduate program. I had registered late, and all the on-campus housing was filled at the university. The only room I could find to rent was from my adviser's father, a World War II veteran named Nate Miller.

Nate was seventy-two. His wife had recently died, so his son thought it might be good for him to have company. Nate had lived in the same bungalow in Buena Park since the war, raised two sons, and enjoyed a quiet life since his days in combat. Other than from high school history classes, I knew little about World War II or what its veterans had been through. I was clueless about what might come next.

Nate kept a big russet Doberman named Diana that did business all over the front lawn. Fairly soon after arriving, I mentioned to my new landlord that it might be appropriate to have the stuff picked up once in a while. "Aw, that ain't nothing," Nate said. "You should see a Kraut's helmet lying on the ground when it's still got his brains in it."

Underneath his pillow Nate kept a loaded pistol. He warned, "If you come home late, make sure you yell so I know it's you. I might blow a hole in your guts." Most evenings Nate fell asleep in front of the TV. The only way into the house was through the front door, near the TV. I'd come home and face a dilemma: should I shout and wake the old man, or let him sleep and risk a bullet?

Nate spoke in monologues, often repeating stories. Most were coarse and ornery tales fit for the pool halls he frequented. His themes usually revolved around how some guy did something dumb and everybody laughed at him, or how some guy insulted somebody else and skulls were cracked and the first guy vowed he'd never do that again. But one story he told was unlike the others:

Nate was fighting in Huertgen Forest, late 1944. It was winter and freezing, with blood on the ground and heavy machine gun fire and artillery resistance. The forest was so ripped full of lead you couldn't even cut down a tree for firewood because you'd break the saw, Nate said.

In a lull in the fighting, a group of the world's toughest soldiers scraped snow from fallen logs, and a chaplain came and held a church service for the men. Some soldiers sat on the logs, some crouched on the snow, some stood. As many times as Nate repeated this story, he always ended with the same line: "I seen a lot of fancy churches while in Europe—huge cathedrals—but that was by far the best church I ever went to."

Nate said it in sincerity, not to disparage cathedrals, but to mark the solemnity of the moment. For all his rough edges, Nate was a reverent man. He loved his country. He loved freedom. There was more to this man than his outer veneer ever let on.

Learning to Live in Gratitude

In 2006 my agent phoned about a book project. Lieutenant Buck Compton wanted to write his memoirs. I agreed to the project immediately, then in a quieter moment wondered what I had done. What did I know about war? I wasn't an expert in military history, like Stephen Ambrose. I wasn't a thirty-year army veteran, like Colonel Kingseed, who penned Major Dick Winters's memoirs. All I knew about war was from renting a room for one semester from Nate Miller.

As work began on Buck's book, strangely, I felt that my ignorance brought vitality to the work. Since I didn't know anything, I needed to ask Buck *everything*. What's a regiment? Why do they award Silver Stars? How does a Thompson differ from an M-1? Buck was ever patient. He'd look at me, sometimes incredulous at the questions I asked, but always open and willing to explain.

As I worked, I found myself looking at the world differently, through the lens of World War II.

A new determination emerged. If the men of Easy Company could run up Currahee, I could certainly go for my morning jog without complaining as much as I usually did.

Challenges were seen in a new perspective. In December I went to a car auction and stood for two hours in the snow as each vehicle came to the block. As I stamped my feet to stay warm, I reminded myself I wasn't in Bastogne with my feet wrapped in burlap bags.

I came to see soldiers as men willing to lay down their lives for the sake of others. They fight for themselves and the generation under immediate attack, but certainly they fight for the futures of free peoples. Decades beyond World War II, I am one who benefited. That I can vote in presidential elections and not bend my knee to Hirohito's grandson is testament to the enduring work of the veterans of World War II. That I can write books for a living instead of sweating in a Third Reich factory is a product of Allied triumph.

What is my hope for my generation? As a whole, we'd probably admit casualness in our patriotism. Most friends I know view Memorial Day as little more than a good day for a barbecue. But I wish we might glimpse anew the freedom we've been handed. I wish we would read books about World War II and watch war movies and talk to veterans and rent rooms from them. I wish we'd pray that future generations will never be called upon to make the same sacrifices as those who gave up everything for the sake of freedom.

And I wish we would live as those who have been given much. That is what I take from men like Nate Miller, Buck Compton, and all the men of Easy Company featured in this book. They have given much so that we might live for what matters.

Memories of My Father

As part of the process of communicating the greater story surrounding the Band of Brothers, I invited three adult children of deceased Easy Company members to tell about their fathers. I recognize the tension that may come from presenting the stories of three deceased men and not of all. It comes not as a result of wanting to exclude anyone, but only from the limits of ink and time. I wish I could have included many more.

One of the living contributors provided a snapshot of the men profiled in regard to their distinctiveness. He asked to be anonymous in his description and wrote: "From long personal experience with Sobel, Luz, and Smith I see each being a one-of-a-kind member of the company. Herbert Sobel clearly stood alone. George Luz, also. He was to me by far the single most popular individual in E Company. His skills as a mimic and morale builder were unique. Burr Smith I remember as probably having the highest IQ of any of us and in a class by himself in imagination and self-dramatizing. Before D-day he had detractors, but not after. His unusual and extreme military success postwar was unlike what any of us knew."

Please enjoy.

Herbert Sobel

Michael Sobel

This is literally how it happened.

It was just before the release of the miniseries in 2001. My mom, in her early eighties, called me from Florida, where she lives and said, "Did you get that newspaper article that I sent you?"

"No, Mom," I said. "What's it all about?"

"Something about this HBO miniseries *Band of Brothers*," she said. "I saw your father's name mentioned in it."

We chatted a bit more. I hung up the receiver, went to the mailbox, and found the envelope with the article in it, which I read and became intrigued. Immediately I went to the local cable company, rented a cable box, and plugged it into my television. As fate would have it, almost immediately when I turned it on, HBO was airing the second showing of the first two episodes of *Band of Brothers*.

I watched and was blown away. My dad had been depicted in the miniseries as an inept ne'er-do-well. My initial reaction was shock. Every kid envisions his father as a kind of Rambo, and I felt my father came across as anything but a hero.

I called my mom back, told her what I had seen, and asked her what she thought. She said, "I got the book and started to read it but couldn't get beyond the first chapter—what they said about your father was just so much garbage."

A short time later I posted a few short lines on the *Band of Brothers* Web site: "I'm the second of three sons of Captain Herbert Sobel. If anybody has any information about what really transpired, I'd be interested to find out."

I was deluged with feedback. The input ranged all the way from "Your father was a chickenshit no-good motherf———" to "Everyone who had been in the service understood that your father's role was not to win a popularity contest, but to harden these men for the combat that he knew was coming." The opinions were diverse and far-ranging. I responded to them all. Initially I took some of the negative comments personally, but later, as I was able to speak to some of the men from Easy Company, I understood more where people got their ideas.

It wasn't all a smooth ride. Shortly after the miniseries aired I got in touch with one of the chief attorneys at HBO, surprisingly with little difficulty. I said I wasn't too thrilled with how my father had been portrayed, and I had gathered information that was contrary to what they had aired. The bottom line, said the attorney, is that "What's done is done," and when somebody is deceased, they're fair game. He was cordial about it, mind you. Our decision as a family at that time was not to press the point or try to set the record straight. Although the negative portrayal hurt our family, we understand that Hollywood needs a fall guy. A while back [Easy Company historian] Jake Powers came to Maui, where I live. He and I sat down for several hours, and he had a plethora of good information as to what really happened.

I found it interesting that after the production the men and their immediate families were flown to various premieres and to Europe by HBO. The Sobel family was never communicated with. My mother is retired military. My older brother is retired military and has the same name as my father. I don't know why we weren't contacted. I guess that although the book was fundamentally sound, every Hollywood drama follows a format, and needs conflict to be successful. My dad was the obvious fall guy.

In 2002 I ended up as an impromptu guest speaker at the Easy Company reunion in Arizona. One of the men's sons hugged me through tears, I can't even tell you who it was, it was such an emotional time, and he said, "My father told me that if I ever had the honor of meeting you to let you know that it was because of your father that I'm alive today." That was pretty much the sentiment of the men I had the honor to meet that day. I receive calls from men who served with my father and who praise him to this day.

On my behalf, there is no animosity toward Stephen Ambrose, HBO, or any of the men of Easy Company—none whatsoever. The way my father was portrayed is subject to personal interpretation. He was a drill instructor. I believe that the men understand what my father's function was and how he operated.

Growing up with Herbert Sobel

Dad grew up in Chicago and attended the strong-disciplined Culver Military Academy in Indiana, where he did well on the high school swim team. He graduated from the University of Illinois. He was six feet tall, a slender build, and bore a striking resemblance to David Schwimmer, who portrayed him in the series.

My dad was home from the war and about thirty-five years old when I was born. He was nine years older than my mom, an American who had worked as a nurse in a hospital in Italy during the war. Later she worked at Hines VA Hospital in Chicago. They met there when Dad visited a fellow soldier who had been wounded. We had three boys in our family and a younger sister who died several days after birth.

My mother was blond-haired and blue-eyed, a very attractive woman. Her family was dirt farmers from South Dakota, German immigrants. She was Catholic but my father was Jewish. Dad's parents were business-people from Chicago, part of the old aristocracy in many ways. Unknown to us when we were kids, his side of the family never really accepted my mom—I guess Jewish families then weren't generally open to their sons marrying Catholic non-Jews. We didn't know that until much later, but I'm sure it created tension between the parents. As kids we were raised Catholic. We attended Mass on a regular basis with my mom. My father attended sporadically. He also went to synagogue occasionally with his sister. There was never much discussion of faith and religion in the home.

As a child, on several occasions I asked my father about the war, but he never had anything to say about it. He could be very private when he chose. My mother told me later that he had never talked to her about the war either. He stayed in the reserves for many years, eventually retiring as a lieutenant colonel.

Dad was very conservative, very Republican, and never missed a day of work. Even when it wasn't popular to drive an economy car, he had a little four-cylinder Metropolitan that he drove to the Chicago L station to ride the train to work. Dad worked as a credit manager for a wholesaler, A. C. McClurg & Co., in downtown Chicago, then for the Mathias Klein Company, which made tools for the telephone industry. Dad's positions were midlevel. He wore a suit and clean, starched white-collar shirts. I don't recall a single day when he was sick or stayed home.

Mom worked, too. Every morning Dad got up early and made breakfast for her. If it was the dead of winter he pulled Mom's car up to the front of the house, cleared off the snow, and turned on the heater for her. Every night after work Dad had a cocktail with Mom and they chatted about the events of the day. We went to family gatherings, where Dad was always well liked and lively. He was a great dad—very loving and attentive. He doted on my mother and was very much in love with her. I never heard him use profanity or witnessed him losing his temper. He never raised a hand to us kids when we didn't deserve it—and there were plenty of times we did deserve it and didn't get it.

We lived in the same house where Dad had grown up as a kid. It was a large, redbrick house with a slate roof, the biggest house on the block, and all the neighborhood kids hung out at our house. On Sunday mornings Dad made pancakes, and there was always a place set for any of the neighborhood kids who straggled by. My father spent a lot of time with us boys playing sports, especially baseball. He always addressed us by the nicknames he had given us: I was Inky; my older brother was Footsie; my younger brother, Skookie.

This is funny: we couldn't have been much older than four, five, and six years old. Every night if we had been good boys during the day, we had the honor of doing twenty minutes of calisthenics with my dad before bed, push-ups, sit-ups, and jumping jacks. If we had been goofing off he wouldn't allow us to do them. He was always in great physical shape and could bang out push-ups, no problem. (It's odd that the series shows him struggling with push-ups.) As kids we did fifty to seventy-five push-ups per night, and Dad did them right with us. It was a game, fun for us. I'm pushing age sixty today, and I can still hit tennis balls at a highly competitive level thanks to the strength and disciplines Dad developed in us as kids.

One incident where I was very appreciative of my father is this: as an eighth grader in Chicago it was cool to be a bit of a tough guy. Everybody was a greaser back then. I was kind of a cool kid and socialized with a lot of girls. At a Friday night dance a skinny kid came up and kicked me in the stomach. I crumbled to the floor, started crying, and was horribly embarrassed. So I told this kid I was going to get him.

Now, I might have fostered a tough-guy reputation, but I had never thrown a real punch in my life. It was January, bitterly cold. I followed the kid outside the dance, and he smacked me in the face. I threw him on the ground, pinned him, and hit him three times in a fury. Blood was drawn, so I got up and walked away.

First thing Monday morning I was called to the principal's office. My dad was also called. He came in from downtown Chicago, about an hour away, for a closed-door meeting with the principal. I was expelled for three days. In those days that was a big deal.

After the meeting Dad and I walked home in the snow without saying a word. At home he asked me to explain the fight. When I was finished he said, "Okay, tonight we're going to go to this kid's house, you're going to apologize to him, and I'm going to talk to his father."

I remember this clearly—that evening as we walked to this kid's house, my dad put his arm around my shoulder. He said, "Son—if you ever get into a fight, you want to win." He thought for a moment, then asked, "You really cleaned that guy's clock, didn't you?" I assured him I had. He continued, "I never want it to happen again. But I'm glad you came out on top." He left it at that—clear in his expectations of me, yet with pride in his voice, too.

We walked to the kid's house. Dad talked to the father. I apologized. On the way home Dad put his arm around me again. This time we walked home in silence. I never got in another fight the rest of my life.

Dad was conservative in his savings and put money aside for all three of his sons to go to college. We were not wealthy, but my father made it known that second only to family, an education was imperative. It was the Vietnam War era. The relationship between my father and me became strained during those years. My younger brother was a diabetic, so he was exempt from the draft. My other brother got a low draft number and enlisted in the coast guard. I grew my hair down to my shoulders and went to Berkeley. I was quite at odds with my father politically, and I know that hurt him a lot. I was arrested for protesting at the 1968 Democratic National Convention in Chicago. I know those years stressed our relationship quite a bit.

My Father's Death

It's tough to know how to tell this. After the Kent State massacre in 1970, I was attending college at Southern Illinois University. As a result of the killings there were student riots going on all over America. I had been involved in some political groups that were unpopular at the time and had decided to lay low for a while. It took the police three days to track down my whereabouts before being able to deliver a message that my father had attempted suicide and that I needed to call home.

It's all a bit of a blur after that. I recall the evening I got home. My mother and I sat at the kitchen table trying to make sense of what had happened. She was inconsolable.

My father had shot himself in the head with a small-caliber pistol. The bullet entered from the left temple and passed behind his eyes out the other side of his head, severing the optic nerves and leaving him blind. I found this rather odd; my father was right-handed.

Because of my political beliefs, I had been out of touch with my dad for some years, so I didn't really know what was happening in his personal life preceding his suicide attempt. I don't know why he chose to do what he did. I asked my mom if she knew, although I didn't want to probe too much. It's true he could be overly private, even controlling at times. To this day she is not certain why he did what he did. She postulated that he thought he had cancer and was unwilling to get tested for the disease. He was not divorced from my mother yet, as some people suggest; that happened later.

Dad was moved to a VA assisted-living facility in Waukegan, Illinois, where he lived out his remaining years. He was fully ambulatory but in and out of being lucid, sometimes in a semivegetative state. He had friends in the VA ward, though the living conditions at the VA were horribly depressing. The place was in a state of disrepair, like the men who inhabited it.

It is true that his immediate family was not in attendance when he died in 1987. To my knowledge there was not a service. Our contact with him had waned over the years, and when he passed, we were unaware of the event. His sister attended to the details. It was days, perhaps even a week, after he died that his sister phoned my mom to let her know. The death certificate listed malnutrition as the cause. He was cremated. He had spent the last seventeen years of his life in the VA assisted-living facility.

I recognize this might sound a bit strange, but my father's death seemed anticlimactic to me. The passage of time had served to distance him from his family. I was living on Maui at the time. My mother and father were divorced by then. She remarried in 1995, at age seventy-five. She married a wonderful man and enjoyed eight fantastic years with Bert before he died. I find it remarkable and heartwarming that she chose to find love again after the heartache she had been through. To this day I admire her inner strength and unwavering support for her sons.

I think my father and I reconciled our differences partially before he died and partially after. One of the last times I saw him in the hospital I gave him a gold coin, a small memento of a trip to Guatemala I had been on, and some money for his personal needs. I think he received it well. I believe now, even in death, my father is closer to me than ever. I respect his strength and guidance. I'm thankful for the father I had.

The Perspective of Years

I think what the *Band of Brothers* has done (as well as movies such as *Saving Private Ryan*) is to reframe the honor due the men and women who serve our country in the military. Look at the way Vietnam ripped this country apart. I was a perfect example of that—strongly disagreeing with the war and even with the soldiers who were in it.

Today, when I realize what these men and women endure for our country, whether you disagree or agree with the wars our country takes part in, the people who serve in our military are heroes. *Band of Brothers* helped heal the ripped soul of this nation. It helped make this country patriotic again. In the big picture, it's a wonderful thing to have happened to us as a nation.

What really brought this together for me personally was this: today I have a six-year-old daughter, Sophia Rose, whom I took to Disney World last December. A job fair for returning veterans (from Operation Iraqi Freedom) was being held in the Dolphin Hotel, where we were staying. My daughter saw a poster for this and said, "Daddy, that's the army, isn't it? I want to meet the army." When I asked why, she said, "Because we sent them cards." This was late evening already. Nearby sat a veteran in a wheelchair. He was young, handsome, and athletic, though missing a leg. My daughter went to him and asked, "You're army—right?"

He said, "Yes, I am."

My daughter hugged him. "Thank you," she said.

Tears welled in the man's eyes.

"Did you get my card?" she asked. "My school sent you a card. It said, 'Thank you for saving our Earth.'"

The guy just about lost it. He said, "You're welcome. Yes, we did get your card. Thank you for doing that."

Sophia chatted with him for a few minutes. It was getting quite late by then. Sophia said, "Daddy, I want to meet all the army."

The man pulled me aside. "Sir, I have to warn you that many of the men here are horribly disfigured—burn victims, triple amputees. I don't know if it's appropriate, but you can make the call." This was just outside the meeting room.

I called my daughter over and said, "Honey, many of these men were badly hurt in the war. It may be frightening for you."

She said, "That's okay, Daddy. I want to meet them."

We went into the hall where the veterans were. The first man my daughter came to was a burn victim whose face had been all but annihilated. She went up to him without saying a word and hugged him. He just looked down at her. "Thank you," she said. The man started to cry.

She went to another man, who was missing a leg. "What happened to you?" she asked. There was gentleness in her voice.

"A bomb went off," the man said quietly.

Sophia hugged him. "You'll be okay," she said, then repeated it.

Sophia went from man to man that evening, hugging them, thanking the veterans for their service. There wasn't a dry eye in the room.

We spent about an hour there the first night. It was about midnight when we left. We spent three more days at Disney World, and each evening when we came back to the hotel she asked to return to the hall and thank more veterans.

That's the picture I hold in my mind today. Regardless of anybody's political views, these men are true heroes, not only as patriots but also as human beings, for who they are, what they have been through, and what they've endured.

Robert Burr Smith

C. Susan Finn

My father never talked about World War II, like many of the men who returned from the war. For years all I knew was that he was in the 101st Airborne, that he jumped out of a plane on D-day, and that he participated in the Battle of the Bulge. He simply didn't talk about his experiences in combat. I knew much more about his later years with the CIA, which is funny because he wasn't supposed to talk about those experiences.

As much as he didn't talk about war, it was always the backdrop of our life. As a kid growing up in the 1960s, I remember my father dragging us to all these World War II movies, especially ones that focused on D-day. I could see he was proud. And I was proud, too—I told people that my father jumped onto the beaches of Normandy, which of course wasn't exactly true—the paratroopers didn't jump onto the beaches. But that's all I knew as a child.

The things I've learned about my father's World War II days have all come as part of an emotional journey for me today. Over the years I've met people, found papers and letters, and read about him in books and magazine articles. Last Christmas, Dick Winters sent many of the families copies of letters and other documents he had collected about the men of Easy Company. There is a great story about my dad from [the late] Carwood Lipton. Bill Guarnere had a copy of it in boxes of papers that he saved and gave it to me. It reads as follows:

> *I had an interesting game with a German gun. It was early in January that Lt. Dike was told by Battalion to establish contact with the unit on our left, across open ground from our position down near Foy—it might have been I Company. Lt. Dike told me to send a patrol over to make the contact, but rather than send someone else I decided to go, myself. I asked "Burr" Smith to go with me.*
>
> *We made it down to the other unit okay and set up communications and outpost positions to be manned at night, but when we started back we found that a German artillery observer had seen us. Luckily, as there were only two of us, he could apparently get only one gun to fire at us.*
>
> *When we got out into the open ground we heard a gun fire off in the distance and heard the shell coming at us. We hit the ground and it exploded near us, but neither of us was hit. It was a high trajectory, fairly low velocity, piece of artillery so we could hear the gun fire in the distance and could hear the shell coming in for several seconds before it hit.*
>
> *We had 600 or 700 yards of open country to go, uphill, so after the shell hit we jumped up and ran toward our positions until we heard the gun fire again, jumping up and running again after that shell hit. We kept this up, jumping up and running, first zigging and then zagging, after each shell hit and hitting the ground just before the next one hit, and it got funnier and funnier. We could visualize that German artillery observer and his gun crew tracking us with their gun, trying to guess whether we would zig or zag. We fooled them with every move and made it back without a scratch.*

To me, that's such a powerful image: Carwood Lipton and my dad running through the woods and getting shot at—but they're making a game out of it. Dad was always like that, so full of life, with so much presence and charisma. He was someone who walked into a room and every eye was drawn to him.

People I hardly know or have never met before tell me that Dad was their hero. Others save his letters—I've collected copies of them written throughout the decades of his life. The other day, completely out of the blue, I got an e-mail from a man who tracked me down through an Easy Company Web site. The man's father came to California from Australia in the 1960s to train with the army rangers. I remembered the man's father when I was about ten when he came to our house, but other than that we've had no contact over the years. In the e-mail the son said, "My father just passed away. He talked about your father until the day he died."

That was the type of impact my father had on people.

Early Life

My father was born May 2, 1924, in Tacoma, Washington, and lived there until about age seven, when his family moved to Los Angeles, where he grew up. My grandfather was a chemical engineer with Kodak. The family had a bit of money. They rented a house at the beach every summer. In many ways my dad had a privileged upbringing.

Dad's full name was Robert Burr Smith. Burr wasn't a nickname, even though some of the men put "Burr" in quotes when they write it. Burr was one of his grandmother's or aunt's names. Dad's father's name was also Robert. Burr is also my son's middle name today.

When my dad was fourteen, as the story goes, he and a friend were fooling around one day acting like German soldiers and painted swastikas somewhere and yelled "Heil Hitler!" My grandmother was furious and sent him to Brown Military Academy in Pacific Beach, California, so he could learn how to be patriotic.

The summer he turned eighteen, Dad enlisted in the army, on August 18, 1942, and quickly signed up to be a paratrooper. He entered from Rochester, New York, where his parents had moved that summer. On the way down to Georgia for basic training he supposedly met and became friends with Warren "Skip" Muck, who was later killed at Bastogne.

Years after the war and just before he passed away, my father started work on a memoir titled "One Last Look Back." He wrote a few pages only, among them a description of Camp Toccoa, where he trained:

W Company, in September of 1942, was a tent city on the grassy slope of a hill just below the regimental medical processing facility. The squad tents, as brand new as the citizen soldiers who occupied them, were aligned to form a company street, but W Company was a company in name only. It served as the regiment's in-and-out processing machine, and it was a fast train in both directions.

The incoming volunteers (mostly draftees, some enlistees, but all volunteers for parachute training) were frantically busy from morning to night . . . drawing clothing and equipment, filling out forms, falling in for meals, marching to examinations, etc. The train was moving much too fast to jump from it and there was never, to my knowledge, a single disciplinary action among the thousand of "in-processees."

Few lasting friendships were made during this period, but I made one which was destined to be one of the strongest of my life, one which ended only with the death of my first "Army buddy" in a foxhole near Bastogne in January, 1945. His name was Warren "Skippy" Muck, an upstate New Yorker of great charm and wit, who drew people to him like a magnet. Quiet, unassuming, totally "real," his strength was revealed in combat, where his 2nd Platoon mortar section earned a fearsome reputation as Easy Company's most effective heavy weapons element. Skippy was a happy guy, and those who knew him basked in the warmth of that happiness and were happy too.

His closest friend, and, inevitably, one of mine, was Don Malarkey, another warm, friendly and happy-go-lucky individual who likewise rose to the top of my list of personal heroes like cream to the top of the old-fashioned glass milk bottle.

Many of the men have told me that when my father first showed up in the army, he came in as this good-looking, well-educated, well-read, Southern California kid—and they all thought he was going to be a real highbrow. Bill Guarnere has said to me that Dad was really skittish when he first showed up, so "Wild" Bill stuck a gun or bayonet under his neck and said, "It's either kill, or be killed, kid." Dad lost his skittishness really fast after that. He won them over and turned out to be a strong soldier in the end, the men say.

My sister Sandra has kept my father's original jump journal. I don't know why Dad stopped writing it other than things got busy with the war, obviously. He writes of his feelings about parachute training:

December 21, 1942: Made my first parachute jump, an experience I'll never forget! Awfully scared, but so was everybody else, so I didn't feel so bad. The sensation of falling through space is indescribable. Just like a dream. The opening shock was slight, but I hit the ground like a ton of bricks!

December 22, 1942: Living on my nerves—how long can I do it? Parachute jumping is terribly exciting, but I can honestly say that I don't enjoy it. It's fun after the canopy opens, but that fun doesn't overshadow the fear that seizes me as I go out the door. Lots of the boys thrive on it, but I'm too damned excitable. I may grow to enjoy it later on, but only time will tell.

December 23, 1942: Two jumps to go to those glorious wings!

December 24, 1942: Made my final qualifying jump today—I'm now a qualified parachutist! The jump itself was the best I've made so far, just a slight opening shock and a very soft landing. My other landings were so hard because I was making my downward pull too soon. One of the men from G Company had a horrible accident today—his right hand got tangled in his suspension lines and pulled off three fingers. He took his agony like a man though—didn't whimper or cry—will I be that brave when I get mine? A man from Headquarters Company froze in the door (just two men ahead of me) but my buddy Skipper Muck kicked him out the door—cruel treatment, but a scared jumper can cause the death of a whole stick if he freezes in the door when we get into action.

July 28, 1943: 12 jumps to date—expect to leave for combat soon.

In the 1960s, author George Koskimaki was writing a book about the 101st Airborne and sent my father a questionnaire. Through Floyd Talbert's brother, Bob, I was later able to get a copy of the questionnaire that showed Dad's recollections of D-day. Dad was originally slated to be in the Easy Company Headquarters plane that went down on D-day [flight 66, with company commander Thomas Meehan and all Headquarters staff aboard], and was pulled off the flight just prior to takeoff by Dick

Winters, thus saving his life. Nobody seems to know exactly why, except the plane was probably overcrowded. Dad flew to Normandy in another plane. Beforehand in the marshaling area, Dad described hearing pop music blaring through speakers before the flight, hit songs such as "Don't Sit under the Apple Tree." The men ate steaks and ice cream as a last meal. Dad got airsick on the way over and threw up shortly after landing in an apple orchard in Normandy. He was a demolitions specialist and was tasked with blowing cables in a certain manhole, but he never reached the vicinity. This was a skill that came in handy later in his job as a case officer for the CIA in Laos.

Shortly after landing he paired up with Bob Rader, who ended up being a lifelong friend. They soon found Frank Perconte, who had been injured in the jump. The three joined with others. They "engaged in a minor firefight with 'White Russians' near St. Come-au-Mont." Then "disengaged and continued to press on toward Vierville." At dawn they joined with Easy Company.

Dad was wounded twice in World War II, once by shrapnel on D-day plus six in Carentan, France, and another time in the attack on Foy, Belgium, on January 13, 1945, earning him two Purple Hearts. After a stay in the hospital with Frank Perconte, who was wounded the same day, he rejoined Easy Company in Germany prior to the end of the war.

After the War

One of the most important things I ever learned about my father's character was found in a condolence letter written in 1944 to the family of the late Salty Harris, one of Dad's good friends who had died in Carentan a few days after the D-day invasion. Dad wrote, "Anything I can say or do is absolutely worthless, I know. The only course open is to pledge myself to the cause of making sure that things he died for are not forgotten."

That statement gave me such insight into my father's motivation for living. His was an ironic calling. On one hand he was a cultured man who enjoyed books, music, art, animals, and the outdoors. On the other hand he dedicated his life to being "an expert in violence," as he later described himself. I truly believe that Dad believed he had a calling to be a soldier, the same way doctors are called into medicine or priests are called into the ministry. He wanted to make the world a safer place for his children, something his colleagues in later years repeated to me often. One of the air force pilots who flew in Laos when my father was there wrote me a letter in 2001 describing this calling:

> *[Your dad] is the closest thing to Superman that I have ever met. You should be very proud of this man—he gave up a normal life that he richly deserved for a higher calling. He is beyond unique. He has a place in my heart forever—I can see him and hear his laugh as if it was yesterday.*

After World War II Dad came home to Los Angeles, where he married my mother, Mary Jane, and they had my brother, Scott, my sister, Sandra, and me. They settled in the San Francisco Bay Area after my brother was born to raise their family. Dad was a lithographer by trade, but he never really enjoyed it. He told me once that he had somehow settled for a life of mowing the lawn and paying the mortgage; at least that's how he felt. He always seemed restless to me, anxious for adventure. My mother often said she thought he had a "death wish." He stayed active in the Army Reserves and rose to the rank of major over the years. In the 1960s he received Special Forces training and became a Green Beret. He was soon recruited by the CIA to be a paramilitary specialist in the "secret" war in Laos, where he went in 1966. His job as a case officer was to assist and train the Hmong hill tribe and other irregular forces to fight the Communist forces during the Vietnam war.

I was able to visit Dad twice while he was in Laos. I saved all of his letters to me during the seven years he was assigned there. He wrote to me about books I should read, or music he was enjoying, college and career advice, or comments on my boyfriends—all the typical father–teenage daughter stuff. In 1969, when things on the American home front were really heating up, I wrote a letter to Dad expressing my confusion. He wrote back to me, commenting on the irony of the times we lived in then:

> *Your observations on the recent violent murders at home are pretty much like mine, I think. These are strange times, babylove—people are mixed*

*up as never before, and the drug thing makes everything just that much
more hideous.*

*My life, my income, and therefore your security, are all directly re-
lated to violence. I would not have this job, nor be away from home so
much, if there was not so much hate and violence in the world. It is odd
(and sometimes deeply disturbing) to realize that my livelihood is gained
from the most basic weakness of mankind—his inability to live in peace
with his neighbors.*

*Someday there may be no need for my kind of person—the experts in
violence—and the world will be a better place when that day comes. I
will be the very first to shout welcome to that happy time, but in the
meantime there are tigers in the jungle, and the defenseless must be
defended—which means killing tigers.*

*I hope you understand baby—I am not really a war-lover or a man
of violence—it's just that I have been trained for many years in the skills
of warfare, and am needed to help other people defend themselves because
they are not trained in these terrible skills.*

Dad seemed to find his life's calling in Southeast Asia, although his
time there was not easy. He was wounded in 1970 and also contracted
malaria, dysentery, and pneumonia. He stayed in Laos until 1974, when
he returned to the United States, settling near the CIA headquarters in
Virginia. While in Southeast Asia, he continued to perform his Army
Reserve duties, and possibly rose to the rank of lieutenant colonel. (We
have had trouble verifying this with the army. My father told me and
several friends that he made lieutenant colonel, but this remains uncon-
firmed, although we had this rank placed on my dad's grave.) Several of
my father's CIA and other military friends tell me today that he used to
talk to them about his days in Easy Company, saying his Easy Company
comrades were the best soldiers he ever fought with. In addition to the
fighting, Dad worked with U.S. relief agencies and family and friends to
get food, clothing, and other donations for the Hmong villages, especially the children. He built a home for several young Hmong soldiers,
orphans that he felt were too young to fight the war, and taught English
to the Hmong children in his quiet evening hours. One of those boys, Da
Yang, became like a son to him, and my sister and I met him on one of

our visits. I recently located Da, and he still calls my father "Dad" and remarks on his kindness. I have a picture of Dad shaking hands with Savang Vatthana, the last king of Laos.

Dad returned to the States and became the CIA's liaison officer to the first newly formed Delta Force, an elite military group that rescues American hostages anywhere in the world. He trained for about two years with Delta Force and took part in their failed mission in 1980 to free American hostages held in the U.S. embassy in Tehran. He fortunately returned safely from that mission. During the debriefings the following week he was proud to tell us he had met President Jimmy Carter.

The weekend after he returned from the Mideast, my father went hang gliding. He did it to relax—that's the type of man he was. He enjoyed hiking, fishing, and camping, even in the snow (which makes sense now that I know more about what Easy Company endured in Bastogne), and being active in the outdoors in some manner. While up in the air, the unthinkable happened: Dad stalled in a wind gradient and plunged about a hundred feet to the ground. After long months in the hospital for bone grafts and nerve splicing, he retired from the CIA on a medical disability and moved west to be closer to us. He wanted to spend his last years with my mother and be near the rest of the family. My father and mother always stayed married, but I know it was a difficult marriage for both of them. He was not a perfect person by any means. I think he was always trying to find himself. Still, in the end, he chose my mother to come home to when he knew he didn't have long to live.

A Long Look Back

While recovering from injuries sustained in the accident, doctors performed another bone graft in his leg, but this one wouldn't take. His body was rejecting the graft, and we discovered that Dad had lung cancer. In the following months I probably spent more time with my father on a day-to-day basis than in my entire adult lifetime to that point. I lived near him in Arizona, and eventually we both moved back in with my mother in San Diego. I sat up nights talking to him about life and death. Oddly enough, we did not discuss his World War II years, although they were heavy on his mind as his friends called and visited him a lot during that time. We talked about movies he wanted to see, books he wanted to read, people he wanted to visit.

Dad knew his time was short. He drove a motorcycle then, and in his last few months often zipped around on the cycle to visit friends from Easy Company, including Buck Compton, who lived nearby, in San Diego County, at the time. He corresponded with or talked on the phone to Dick Winters, Don Malarkey, Bill Guarnere, Bob Rader, Mike Ranney, Pat Christenson, Bull Randleman, and many more. The guys wrote to encourage him, saying, "Hang tough." I still have all those cards and letters from those times. Many of the men of Easy Company have since told me that they came to visit Dad in his last weeks. Others tried but never touched base. The devotion of the men really means a lot to me. I think my father would be astonished but proud that I became friends with many of those men and their families in later years.

Dad fought the cancer tooth and nail. He had spent so many years in near-death situations that to die of cancer felt degrading. "To die over a lousy pack of cigarettes is just plain embarrassing," he told me once. As sick as he was, he kept lists in his pockets of things he wanted to do, trips he wanted to take, household remodeling tasks, letters to friends he wanted to write.

The illness left Dad so tired and depressed. "If this isn't dying, what does dying feel like?" he said to me once. Around Thanksgiving of that year he decided to go hang gliding again. He wanted to fly in the air one last time. When he walked out the door, my mother and I both wondered aloud if he was going to jump off a cliff and end his life, choosing to die on his own terms. Three days later he returned from his trip, and I was relieved. "I'm so weak," he told me, "I'm just so weak." He was crying.

Right around then he called many of his closest friends and said, "I just wanted to say good-bye." He just needed to hear their voices one last time. Many of them didn't really believe he was so near the end. I think my father's life was blessed with deep, lifelong friendships. People either worshipped him or didn't care for his personality. He was opinionated and had a temper, but predominately he was very beloved and made a lasting impact on people's lives.

My father died an ugly, painful death, just horrible and slow, terrified as he coughed up blood and pieces of lung tissue for days at the end. He was coherent and talking until the night before he died. I feel so fortunate that I was able to tell him that I loved him and that he was my best friend. He died January 7, 1983, at age fifty-eight. I was with him until just moments before he took his last breath.

He was cremated and interred at the military cemetery at Fort Rosecrans National Cemetery in San Diego. The cemetery sits on a beautiful bluff looking over San Diego Harbor on one side and the Pacific Ocean on the other. I think he would like it there. I live in Wisconsin now but try to visit my mother once a year and always stop by to put flowers on Dad's grave. Alex Penkala, who died in Bastogne, has a nephew, Tim Penkala, who lives in San Diego. Every year on Memorial Day, Tim and his daughters place flowers on my father's grave site as a tribute to my father and the men of Easy Company.

I have a copy of a letter written from Easy Company veteran Mike Ranney to Dick Winters eighteen days after my father died. It is perhaps the memory I hold closest. It sums up his life and the men he served with so well. Mike wrote:

> *Still have trouble realizing that old Burr is really gone. I flew down to see him in early December and spent most of an afternoon swapping lies about Easy Company, Toccoa, Currahee, and those old memories. Came home to Oakland understanding that Burr had "come home to die," but the finality of the news still was a shock. But he was in a place of kindness, with his wife, Mary Jane, and both daughters living in San Diego. His son, Scott, lives not too far away.*

Mike went on in the letter to talk briefly about seeing Bob Rader, then some medical tests he himself was going to have. Then Mike ended with those lines that have become so famous now. In the miniseries, Dick Winters quoted him:

> *In thinking back on the days of Easy Company, I'm treasuring my remark to a grandson who asked, "Grandpa, were you a hero in the war?"*
> *"No," I answered, "but I served in the company of heroes."*

George Luz Sr.

Lana Luz Miller and George Luz Jr.

Everybody who knew George Luz Sr. loved him. Our dad would do anything for anybody. He was sincere, kind, and caring, a behind-the-scenes man who shunned attention. He did things solely because they were the right things to do, and when he did someone a favor, he expected nothing in return.

Dad was born June 17, 1921, in Fall River, Massachusetts, and grew up in a large family, with six sisters and three brothers. The family soon moved to West Warwick, Rhode Island, a small town built around pockets of ethnic neighborhoods. His parents spoke Portuguese only, and when Dad went to first grade he didn't speak English yet. He learned quickly.

Dad quit school in the eleventh grade to help support the family. (In the 1970s he went back to school and got his GED.) Soon after high school he joined the army. Dad was a private with Easy Company when they formed in Toccoa. He parachuted into Normandy and Holland and fought in Bastogne and on into Germany. He was known for his sense of humor and ability to do imitations of other people. We think he was a sergeant by the end of the war, though we haven't been able to verify that. Like many of the men, our dad's stripes were removed and reinstated several times for doing crazy things. His grave reads: "PFC George Luz."

When he got out of the service he married our mom, Delvina, the younger sister of one of Dad's neighborhood friends. Dad was six years older than Mom. They had grown up in the same neighborhood, but because of their age difference had never hung around together as kids. During the war our mother had worked in a factory that made pilots' flight jackets. Later she worked as a seamstress for high-end clothing companies.

Dad worked a few different jobs out of the service, then landed an apprenticeship in the textile industry as a lace weaver. He completed the apprenticeship and was offered a job in a mill. It wasn't long until Mom and Dad saved enough to put a down payment on a house. The house cost eleven thousand dollars. Its price became a running joke in the family: later in life, Dad wanted to buy my mother a different car. She said, "I don't care what it is—as long as it doesn't cost any more than what we paid for the house."

Dad was well liked in the neighborhood. He was on the volunteer fire department and president of a Portuguese club called the Holy Ghost Association. Each Labor Day the association held carnivals, banquets, and a big feast. Dad marched proudly in each Labor Day parade in his white tuxedo. His friends all called him Georgie *Luge,* (pronounced like the Olympic sport, which is how the Portuguese said our name). He always had a lot of friends.

Since Dad had nine brothers and sisters and Mom had eleven brothers and sisters, we always had terrific family parties, picnics, and barbecues. Social activities meant getting the family together. Sometimes we got a softball game going at a park, or we went to one of the local beaches. Whenever we gathered there was always a lot of food. We cheered for the New York Giants for football, the Red Sox for baseball, and the Bruins for hockey.

When I (Lana) was about ten we always went out for breakfast on Sunday mornings at a place called Palm's Drugstore after going to Mass at St. Anthony's Church. At Palm's Drugstore we feasted on Ring Dings, Devil Dogs, Twinkies—it was the only time we were allowed to eat junk food for breakfast. After eating we went to the house where my father grew up: my father's sister lived there then; they called it The Homestead. Cousins and I went to the local theater, where they played Disney movies on Sunday afternoons.

Mom and Dad never argued in front of us. And you could never play one against the other. But they could both be strict. When I (George Jr.) was twelve years old, a friend and I were out having fun at one of the local golf courses riding around on a cart. The cart ran out of gas, and I ended up coming home quite a bit later than expected. The rule was that we had to come home as soon as the streetlights came on. That night, when I came home, Dad let me know I hadn't made the right choice. He didn't smash me or anything, he just gave me a verbal tongue-lashing. I was grounded, and *that better not happen again.*

I (Lana) butted heads with my father more often. When I was a teenager I never knew why everyone always said my dad was so great. He was just the guy who told me I couldn't go out to a particular movie or whatever. I'm so glad I got to grow up out of that and get to know my father when I was an adult. Then I could understand why people loved him so much.

One year, our mother's sister was having financial difficulties. There were six kids in her family, and it bothered our father to know there wasn't enough money to buy Christmas presents. So he bought presents for all his nieces and nephews. It couldn't have been easy for him—he had his own family—but he just said, "There is no way these kids aren't going to have toys for Christmas."

Mom and Dad seemed to be able to stretch a buck in a million ways. Growing up, we always had everything we needed. They were able to put money away for their retirement. They traveled to reunions every year. They flew out to see our older brother in California a lot. For their thirty-fifth wedding anniversary they traveled to Portugal for three weeks and took one of Dad's sisters and me (Lana) with them.

Dad always lived life at full blast. After working in the textile industry, he worked for the State of Rhode Island as a machine mechanic, then for a company called Little Rhodie, a maintenance company, which did preventative maintenance on pumps and motors. When he turned sixty-five he tried retiring, but that lasted a month or two; then he went back to work. He worked twelve more years after that.

Dad was always physically strong. I (George) remember doing a roofing job on our home when Dad was in his fifties. He could still carry a ninety-pound bundle of shingles on each shoulder up a ladder. My brother-in-law Albert was amazed. Forget two bundles—Albert and I could barely carry one. Two months before Dad died I was doing a roofing job on my house with my buddy, Rene. Dad showed up unannounced with his hammer and pouch, worked all day, ate a slice of pizza, then said, "Well, I have to go home, pick up Mom, and get ready for church." That was Dad.

It's funny—while we kids were growing up, he was never a huggy-kissy father, but as time went on he really softened. By the time he had grandchildren, it wasn't unusual to see him crawling down the hallway on his hands and knees after the grandkids.

In the earlier years Dad was never one to hand out praise or congratulate you on a job well done, but he was proud of his family. I (Lana) am not sure he ever told his oldest son, Steve, how proud he was of him, even though I know he was. Many times in later years I heard Dad tell people of Steve's accomplishments.

Steve has always felt a strong bond with the men of Easy Company. In the early 1970s, after getting out of the air force, Steve and his young family moved to California, where his wife, Sue, was originally from. Steve put himself through college, got a job with the California Highway Patrol, and lived well. He was responsible for locating Floyd Talbert after years of my father and others from E Company trying to locate him. Talbert had dropped out of sight after the war. After Steve located him, he came to the next reunion. Not long after that reunion, Talbert passed away.

Growing up in Easy Company

Unquestionably, part of what made Dad's character was the men he served with in Easy Company. In 1992, at the *Band of Brothers* book opening in New Orleans, all the men got a chance to speak. Dad got up and said, "Nothing against my wonderful wife, Del, who I've been married to for forty years, but the three years I spent with these men were the best three years of my life." At the end of saying that, he choked up.

It seemed the men of Easy Company were always part of our family's life. In the early 1950s, Mom and Dad went to the reunions of the 101st. The gatherings were quite large, so Easy Company started having its own reunions, and Mom and Dad always went.

The reunions were part of our lives as kids as well. I (George Jr.) was nine in 1965 when I went to my first reunion. I didn't go every year, but I went to several growing up. At that first reunion we drove all the way from Rhode Island to Kentucky, where it was held. My father didn't stop the whole way—he drove straight through the night. Mom vowed that it was the last time they would ever drive to a reunion. I doubt if I fully appreciated the quality of the men who were there. The reunion was held at a Holiday Inn. There was one other kid my age there. We hung out in the pool the whole time, just having fun. We went to Fort Campbell, Kentucky, where I got a chance to shoot an automatic weapon in the tripod position, which I thought was pretty cool for a kid to get to do. One of the men, Phil Perugini, and his wife, Josephine, had taken a train from New York to the reunion. My father said, "We're going that same way back; why don't you come with us." So the Peruginis did. We had this brand-new 1965 Chevy Bel Air station wagon. My older brother Steve didn't come on that trip, so it was Dad and Phil in the front seat with my mom; Mrs. Perugini and Lana sat in the backseat. I was relegated to the back part of the station wagon, with all the luggage. That wasn't much fun for me. I had a propensity to throw up.

I (Lana) remember going to one reunion, in Nashville. I had just started a job and couldn't take time off, so Dad left me money for me to take a flight down for the weekend. My father and Bill Guarnere came to pick me up at the airport. I sat between them in the front seat. Bill was driving. The car had a stick shift, and Bill only has one leg, so it was kind of a wild and hairy ride from the airport.

Bill and Dad were always good friends. When Dad died, Bill drove over to Rhode Island from Philadelphia for the funeral. My mother always thought Bill was kind of loud and brash (and he is—he says words like "broad"). Well, Bill came to the door because he was staying at the house and Mom asked, "Is there anything you need to get from the car?"

"Naw," Bill said. He had his suit over his shoulder. "I got my suit here, an extra pair of underwear in one pocket, and an extra pair of socks in the other. That's all I need—I'm all set!"

During the wake, Bill went outside and had a cigarette. My daughter was outside then, and Bill showed her how to "field-strip" a cigarette (as if she really needed to know). I guess cigarette butts aren't biodegradable, so you stub out your burning cigarette, remove the filter and put it in your pocket, tear the paper, scatter the tobacco, then roll up the paper into a tiny ball and throw it away.

Or in Bill's case, you eat the paper—which he did.

You've absolutely gotta love Bill Guarnere.

A Life Cut Short

Right before the industrial accident in 1998 that took Dad's life, our older brother Steve had come out from California to visit. When Steve left to go home, we all went to the airport to say good-bye; those were the days when you could go all the way to the gate. My brother got on the plane. Normally Dad would have left immediately at that point, but for some reason that day, he stayed. Dad stood there for the longest time, just looking at Steve's plane. He stayed until the plane took off.

Dad died on a Thursday. It's a habit of mine (George Jr.) to go to my mom and dad's house every Wednesday for spaghetti and meatballs. Mom does my laundry. That previous night had been just like every other night. I went to the car, looked back up toward the house, and said, "Good night, Dad."

He said, "Good night, George." That was my last memory of him alive.

Our father's last day was just like every other day. If a person has cancer or something, there's time to say good-bye, but when a person dies in an accident, it's life as usual up to that point. At age seventy-seven he was still working part-time, three days a week as a mechanic. When he left that morning after kissing Mom good-bye, he said, "I'll see you later, Del; we'll meet at Jess's at about two-thirty for coffee." Dad went to work that day with the full understanding that he and Mom would meet again that afternoon.

Later that day I (George Jr.) received a call from Mom saying that Dad had been hurt and was in the hospital. Naturally, hospitals don't tell you what's really going on—they don't want to freak you out when you're driving over there. So I picked up Mom, tried to be strong for her, and drove to the hospital. At that point we thought it could have been anything.

I (Lana) received a call saying that there had been an accident over at the laundry. My husband came and got me. I prayed all the way over to the hospital.

Dad worked on large industrial dryers. One of the dryers, about seventy-two hundred pounds, had slipped off its supports and had fallen on him. Doctors said he died instantly.

It's shocking when you lose someone like that. Horrible, really. One of the hardest things I (George Jr.) had to do was call my older brother Steve in California and tell him that Dad was gone. That was so tough.

The next few days felt surreal. You're kind of there and kind of not. The first night, I (Lana) stayed with my mother, because somebody needed to be there. I remember hearing her cry all night—that's how it went. The next morning we woke up and there were tons of things to do. George's wife, Susan, had lost her parents not long before, so she had a handle on what needed to be done and basically ran with it, went to the church, got the readings, songs, and passages lined up.

My older brother and I went to the funeral parlor to make the final arrangements. I couldn't imagine the funeral parlor playing all that generic music at the wake. I just love Big Band music from the 1940s, the music of my father's era. I had a Glenn Miller CD with me, so I asked the funeral director if it would be okay if we played that for background music. The music turned out to be perfect. CJ, my youngest (my father absolutely loved him), drew some pictures that we put in the casket.

For Dad's wake, a line of people stretched out the door of the funeral parlor and around the block; sixteen hundred people came to his funeral to pay their respects. There was not enough room for everybody.

Dad was buried with his medals on his chest, a Purple Heart, a Bronze Star, and others. We had no idea that he had medals. He had never told us about them. He was buried at the Veterans' Cemetery in Exeter, Rhode Island. It's a beautiful spot with a lot of flowers around. They make it beautiful there.

Paying Tribute

At the funeral, I (George Jr.) sat in the front row of the church with my mom, wife, sister, brother, and family. Person after person came by and told us how much my father meant to him or her. One man I didn't know touched the top of the casket and said with tears in his eyes, "Good-bye, George"—that really touched me. I had no idea who the man was, but Dad had obviously meant a lot to him.

Strange that it took my father's death for me to really understand the impact he had on people. Right there at the funeral I said to myself, From here on I want to be the best I can be, someone I hope he would be proud of. I wanted to do something more with my life to measure up to what my father did with his.

One of the hardest parts for me was simply realizing he wasn't there anymore. I'd think of something during the day and want to call my dad to talk, but then have to stop and realize he was really gone. In 2000 my sister and I were able to convince Mom to attend the Easy Company reunion in Biloxi. Mom had one condition: "as long as we go as a family," and we did. I went so I could reconnect with the men who had meant so much to my father. When I saw Johnny Martin, he recognized me right away, and he welled up. Babe Heffron came over and told me how great my dad was. Jack Foley told me that every unit needs a George Luz. While at a conference at the Army War College in Carlyle, I and my friend John had the privilege of having dinner with Ethel and Dick Winters. My mom and dad admired and loved them both very much. I hadn't seen Dick since the 1981 reunion in San Diego. To me, connecting with the men felt like connecting with Dad again.

I (Lana) paid tribute another way. Three years after Dad died, the *Band of Brothers* miniseries came out. Some people in West Warwick got cable just because of that series. At first, watching the series felt private to me. So my mom came up and we watched it at my house. Then we decided we needed to do something larger. We rented the Elks Hall and a big-screen TV with surround sound and gathered family and friends. I took snippets of all the scenes actor Rick Gomez was in (who played my dad) and spliced them together. We watched the clips and then played the final episode. It was just wonderful. I think Dad would have really enjoyed being there—he would have loved seeing all his friends and family, watching it together.

This memory puts my father's life into perspective for me—sure, life continues, but losing a parent is about the hardest thing I've ever gone through. As a child I remember lying in bed at night saying my prayers and asking God to let me die before my father died. Isn't that strange? I didn't know what I'd do without my father. I just couldn't fathom life without my dad.

In many ways that's still how I feel today. Not that I want to be gone, but I truly miss my father. It's hard to imagine life without him. I know a lot of people feel the same way. George Luz Sr. was a great man. He is truly missed by many.

Easy Company's Campaigns 1944–1945

July–Nov. 1942: 506th PIR activated at Camp Toccoa, Georgia. Basic Training. Hike from Toccoa to Atlanta in late November.

Dec. 1942: Parachute training at Fort Benning, Georgia. Additional training at Benning through February '43.

Feb.–May 1943: Additional training exercises at Camp Mackall, North Carolina. More training jumps.

June–Aug. 1943: Additional training in Kentucky and Tennessee, then to Fort Bragg, North Carolina.

Sept. 1943: Regiment moves to Camp Shanks, New York, boards SS *Samaria* for England. Arrive in Swindon and moved to Aldbourne.

Sept. 1943–May 1944: Additional training in Aldbourne. In May moves to marshalling area near Exeter, England, then to Upottery Airfield.

June 6, 1944: Jump into France. June 7–8 various battles in Normandy.

June 8–16, 1944: Battle for Carentan.

June 29, 1944: Company is relieved and returns to Aldbourne.

Sept. 17, 1944: Company jumps at Zon, Holland, and advances into Eindhoven, heading for Arnhem. Series of intense battles along "Hell's Highway" throughout September.

Oct. 3, 1944: Company is relieved from duty around Eindhoven and transported by truck to the Island, the area between the Waal and the Neder Rhine. Patrols and battles until November when Company is relieved and sent to Mourmelon, France.

December 17, 1944: Company sent to Bastogne, Belgium, to fight in Bois Jacques woods.

January 13–16, 1944: Fighting around Foy, Noville, and Rachamps.

Jan. 19–Feb. 25, 1944: Company is relieved and moved to Hagenau. Fights along the Moder River.

March 1945: Now back in Mourmelon, the entire 101st Airborne Division receives the Presidential Unit Citation. This is the first time an entire division has been honored this way.

April 1945: Company heads into Germany. Finds concentration camps. Occupies Berchtesgaden.

April 6–10, 1945: Company moves to Kaprun, Austria. Begins occupation duties.

May 8, 1945: Victory in Europe day.

May–November, 1945: High-point men are rotated home.

APPENDIX II: SUMMARY OF CONTRIBUTORS' INVOLVEMENT IN CAMPAIGNS

Contributor, Current Hometown	Wartime Rank	Toccoa/ Replacement	Normandy	Holland	Bastogne/ Belgium	Hagenau	Ruhr and Germany	Austria
1. Rod Bain *Anchorage, AK*	T/5	Toccoa	x	x	x	x	x	x
2. Don Bond *Albany, OR*	Pvt.	Replacement				x	x	x
3. Roy Gates *Santa Rosa Beach, FL*	2nd Lt.	Replacement					x	x
4. Forrest Guth *Hockessin, DE*	Sgt.	Toccoa	x	x	x	x		
5. Ed Joint *Erie, PA*	Cpl.	(Joined at Mackall)	x	x	x		x	x
6. Joe Lesniewski *Erie, PA*	PFC	Replacement	x	x	x	x		x
7. Dewitt Lowrey *Montgomery, AL*	PFC	Toccoa	x					
8. Clancy Lyall *Lexington Park, MD*	Sgt.	Replacement	x	x	x	x	x	x
9. Al Mampre *Skokie, IL*	S/Sgt. [medic]	Toccoa		x	x	x	x	x
10. Earl "One Lung" McClung *Pueblo West, CO*	Cpl.	(Joined at Fort Bragg)	x	x	x	x	x	x

Contributor, Current Hometown	Wartime Rank	Toccoa/ Replacement	Normandy	Holland	Bastogne/ Belgium	Hagenau	Ruhr and Germany	Austria
11. Norman Neitzke *Menomonee Falls, WI*	PFC	Replacement				x	x	x
12. Ed Pepping *Whittier, CA*	PFC [medic]	Toccoa	x	x				
13. Frank Perconte *Joliet, IL*	PFC	Toccoa	x	x	x		x	x
14. Darrell "Shifty" Powers *Clincho, VA*	Sgt.	Toccoa	x	x	x	x	x	x
15. Frank Soboleski *International Falls, MN*	S/Sgt.	Replacement		x	x	x	x	x
16. Herb Suerth Jr. *Wayzata, MN*	Sgt.	Replacement			x			
17. Amos "Buck" Taylor *Stuart, FL*	T/Sgt.	Toccoa	x	x	x			
18. Ed Tipper *Lakewood, CO*	PFC	Toccoa	x					
19. Bill Wingett *Salem, OR*	PFC	Toccoa	x	x	x	x	x	x
20. Henry Zimmerman *Oak Island, NC*	PFC	Replacement			x	x	x	x

Understanding Easy Company's Placement: Easy Company, 506th Regiment, 101st Airborne, World War II

101st AIRBORNE DIVISION/THE "SCREAMING EAGLES"
12,000–15,000 men
General Maxwell Taylor commanded the four regiments that made up the 101st Airborne Division. The United States began World War II with 6 divisions (5 infantry and 1 cavalry). By the end of the war, there were nearly 100 divisions.

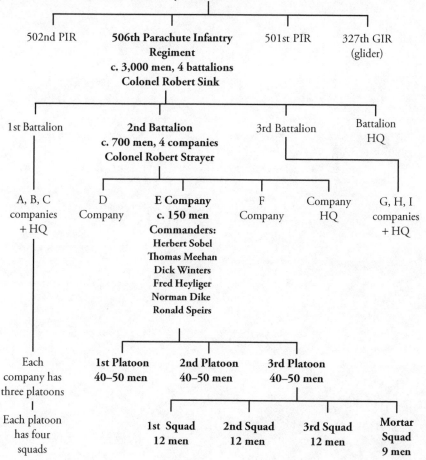

502nd PIR

506th Parachute Infantry Regiment
c. 3,000 men, 4 battalions
Colonel Robert Sink

501st PIR

327th GIR
(glider)

1st Battalion

2nd Battalion
c. 700 men, 4 companies
Colonel Robert Strayer

3rd Battalion

Battalion HQ

A, B, C companies + HQ

D Company

E Company
c. 150 men
Commanders:
Herbert Sobel
Thomas Meehan
Dick Winters
Fred Heyliger
Norman Dike
Ronald Speirs

F Company

Company HQ

G, H, I companies + HQ

Each company has three platoons

1st Platoon
40–50 men

2nd Platoon
40–50 men

3rd Platoon
40–50 men

Each platoon has four squads

1st Squad
12 men

2nd Squad
12 men

3rd Squad
12 men

Mortar Squad
9 men

Known Members of Easy Company, 506th Parachute Infantry Regiment, 101st Airborne Division*

Aldrich, PFC
Alley, James H. Jr., Sgt.
Andrews, Owen L., Pvt.
Ansell, Keith

Bain, Roderick G., T/5
Baker, Pvt.
Baldwin, Kenneth T., Cpl.
Ballew, Raymond L., PFC
Barnwell, Archibold
   Smith, 2nd Lt.
Bay, Conrad, M., PFC
Bealke, Frederick G., Pvt.
Becker, Paul L., Sgt.
Bellino, Salvator F., PFC
Benton, James V., Cpl.
Berg, Richard F., Pvt.
Bernat, Edward J., PFC
Blake, Homer T., Pvt.
Blithe, Albert, PFC
Bloser, Robert J., Pvt.
Bond, Donald S., Pvt.
Boyle, Leo D., S/Sgt.
Bray, Richard L., Pvt.
Brewer, Robert B., Col.

Broska, Charles F., Pvt.
Bruce, Earl V., Pvt.
Burden, PFC
Burgess, Thomas H., PFC

Campbell, James
Campbell, James D., Cpl.
Capoferra, John J.
Carillo, Leopollo P. [Alex],
   T/5
Carlino,Matthew J., PFC
Carson, Gordon F., Sgt.
Childers, Ora. M., Pvt.
Chow, Pvt.
Christenson, Burton Pat.,
   T/Sgt.
Cipriano, Robert, Pvt.
Clark, Maxwell M., PFC
Cobb, Roy W., PFC
Coleman, James F., Pvt.
Collette, Vincent S., PFC
Collins, Herman F., T/5
Comba, James
Compton, Lynn. D.
   [Buck], 1st Lt.

Connell, John G., Pvt.
Conway, Pvt.
Coombs, James [Tex], Sgt.
Coviello, Phillip, Pvt.
Cowing, Robert H., 1st Lt.
Cowthu, Samuel M., Pvt.
Crosby, Seth O., PFC
Cunningham, Bernard S.,
   Sgt.
Cushman, Pvt.

Damon, Pvt.
Dassault, Barry J.
Davenport, Richard P.,
   PFC
Davis, James K., 1st Lt.
De Tuncq, Edward R.
Dickerson, Jay S., Pvt.
Diel, James L., 2nd Lt.
Dike, Norman S. Jr., Capt.
Dittrich, Rudolph R., Pvt.
Doe, John, Pvt.
Dominguez, Joseph P.,
   PFC
Donahue, Edward J., PFC

Dukeman, William H. Jr.,
Sgt.

Eckstrom, Carl F., PFC
Eggert, Walter F.
Elliott, George L., Pvt.
Ellis, Taskel, Sgt.
Eschenbach, Chester, Pvt.
Eubanks, John L., Pvt.
Evans, William S., 1st Sgt.

Fenstermaker, Carl L.,
PFC
Fernandez, PFC
Fieguth, John F., Cpl.
Flurie, Gerald, L., PFC
Foley, Jack E., Capt.
Ford, Norman A. [cadre,
2nd Pl.], S/Sgt.
Freeman, Bradford C.,
PFC

Garcia, Antonio, PFC
Garrod, Richard R., PFC
Gates, Roy, 2nd Lt.
Gathings, Johnnie E., PFC
Geraghty, John L., Pvt.
Gier, William D.
Giles, Terry G., Pvt.
Gilmore, Eugene S. [Bob],
Pvt.
Ginn, Jack O., PFC
Glass, Milton B., Pvt.
Gordon, Walter S. Jr.
[Smokey], Cpl.
Grant, Charles E. [Chuck],
Sgt.
Grant, Frank B., Pvt.
Gray, Everett J., PFC
Griffith, Genoa H., Pvt.
Grodski, Stephen E., Pvt.
Guarnere, William J.,
S/Sgt.
Guth, Forrest L., Sgt.
Guy, Lloyd D., Sgt.

Hagerman, Stanley L.,
Pvt.

Hale, Earl L., S/Sgt.
Hale, Franklin W., Pvt.
Haley, Robert, Lt.
Hanes, Sgt.
Hansen, Herman E., T/5
Hansen, Walter E., PFC
Hargroves, Elwood, Pvt.
Harrell, Thomas A., Pvt.
Harrellson, Siles E., PFC
Harris, Terrence [Salty] C.,
S/Sgt.
Hartley, Dale L., PFC
Hartsuff, George B., Pvt.
Hashey, Lester [Hash],
1st Sgt.
Hawkins, Verlin V., Pvt.
Hayden, Sgt.
Hayes, Harold G., Pvt.
Haynes, Sgt.
Heckler, Cyril B., Pvt.
Heffron, Edward J. [Babe],
PFC
Henderson, J. D., Sgt.
Hendrix, Walter [Black
Jack], T/Sgt.
Hensley, Robert C., Pvt.
Herron, A. P., PFC
Hertzog, Elwood, PFC
Hester, Clarence, Lt. Col.
Hewitt, George W.
Heyliger, Frederick T.
[Moose], Capt.
Hickman, PFC
Higgins, George, Cpl.
Hite, Paul A., Pvt.
Hogan, Joseph E., PFC
Holbrook, Owen V., Pvt.
Holland, John R. [medic],
Pvt.
Holton, David L., Pvt.
Hoobler, Donald B., Cpl.
Howard, Walter G., PFC
Howell, Clarence S., PFC
Howell, William A., T/5
Hudgens, Bruce A., Pvt.
Hudson, PFC
Hudson, Charles A.,
2nd Lt.

Hughes, Richard H. II,
1st Lt.
Hughes, Richard J., Pvt.
Huntley, Warren C., PFC
Hussion, Charles F., Pvt.

Irish, Sherman M., Sgt.
Ivie, Eugene E., PFC

Jackson, Eugene E., Pvt.
Janovec, John A., PFC
Jarrett, Robert, Pvt.
Johnson, Coburn M., PFC
Joint, Edward J., Cpl.
Jones, George E., PFC
Jones, Hank, 1st Lt.
Jordan, Joseph M., PFC
Jordan, Vernon, Pvt.
Julian, John T., PFC

Kiehn, William F., Sgt.
King, Donald L., Cpl.
Kohler, PFC
Korb, John R., Pvt.
Kratzer, William N., Pvt.
Kudla, Steven A. [cadre,
3rd Pl.], S/Sgt.

Lager, Harry, PFC
Lamoureux, Paul E., PFC
Lampos, Lewis [Bob], Pvt.
Lavenson, George, 1st Lt.
Leonard, Robert T., PFC
Lesniewski, Joseph A.,
PFC
Liebgott, Joseph D., T/5
Lindler, Quinton E., PFC
Lipton, C. Carwood.,
1st Lt.
Longo, Philip E., Pvt.
Lowrey, Dewitt, PFC
Lusty, John, Pvt.
Luz, George, T/5
Lyall, Clarence O., Sgt.
Lynch, John C., 1st Sgt.

Mahmood, A., Pvt.
Maitland, Thomas, Cpl.

Malarkey, Donald G.,
T/Sgt.
Mampre, Albert L.,
S/Sgt.
Mann, Robert A., 1st Sgt.
Marsh, Robert K., Sgt.
Martin, John W., Sgt.
Martin, Walter E., Pvt.
Massaconi, Michael V.,
Pvt.
Mather
Matheson, S. L., Maj. Gen.
Mathews, Robert L., 2nd
Lt.
Matthews, Jack F., Pvt.
Matz, Leo J., Lt. Col.
Mauser, Edward A., PFC
Mauzerall, Arthur J., PFC
Maxwell, Robert, Pvt.
Mayer, John G., T/5
Maynard, William C., T/5
McBreen, John, PFC
McCauley, Carl F., Pvt.
McClung, Earl J. [One
Lung], Cpl.
McCreary, Thomas A., Sgt.
McGonigal, William T. Jr.,
PFC
McGrath, John, T/5
McKay, Walter L., PFC
McMahon, James A., PFC
Medved, William E., PFC
Meehan, Thomas, 1st Lt.
Mellett, Francis J., Cpl.
Melo, Joachim, Pvt.
Mendoza, Ynez M., Pvt.
Menze, Vernon J., PFC
Mercier, Kenneth D., Sgt.
Meth, Elmer T., Pvt.
Meth, Max M., Pvt.
Metzler, William S., PFC
Miller, James W., PFC
Miller, John N., PFC
Miller, William T., PFC
Milo, Franklin, Pvt.
Minne, Elmer T., Pvt.
Montes, Alfred B., Pvt.
Moone, Donald J., Pvt.

Moore, Walter L., 1st Lt.
More, Alton M., PFC
Morehead, Harvey H.
[cadre], 1st Sgt.
Morris, David, E., PFC
Morris, William E., Pvt.
Motowski, Stanley F., Cpl.
Motz
Moya, Sergio G., PFC
Muck, Warren H. [Skip],
Sgt.
Murray, Elmer L. Jr., Sgt.

Neitzke, Norman W., PFC
Nelson, Henry E., PFC
Neumann, Pvt.
Nevenfeldt, Gordon, Pvt.
Nixon, Lewis [Black-
beard], Capt.

O'Brien, Francis L., 1st Lt.
O'Keefe, Patrick S., Pvt.
Oats, Ernest L. [medic],
PFC
Oien, Gordon H., Pvt.
Orth, Ralph J. [medic],
PFC
Owen, Richard E., Sgt.

Pace, Cecil M., Pvt.
Pace, Ledlie R., T/5
Peacock, Thomas A., 1st
Lt.
Penkala, Alex M. Jr.,
PFC
Pepping, Edwin E., PFC
Perconte, Frank J., PFC
Perkins, Ben M., 1st Lt.
Peruginni, Philip P.,
PFC
Petty, Cleveland O., PFC
Pickel, Roy E., Pvt.
Pierce, David R., Pvt.
Pisanchin, John E.,
1st Lt.
Plesha, John Jr., Cpl.
Pomely, Pvt.
Potter, George L. Jr., Pvt.

Powers, Darrell C.
[Shifty], Sgt.
Pyle, Charles W., Pvt.

Raczkowski, Alex R., Pvt.
Rader, Robert J., S/Sgt.
Rajner, George J., Pvt.
Ramierez, Joseph, PFC
Randleman, Denver [Bull],
Sgt.
Ranney, Myron Mike, S/
Sgt.
Reese, Lavon P., Cpl.
Rexrode, Charles E., 2nd
Lt.
Rhinehart, Charles E., T/4
Rice, Farris O., PFC
Richey, Ralph D. Jr.,
Major
Riggs, Carl N., Sgt.
Robbins, Woodrow W.,
PFC
Roberts, Murray B., S/Sgt.
Robinson, Harvey G., Cpl.
Roe, Eugene G. [medic],
T/5
Rogers, Clifford E., Cpl.
Rogers, Paul C., Sgt.
Rossman, John W., PFC
Rotella, Gregory C., Pvt.
Roush, Warren R., 1st Lt.
Rowles, Richard C., T/4

Sabo, Edward F., PFC
Sarago, James
Sawosko, Carl C., PFC
Schmitz, Raymond G., 1st
Lt.
Schuyler, Elmer N., PFC
Serilla, William D., Pvt.
Sewell, John P., Pvt.
Shames, Edward D.,
Col.
Sheehy, John L., PFC
Sheeley, John P., PFC
Shindell, John E., Pvt.
Shirley, Urbon M., Pvt.
Sholty, James B., Sgt.

Sisk, Wayne A. [Skinny], Sgt.
Smith, Campbell T., T/5
Smith, Garland R., PFC
Smith, George H. Jr., Pvt.
Smith, John D., Pvt.
Smith, Robert Burr, Lt. Col.
Smith, Robert T. [supply sgt.], S/Sgt.
Snider, Gerald R., PFC
Sobel, Herbert M., Major
Soboleski, Frank
Sowell, James L.
Speirs, Ronald, C. [Killer], Major
Spina, Ralph F. [medic], PFC
Stafford, Ralph I., T/5
Stedman, Joe E. [cadre, 1st Pl.], S/Sgt.
Steele, Robert L.
Stein, Edward H., Cpl.
Stickley, Joseph, Pvt.
Stokes, J. B., Sgt.
Stoney, Benjamin J., T/4
Strohl, Roderick G., PFC
Suerth, Herbert J., Sgt.
Sullivan, Paul J., PFC
Supko, Paul
Sweeney, Patrick J., 1st Lt.

Talbert, Floyd M., 1st Sgt.
Taylor, Amos J. [Buck], T/Sgt.
Telstad, Elmer L., PFC
Thomason, George W., Pvt.
Thompson, Raymond H., Pvt.
Tipper, Edward J., PFC
Tokarzewski, Felix J., PFC
Toner, John, Pvt.
Toye, Joseph D., Sgt.
Trapuzzano, Ralph J., PFC
Tremble, Eugene R.
Tremonti, Norman, Pvt.
Tridle, Clarence M., Sgt.

Uuban, Andrew, PFC

Van Klinken, Robert, PFC
Vest, Allen E. [Jaws], PFC
Vittorre, Alexander, PFC

Wagner, Paul, PFC
Wagner, William H., T/5
Warren, Thomas W., PFC
Webb, Harold B., PFC
Webb, Kenneth J., PFC
Webster, David Kenyon., PFC

Welling, James W., PFC
Welsh, Harry F., Lt. Col.
Wentzel, Jerry A., T/5
Wentzel, Walter H., Pvt.
West, Daniel B., PFC
Wheeler, James W., Pvt.
Whitecavage, Joseph P., S/Sgt.
Whitwer, Roland M., PFC
Whytsell, Elijah, Pvt.
Wimer, Ralph H., T/5
Wingett, William T., PFC
Winn, Melvin W., PFC
Winters, Richard D., Maj.
Wiseman, Donald S., Pvt.
Woodcock, William H., PFC
Wright, Richard M., Sgt.
Wynn, Robert E. [Popeye], PFC

Yochum, George F., PFC
York, Ronald V.
Youman, Arthur C., Sgt.
Young, Jerry G., Pvt.

Zastavniak, Frank J., PFC
Zimmerman, Henry C., PFC

*Source: Men of Easy Company Association.

Killed in Action, Easy Company, 506th Parachute Infantry Regiment, 101st Airborne Division*

Robert J. Bloser	June 7, 1944
James D. Campbell	October 8, 1944
Herman F. Collins	June 6, 1944
James L. Diel	September 19, 1944
William H. Dukeman	October 5, 1944
George L. Elliot	June 6, 1944
William S. Evans	June 6, 1944
Everett J. Gray	June 8, 1944
Terrence C. Harris	June 18, 1944
Harold G Hayes	December 1944
A. P. Herron	January 13, 1945
Donald B. Hoobler	January 3, 1945
Richard J. Hughes	January 9, 1945
Eugene E. Jackson	February 15, 1945
John A. Janovec	May 1945
Joseph M. Jordan	June 6, 1944
John T. Julian	January 1, 1945
William F. Kiehn	February 10, 1945
Robert L. Matthews	June 6, 1944
William T. McGonigal	June 6, 1944
Thomas Meehan	June 6, 1944
Francis J. Mellett	January 13, 1945
Vernon J. Menze	September 20, 1944
William S. Metzler	June 1944
James W. Miller	September 20, 1944

John N. Miller	June 6, 1944
William T. Miller	September 20, 1944
Sergio G. Moya	June 6, 1944
Warren H. Muck	January 10, 1945
Elmer L. Murray	June 6, 1944
Patrick H. Neill	January 13, 1945
Ernest L. Oats	June 6, 1944
Francis L. O'Brien	December 1944
Richard E. Owen	June 6, 1944
Alex M. Penkala	January 10, 1945
Carl N. Riggs	June 6, 1944
Murray B. Roberts	June 6, 1944
Carl C. Sawosko	December 1944
Raymond G. Schmitz	September 23, 1944
John E. Shindell	January 13, 1945
Gerald. R. Snider	June 6, 1944
Benjamin J. Stoney	June 6, 1944
Elmer L. Telstad	June 6, 1944
Robert Van Klinken	September 20, 1944
Thomas W. Warren	June 6, 1944
Harold D. Webb	January 13, 1945
Kenneth J. Webb	January 13, 1945
Jerry A. Wentzel	June 6, 1944
Ralph H. Wimer	June 6, 1944

* Source: Men of Easy Company Association.

INDEX

Page numbers in **bold** indicate tables or charts; those followed by "n" indicate notes.

ABOUT THE AUTHOR

Marcus Brotherton is a journalist and professional writer, and the author or coauthor of seventeen books. He has collaborated with Dr. Nancy Heche (mother of actress Anne Heche), international humanitarian Susan Scott Krabacher, and most recently with Lieutenant Lynn "Buck" Compton on his memoir *Call of Duty*. Marcus lives with his family in Washington State.

www.BandOfBrothersBooks.com

Printed in the United States
by Baker & Taylor Publisher Services